JOURNEY TO JAPAN
A LIFE-SAVING MEMOIR

A Story of Compassion and Perseverance

By
Sarah Deschamps

Dedication

To Emma, who bravely watched it happen

To Lily, who fought to survive

To Fred, who fiercely protected us all

Prologue

One evening in January 2000, the opportunity of a lifetime fell into Fred's lap. He ran in the door, "You'll never, ever guess what happened!" I braced myself, not knowing if this was going to be good or bad news. "The position in Tokyo opened up, and they are offering it to me, to us!" He was almost stumbling over his words. The Pacific Division of Northwest Airlines, where he had worked for eight years, was looking for someone from headquarters in Minnesota to run the financial operations and administration for the entire Pacific region in Tokyo. This was a position Fred and I had talked about enthusiastically for many years. We couldn't believe this dream might come true for us.

Fred called from work the next day to tell me about the offer. "They're going to promote me from Director to Managing Director. We'll live in the apartments Northwest owns in Tokyo. My salary will be adjusted so we can afford to live in Japan."

I hesitated with my next question. We were five months pregnant with our second child, and moving to Japan would mean delivering a baby in Tokyo, in a Japanese hospital. "What did they say about giving birth?"

"There are phenomenal English-speaking doctors and American-style hospitals in Tokyo. The company's international medical insurance is outstanding."

We knew the pregnancy was the one thing that might keep us in Minnesota. I had tossed and turned all night, excited about the adventure for our family but concerned about the birth.

We fondly remembered that our first daughter had been born uneventfully two years before in Minneapolis, and it seemed, based on what

Fred had learned, like this baby's birth would be uneventful too. Fred signed the contract. We were in!

Chapter 1

Fred and I met in 1985 in Saint Paul, Minnesota, at Macalester College. Fred was from Belgium, and I was from across the street. On our first date, we went to a Japanese restaurant near campus. Fred proclaimed, "I took you to a Japanese place because I want to live in Japan someday."

I loved to travel. When I was a child, my parents found ways for us to explore Europe and Australia. In college, I had taken every opportunity to leave Minnesota. I spent January terms in Spain, in New York at the United Nations studying at the Embassy of the Soviet Union, and my senior year in China. I studied in Bogotá, Colombia for a semester during my junior year. Japan intrigued me. The moment Fred mentioned it, I was all in.

In 1992, we began our married life in Saint Paul. I worked as a Spanish teacher and administrator at Saint Paul Academy and Summit School, and Fred worked for Northwest Airlines. A crucial benefit of working for an airline was that employees could travel for free almost anywhere they wanted, almost any time. So, we traveled. All the time. We honeymooned in Bali, and for the next two years, we saved money all year to travel to Thailand and the Philippines, always stopping in Japan on the way.

Since we had free flights and a free place to stay in Belgium, Fred would call me on Thursday afternoon at school, "the flights to Brussels look good for tomorrow night with a return on Sunday. What do you think?" We would meet at the airport, fly all night, and spend Saturday with Fred's family and our friends at our favorite Belgian restaurants eating *steak frites* and drinking one of 300 different kinds of Belgian beer. We both felt the need to explore and constantly embrace another culture. When we returned to work on Monday morning, we loved it when our colleagues asked casually, "what did you do this weekend?"

Chapter 2

I burst into my next obstetrician's appointment. "Guess what? We're moving to Japan, and we get to have our baby there!" I wiggled up onto the examining table so I could be face-to-face with the doctor. I had pictured his excitement in my head all the way to the clinic. I was ready to hear how thrilled he was for me.

He wasn't. He seemed oblivious to my exuberance. Looking away from me, he said matter-of-factly, "Sarah, I don't know of a single other expectant mother who would make an international move to a place where they don't speak English. It's too much stress to add to a pregnancy." He glanced up and saw my raised eyebrow and pursed lips. I was taken aback. It was out of character for him. He should know me better than that. During my first pregnancy, he had heard me gush about the twelve trips we had taken during those nine months. He knew we loved adventure. This time was even more exciting because the baby would have a Japanese birth certificate. I suppressed the urge to mutter something rude. He cleared his throat and changed his tone. "Um, I know you will find good medical care in Japan. We'll do what we can in our clinic before you leave."

He paged through my chart. "You're almost five months along, so I think we should have you do a second ultrasound. That way, you'll have current and quality information to bring to your doctor in Japan. I'm certain it will confirm what we already know, the baby is healthy, and the pregnancy is progressing normally." I nodded, hopped down off the exam table, pushed out my baby belly, and thanked him. I left the doctor's office filled with even more confidence about our decision. I told Fred about the appointment and how even though he didn't wholeheartedly support our decision, the doctor was willing to put everything in place for us to move during the pregnancy.

Instead of moving right away, our plan had been that the three of us would move to Tokyo at the beginning of May. I wanted my teaching and work responsibilities to come to a natural conclusion, and this would allow for most of my pregnancy to happen in Minnesota. Northwest had a different idea. The person currently in the job in Tokyo was about to leave, and they wanted Fred to get to Japan as soon as possible. We made the difficult decision to separate our family. We justified it by thinking that Fred could set up the apartment for us, find a doctor for me and figure out the logistics of the move. Emma, our two-year-old daughter, and I would follow in three months. We learned that airlines allow pregnant women to fly internationally for up to seven and a half months. The baby was due June 21st, so we picked May 7th to travel, the last possible day.

Ten days before Fred had to leave for Tokyo, I had an appointment with the ultrasound technician. Fred was swamped at work trying to wrap up his old job and get prepared for the new one. We thought it would be routine and they would just hand me the cute black and white ultrasound photos of the baby in amniotic fluid waving as they had at the previous ultrasound, so I went to the appointment alone.

"Sarah Dee-Champs," said someone standing in a white lab coat at the door to the waiting room. I was constantly being called a name other than Deschamps, Day-Shaun, the correct Belgian pronunciation. I was used to people standing, ready to call my name, and then hesitating. I usually said, "I'm here," before they even tried. I got up and followed the technician.

"Hi, I'm John, and I'm going to do your level two ultrasound today." He seemed like a kind man. John had me lie down on my back on the examining table next to the ultrasound machine. He started the procedure, pointing to the computer screen. "Look, here are the baby's head, legs, and arms. You can even see the fingers and toes." He then turned on the microphone in his wand. "That is her heartbeat." It sounded perfect, just as it had earlier in the pregnancy. It reassured me and made my own heart sing. We were so happy we were going to have another girl, and she was fine!

I watched on the monitor as John typed my name and "Baby Deschamps" in the upper left-hand corner of the screen. Since I was further along in my pregnancy and the first ultrasound had been normal, this time the technician was supposed to take a deeper look inside the baby to check the health of her brain, organs, blood flow, and heart. John took pictures with the machine spitting them out as he moved the wand from one side to the other. Then, abruptly, he stopped. Without saying a word, he stood up and walked out of the room. I was surprised but not concerned. Was the machine not working? Did he need to ask about exactly what pictures the doctor wanted?

After a few minutes, a doctor I didn't know entered the room. He was tall with a starched blue shirt, blue striped tie, and white lab coat. In a brusque voice he said, "I'm here to put a second pair of eyes on your baby." He tilted the computer screen away from me. The doctor watched as the technician put more gel on my stomach and began to move the wand again. "Sarah, can you turn on your left side? Good. Now back to the middle." They were not telling me what they were seeing. The happiness I was feeling only minutes before drained out of me.

My hands started to shake, and my heart started to race. I was glad they weren't taking my blood pressure because it would have been high. For what seemed like hours, I moved and turned as they instructed. I said nothing, wishing that Fred was there with me. This would be the first of many times I wished I was not alone.

Finally, the doctor turned the screen back around so I could see it. He took the wand from the technician and spoke slowly and deliberately. "There is something unusual in the baby's lower abdomen. Let me show you what we're seeing." I saw her head, body, legs, and arms again. With a quick jerk of his hand, he turned up the volume on the microphone. Her heartbeat thumped back at me, making that strong, reassuring rhythm, *ba-boom, ba-boom, ba-boom.* What could possibly be wrong? It all sounded and looked good to me.

He moved the wand to a different place on my stomach, pushing harder than I thought necessary. The outline of the baby's delicate body disappeared. It seemed like we were now seeing inside her. There were different black and gray shapes, all pulsing and moving to the beat of her heart. There was a click on the keyboard, and then I saw bright colors. The shapes that had been dark before now had yellow, red, and blue lines snaking through them, looking like rainbow-colored spaghetti. It was pretty but didn't resemble a baby.

6

The doctor pointed to one of the shapes. "See this? This is the one we're worried about. Inside her belly." Instinctively, my own belly tightened. I saw what he was pointing to, but I thought it looked like all the other shapes. I'm sure I looked confused. The doctor tried again. "There's a dark shadow in the lower abdomen. Right here." He poked so hard on the screen it wobbled. He looked at me and could see my blank face, but he didn't change his tone or demeanor. He said nothing as if he had explained enough for me to grasp the concept.

I desperately wanted to see a dark shadow or even make out the shape of an abdomen. I discovered too late that it was hard to interpret images on an ultrasound machine, at least for me. I nervously scanned the screen back and forth, tilting my head while I still was on my back, uncomfortably sprawled out on the exam table. I was trying so hard to find anything that resembled a shadow. I looked at the doctor for help but got none. There was an awkward silence.

I prided myself as someone who could figure out difficult things, but this time I just lay there feeling like a fool. I knew I had to understand, but I couldn't.

Slowly, the room came back into focus. There were two men looming over my exposed, vulnerable body. My mind flipped defensively from bewilderment and embarrassment to resentment. I shut them out, choosing not to believe what they were saying. They were the experts, and I was the patient. It was their job to calmly explain to me what was wrong until I understood. Even worse, I remembered that I had been reassured by multiple tests during the first months of the pregnancy that the baby was healthy. They were now making me second-guess everything.

The doctor was looking straight at me. I was sweating and breathing heavily, with tears of confusion streaming down my face. "Sarah, it may not be anything. The baby is so small and in too tight a position in the uterus, but we are concerned." He added offhandedly he could only see one kidney.

I muttered, "okay." I had heard, 'dark shadow, missing kidney, may not be anything.' I hung onto those last four words.

7

Without acknowledging the fear written all over my face, not even bothering to hand me a tissue, he said, "you should wipe the gel off your stomach, and then we can talk." My mind wasn't focused. I should've been questioning what he said, but instead I was questioning what he did. I didn't know or trust this doctor. I hadn't seen him during Emma's pregnancy. I realized I wouldn't even know how to tell Fred what I had been told because I didn't understand any of it myself.

The rest of the visit was a blur. I don't remember wiping off the gel or anything the doctor told me afterward. He didn't try again to explain the ultrasound's findings, and I didn't ask. He wasn't going to be the one to help me. I clearly heard that I was being referred to the University's medical center, where they take care of high-risk pregnancies. I stuttered that I was moving to Japan, and he said, "I'll put it in my referral notes. I suggest you go as soon as possible."

I made the appointment at the high-risk pregnancy clinic before I left the office. They scheduled it two days before Fred was planning to leave for Tokyo. As I was walking out, the doctor handed me several ultrasound photos, each supposedly showing a murky dark shadow. I shoved the pictures in my bag.

In the car, my head pounding and hands shaking on the steering wheel, I allowed myself to think through every second of the pregnancy, trying to pinpoint an instance when a dark shadow might have entered the baby's belly. I reviewed all of the days I taught, all the kids with coughs in my classes, and the late-night papers I graded. I thought about the precautionary tests I had taken and all the doctor's appointments where I was told the baby was healthy. I thought about my food, my exercise, and the movement of the baby. I couldn't think how this could have happened to our child. I needed Fred.

I called him at his office. My worries about what I had just heard and anger at the doctor were pulsing through me. I blurted out, "Come home now. There's something very wrong."

I stood frozen at the door, waiting for the twenty minutes to tick by for him to arrive. He rushed in and hugged me. "What's going on?"

8

"During the ultrasound, the doctor saw something wrong in the baby's abdomen. He called it a dark shadow." I shoved the now crumpled images at him.

He looked at the pictures with a confused expression, just as bewildered as I was. "How do you look at these? Where exactly is the shadow? How sure is the doctor?"

He then started to wonder as I had, "Do you know this doctor? Is he a specialist in ultrasound images? In abdominal issues?"

We stood there for a long time shuffling through the pictures pointing at something and then dismissing it as nothing. The longer we shuffled, the more confused we became.

We finally put the images down and realized we had to revisit our decision to move to Japan. It was incomprehensible that this was happening. Fred's flight was booked, our plans were set, and our new and exciting life on the other side of the globe was waiting for us. It was our dream. We had to get there. A murky, unidentified shadow in the baby that the doctor said might not be anything couldn't stop us; at least we didn't want it to.

Maybe it was naiveté or our bullheaded determination, or maybe we were just too young to understand the dire situation we might be facing, but after the doctor's behavior, we both felt a shift inside ourselves. We began to think that maybe the doctors in Japan wouldn't treat us this way. Maybe they would have the time and patience needed. A small crack formed in our firm belief that the U.S. had the best medical care. Perhaps, instead, we could find the best in Japan.

When I think of this moment, it still makes my heart quicken. I didn't have the courage to ask that doctor a single question. I should've demanded that he stay in the room until I understood, but I didn't say a word. It was the first time I experienced bewildering shock and disbelief and an inability to act. It wouldn't be the last.

Chapter 3

One of the things that initially attracted us to each other was our mutual determination to leave our birthplaces. We found it thrilling to live far outside our comfort zone. We had both lived abroad, me in Colombia and Fred in the United States, and throughout our relationship, we spoke enthusiastically about living abroad in a place neither of us knew.

In 1988, after finishing at Macalester, I moved to California to attend graduate school in education at Stanford University. As a Belgian male, Fred had to do a year of mandatory military service in Northern Belgium. For a mathematics major, the switch from solving problems in differential equations, which he loved, to recreating the liberation of Belgium in World War II by running 30 kilometers in the August heat with full military gear on his back was head-spinning at best.

When I finished my master's degree at Stanford, I moved to Brussels to be with him. I worked at a Belgian textile mill. Early each morning, I took two trains traveling for an hour and a half far into Flanders for a job that amounted to serving coffee and sending faxes. Nothing that I had learned in college or graduate school was required.

For me, it was a powerful feeling to be in a country that was so different from my own. I had to overcome a cultural and linguistic barrier each day. To call Fred at the army base, I had to use the six Flemish words I had memorized, "*vijf en twintig drie en dertig, Sergeant Deschamps, alsjeblieft.*" (Phone extension 25, 33, Sergeant Deschamps, please.) I held my breath, hoping he would come on the phone because I didn't know a single other word of Flemish.

Fred studied for the GMAT, the entrance exam for business school in the U.S., while he was at the army base on night patrol. In 1989 in Northern Flanders at Bataljon Bevrijding, there were no enemies to fight. As he guarded the grounds, he always had *The Official Guide for the GMAT* tucked under his arm and a flashlight at the ready so he could study. Under the circumstances, it was impressive that he got an almost perfect score on the exam and decided to attend the Kellogg School of Management at Northwestern University. Once again, we decided to begin another adventure together. We left Belgium and headed back to the United States.

Chapter 4

As we waited for the visit at the University's high-risk pregnancy clinic, each evening I went into Emma's room after she was fast asleep. I kissed her sweet cheeks, listened to her breathe, and marveled at how beautiful she was. I said in my head, "Emma is healthy. I have always been healthy. Fred is healthy. Both of our families are healthy, so this baby is healthy too."

At this point, Fred was understandably anxious and stressed. He had to be ready for his new demanding job, and before he left, he wanted to know that Emma, the baby, and I would be all right.

In contrast, I was calm. I knew the baby would be fine. I decided to remain skeptical of what the doctor had said. It seemed like the prudent response. He had told me that the shadow might be nothing. We had no information beyond his hunch, which I doubted anyway, to indicate there was a problem. I told Fred I'd like to go to the high-risk medical center by myself. I explained rationally that I was sure they'd clear up any misunderstanding about our baby. Out of respect for my wishes and so he could get one more project done before leaving, he let me go alone.

It turns out receptionists in high-risk pregnancy clinics are the nicest people. They are gentle, reassuring, and understand you don't know what to expect. "Welcome! I hope you easily found our clinic. I love the dress you're wearing. There is water on the shelf over there and some healthy snacks in case you are hungry." I relaxed. This seemed like a good place to be, even though the name implied otherwise.

The waiting room was pristine. There was background music, lamps with soft lighting, and the couches could fit two people comfortably, so couples were quietly sitting together with their arms around each other. I stood by myself.

"Sarah...Des...Champs." Ugh, a bad beginning. The nurse brought me back to a room that looked more like a sterile operating room than a doctor's office. It had a solid metal examining table in the middle of the space with nothing covering it, not even waxy white paper. The walls were red brick, and the floor was concrete. It felt cold, as if the air conditioning had been turned way down. The lights were bright fluorescent overhead, and there was a high lab stool placed in front of the metal examining table. It was quite a contrast to the soothing waiting area.

Before the doctor appeared, I put on the paper gown the nurse had given me with the opening at the front. I sat down on the metal table. I shivered. My fingers were freezing and looked like they were turning blue. I could tell, based on the setup in the room, I was to be a patient lying on the table in my embarrassing gown, and the doctor would be in charge. I was suddenly terrified that I was so vulnerable. It felt ominously similar to the situation with the ultrasound doctor.

There was a knock at the door. I whispered, "Come in." A woman in her thirties, close in age to me, entered the room. She had long straight brown hair and a bright red silk shirt that was open at the neck, revealing too much cleavage for this sterile environment. She confidently walked over to me in black stiletto heels. I flinched. It was then that I noticed she had a large gold cross gently pulsing on her chest like a steady heartbeat as she walked. As if the entire setting wasn't already too much, I was surprised to have a doctor so visibly display her religion in a medical office.

She shoved her hand toward me, requiring a formal and strong handshake, "Hello." She didn't say her name, didn't attempt to pronounce mine, and got right down to business. "Please lie down so I can look at you." I obediently lay down flat, shivering as I lowered my body. She looked at my stomach, not even touching me. She left my gown open over my belly and inched herself toward my head as her spiky shoes *clickety clicked* loudly on the cement floor. I felt so insignificant and inconsequential, almost irrelevant. "I've read the report from your doctor and have looked extensively at the ultrasound you had done a few days ago." She moved the metal stool closer to my head and sat down. She was now towering above me. "Things don't look good. I can't tell exactly what the problem is, but there is a dark shadow in the lower belly of the baby. It indicates there might be something wrong." She didn't blink or take a breath. "There is nothing we can do. We'll monitor your pregnancy and wait until the birth to confirm our suspicions."

She couldn't be saying this. She was supposed to tell me that everything was fine. She talked for several minutes using the same words as the ultrasound doctor. They floated above me until she said something I clearly heard.

"I understand you are planning on moving to Japan for the birth. I am adamantly against this." The word *adamant* hit me. Who was she to be adamant about anything related to my baby?

"The Japanese medical system is not capable of helping a woman with a high-risk pregnancy. You will be making a mistake. We need you here. We need to be in control."

With each word, she leaned closer to me, hovering above my face. As she said *control*, her gold cross dangled over my face, almost grazing the top of my nose. Then, as quickly as it began, she stood up, making the rubber legs of the stool *thump, thump, thump* across the floor. I didn't have time to form a question; she was at the door in an instant. She held it open, exposing me to the hallway, and glanced back at me, saying, "make an appointment in a month," and walked out.

My reaction to her was intense and immediate. I wanted out. I ripped off the gown and violently yanked on my clothes, completely lost in my fury. This appointment was supposed to clarify everything for us. Instead, she made things worse, exponentially worse. Now, not only was I uneasy about the baby, but I didn't have a doctor I trusted that could provide the kind of information and care I needed. I literally ran past the receptionist, making my mind up as I fled. This clinic wasn't going to touch our baby or me.

I didn't agree with her denigration of the medical system in Japan. Fred had spoken to Northwest Airlines colleagues he trusted who had recently given birth in Tokyo. There was one doctor in particular who delivered most of the babies for foreigners. He had gone to medical school at Yale and had his own American-style office in the heart of Tokyo. Fred heard glowing

14

reports about the team of nurses who worked with him. His colleagues confirmed the doctor had all of the latest medical equipment right in his office.

By the time I got home, I was even more eager to move to Japan. If nothing else, I held onto the belief that doctors in Tokyo wouldn't speak to a patient in such a condescending way.

There might be something wrong with our baby, but we'd be finding out what it was in Japan. With our decision made, Fred left for Tokyo.

After all these years, one thing from that appointment has haunted me. Having that doctor's large gold cross hang closer and closer to me as she became more animated about what I had to do, shook me. I kept wondering if she was so focused on controlling my pregnancy because of her medical beliefs, or was it her religious ones? Instead of wanting to perform more ultrasounds or more tests or give more of a diagnosis, did she believe it was God's will that would determine what would happen to our baby?

Chapter 5

With Fred gone and so far away, the conviction I had about our decision to move to Japan began to waver. I tried not to worry. I rubbed my belly all the time, assuring the baby that we'd take care of her no matter what. I found myself talking out loud, using different voices like Obi-Wan Kenobi with his authoritative whispery voice, "Remember...the Force will be with you, always." It didn't help my stress level, but it served as a good distraction and made Emma giggle.

I took Emma to her pediatrician to make certain all of her immunizations were up-to-date and that we had her medical records to give to her new doctor in Tokyo.

Two-and-a-half-year-old Emma strutted proudly into the examining room, greeting the doctor with, "Hi! We are moving to To-key-yo, Japan. Mommy has my baby sister in her tummy. We are taking her with us." The doctor chuckled.

Emma was incredibly smart and constantly delighted us. By the time she was one year old, she was speaking in full sentences. By the time she was two, she had memorized every word on every page of over 50 children's books. She'd eagerly grab a book from the overflowing pile and sit up straight, holding it in her lap. She could recite the stories of *Babar*, *The Cat in the Hat*, *Blueberries for Sal*, and her favorite, *Green Eggs and Ham*. Emma turned the pages while saying the exact words on each page, *"Do you like green eggs and ham? I do not like them, Sam-I-am."* Then she'd pause, shake her head vigorously, stick out her tongue, and say each word with a staccato, *"I Do Not Like Green Eggs and Ham!"*

The doctor told me what we already knew. "Emma is a very healthy, extremely intelligent little girl. It is rare for a two-year-old to speak in complete sentences and to have such a broad vocabulary." He bent down and gave her a high five. "Emma, you are ready to make your big move. Go and learn some Japanese for me!"

I trusted and liked her doctor, so at the end of our appointment, I told him about the baby. "The doctors are saying there is a dark shadow in her lower abdomen, and she might be missing a kidney." I quickly added, "They also say it might be nothing."

He looked at me and smiled. "Sarah, it's always a bit difficult to see deeply inside when the baby is so small. Kidneys aren't easy to spot, and lots of people grow up never knowing they are missing one." I forced out the air I had been holding in. I had another data point from a trusted doctor on the positive side of the very precarious teeter-totter balancing which way our lives would go.

During those weeks of waiting, I was exhausted and consumed by worry. Finally, in the middle of one of my sleepless nights, I forced myself to realize no matter what the outcome was, we wouldn't know anything about the health of the baby until she was born. All the doctors were in agreement about that. So, I shifted my thinking away from the baby to our exciting new life in Tokyo.

I went back to my regular obstetrician after the frightening high-risk one. He knew I had seen the doctor there, had gotten her report, and wondered why I was back. "I want you to know we are going forward with our plans to move to Tokyo. At the other clinic, I was told there was nothing that could be done for the baby until she was born, so I want to see you instead." I never told him about my experience; it wouldn't change my situation. He said he'd be happy to see me until we left. After that, he did all the monthly tests and visits that happened during any pregnancy. He always confirmed the baby was growing and moving as she should.

Emma and I missed Fred. He was such an important part of our stability and happiness. It was hard to have him gone. Emma adored her father. She loved to ride high on his shoulders on our family outings, kicking her feet up in the air and pointing out everything we passed. Fred introduced her to *Blues Clues*, and they sat together on the couch animatedly figuring out the clues.

Fred was a math major at Macalester, and it felt like he was always a step or more ahead of anyone else. One day during senior year, he said, "Sarah, I figured out that 1+1 actually does equal two."

"What did you say?"

"I know you know that, but I found a way to *prove* it." He had a sparkle in his eye at the complex problem he had solved.

He was tall and thin and had been a sailor, swimmer, and basketball player when he was young. Electronic music was a passion. He created his own in the style of the French master, Jean-Michel Jarre. Fred was trilingual and had a flair for writing in any language. Love notes and poems with decorative drawings often appeared in my student post office box.

He loved Belgium, but even as a young boy, the thrill of America tugged at him. There was something exotic and tantalizing about it. When the opportunity to attend college in the U.S. came along, he embraced it and never looked back. America was the land of opportunity. It ultimately even provided a way to explore his other passion, Japan.

Fred's roommate at Macalester was from Japan. Hiro was a joyful person who was at Mac for a year of study abroad, coming from a very prestigious university in Tokyo. He tantalized both of us with stories of his culture and country, so when we arrived in Japan, our friendship with him deepened. Fred spoke at his wedding, and he and his new wife helped us to get to know our new home.

On our weekly landline phone calls, I could hear the excitement in Fred's voice. "Sarah, Hiro has introduced me to so many things. You are absolutely going to love Tokyo. One wild thing is that I pick up lunch on my way to work at a *konbini* convenience store, like 7-Eleven."

I interrupted, "What? 7-Eleven? Do they have hotdogs turning on that questionably hygienic rotisserie at the front counter? Yikes!"

"It sounds strange, but the stores are great, immaculate. They have sushi, can you believe it, at a convenience store? I love their ramen noodles and *onigiri*, rice balls with fish inside. The restaurants are incredible. Since I don't know any Japanese, it is strange sometimes to try and order. I use lots of hand gestures. It is all delicious, *Oishi*. That's my new Japanese word. The subway is spotless, and inside the train, it's quiet. I'm pretty sure there are rules for kids about not standing on the seats or running in the subway trains."

"Oh no! Emma has her own rules, and they don't involve sitting still!"

Fred was thrilled with his new job and was thriving in the dynamic environment of an American company abroad. In his role running finance and administration for Northwest Airlines in the Pacific Region, he not only spent time in the Tokyo office, but he traveled extensively to support the general managers all around Asia. Fred had never been one to just do his job; he dove in and swam deep. He often worked long hours spending parts of the Christmas and Easter holidays at the office doing last-minute analysis or finishing a report. In his new role in Tokyo, just as he had in Minnesota, he happily devoted himself to work.

The first week in May was a whirlwind, with everything needing to get wrapped up before we left on the seventh. I had my last doctor's appointment in Minneapolis. The doctor started the appointment in his usual clinical way. "The baby is breech, with her head up. It is quite normal, with six weeks remaining in the pregnancy. Most babies start to turn and put their heads into position as they get ready to be born. You should be fine on the flight since you are still several weeks from your due date." Then he paused.

He looked me in the eye with compassion and kindness. "I have something I want to say. Most importantly, I wish you good luck. I want this to go well for you because you have more enthusiasm and determination than anyone I have ever met. We still don't know if there is anything wrong, especially since it seems that the baby is growing exactly as she should. I really want this to turn out well for you." He handed me a letter saying I could still travel on an international flight.

Fred returned home to much fanfare. Emma and I stood waiting for him waving small American and Japanese flags at the exit to customs and immigration at the Minneapolis airport. He ran out. Emma exuberantly jumped into his arms with the flags flying in every direction. She talked all the way home about our preparations for the move. "Daddy, our house is messy with stuff for Japan. Mommy gave me my own suitcase. I practiced getting into it. I fit! It was cozy."

Fred looked at me, astonished. "Emma, I can't believe how well you are speaking! You've grown so much since I left."

It was fun to hear Emma express the excitement she and I had been talking about while Fred was away. She pointed to my belly. "Look at the baby! That's my sister. She is so big. Mommy and I have been picking out names. I want to name her *Sam I am*." Fred and I looked at each other and laughed.

I quit my job. Teaching and being part of a school thrilled me. I got a kick out of middle school students, always doing my best to make learning Spanish exceptionally fun. After seven years at Saint Paul Academy and Summit School, it made me sad to leave it all behind. I had accomplished a lot and matured as a person and educator, but having this next adventure for our family tugged at me enough that it felt like the right time to go.

The moving van arrived. We watched all of our belongings get loaded onto a truck, knowing it would then be loaded onto a plane and flown all the way to Japan. I couldn't wait to see our things on the other side. Another family bought our house three days after we put it on the market. They were overjoyed to raise their family there. We were happy to let it go.

On May seventh, 2000, we headed to the airport. My parents came with us. We were sad to leave them. They had been an integral part of our lives in St. Paul. They took care of Emma, had meals with us often, and were our greatest fans. It was hard on all of us that we had chosen to move, especially since we had another baby on the way. Goodbye felt more permanent than it had at any other time in my life. For college, I had gone half a block away. For graduate school, I had gone halfway across the country. But this time, our entire family was moving halfway around the world. As the three of us walked down the jetway, the others boarding the plane gave us space. We were obviously doing something quite significant. Fred picked up Emma so she could wave and blow kisses to Grandma and Grandpa. She said softly, and then louder and louder, "Goodbye, Grandma and Grandpa, I'm moving to Japan. I love you." Then we disappeared inside the 747 airplane. Our next step in an airport would be in Tokyo.

Once we were settled in our seats, I tucked the letter from my doctor into my passport. It confirmed that I could still fly, but at seven-and-a-half months, I was at the limit. Emma seemed at peace about the trip, but I was glad we had purchased many small presents for her to open during the twelve-hour flight. Fred excitedly grabbed my hand as the plane went down the runway. Japan, here we come!

Chapter 6

It felt like the flight was closer to twenty-four hours than twelve. When we finally arrived, there was no waving, no blowing kisses, and no grandparents. We were bleary-eyed and exhausted. As we walked off the plane, I focused on putting one foot in front of the other until we saw the Japanese stamps on our passports. That made it real. After everything that we had gone through, all of the doctors and worries, and stress, we had made it happen for our family. We were about to start our adventure in Japan.

Fred got our luggage from the carousel and pulled out a cart. He placed all six suitcases and carry-on items on it. He set Emma on top, like a princess on her throne. The Japanese agents glanced at our belongings, smiled at Emma, and waved us through.

It dawned on me as the glass doors opened from customs that aside from *arigato* (thank you), I didn't know a single word of Japanese. Even though I was a language teacher, I hadn't focused on learning the language. I was going to be walking around the streets of Tokyo telling people, 'Thank you.' I silently nodded my head, congratulating myself because if you had to have one thing to say, "thank you," worked.

During the two-hour taxi ride from Narita airport, Emma and I were now wide awake and riveted, looking out the window at the last of the evening light. At first, the buildings were huge, towering, gleaming skyscrapers that you'd find in any city. As we traveled further, the buildings got smaller and finally settled into one or two stories. There were storefronts and homes next to each other; most were modern and comprehensible to a foreign eye. Others looked like they were from a hundred years ago, with dark wood roofs and sliding wooden windows covered in white shoji paper so you couldn't look inside. I spotted one of Fred's famous *konbini*, 7-Eleven, on a corner and gasped that it was right there in front of me.

The taxi finally stopped. We arrived at 17-10 Sarugaku-cho #1A, Shibuya-ku, 1500033, our new address. We got out and stopped at our apartment's dark green, very heavy, earthquake-proof front door. Fred had the key ready. As he swung open the door, he held out his arms in triumph. "Welcome home!"

Overcome by what we had just done, tears were streaming down my face. I hesitated before taking a step inside. Emma and Fred were next to me, we were together, and I grabbed their hands. A thrilling shiver raced through my body and burst out in a resounding cheer. I threw our arms into the air and started whopping and hollering and jumping up and down. We were here.

Fred told me the Northwest Airlines compound was gigantic, which was unheard of in Tokyo. Not only did it have an apartment building for all of the foreign employees, but it had a yard the size of a soccer field, complete with a forest with spectacular tall trees and boulders at one end. Northwest had been given the property by the Japanese government in exchange for helping to establish Japan Airlines after World War II.

Since the massive piece of land was legendary in the city of Tokyo, I wanted to see the yard right away. We walked through our small living room and slid open the floor-to-ceiling glass doors leading out to the terrace. I inhaled deeply, thinking there would be fresh air. Instead, I was struck by a very pungent scent. "What is that awful stink? It smells like vomit!" Fred was behind me. Stepping forward, the smell got worse, and I crinkled my nose. With the streetlights shining down, I could see a row of trees in front of me. I bent down and picked up a fan-shaped leaf from the ground. It was from a Ginkgo tree.

From behind me, Fred yelled, "It turns out there are male Ginkgo trees and female ones. In the spring, the females have berries, and they have an unusual scent. Welcome to spring in your Japanese home!"

I ran back inside the apartment to get away from the smell. Fred quickly slid the doors closed and motioned for me to come into the galley kitchen, "Look, it's small, but there are plenty of cupboards, and the stove and refrigerator are American-sized." He opened the cupboards and drawers and showed me the silverware, plates, bowls, pots, and pans that he had rented for us, knowing our shipment would not arrive from Minnesota for several weeks. He had also rented a couch, television, dining room table and chairs, and beds for each of the rooms.

Fred walked down the hallway with Emma, "Look! This is your room. Soon all of your things from home will be right here. What do you think?"

With a radiant smile on her face, Emma started twirling and shouted, "I love it."

While Emma and I did a bit of unpacking, Fred went to the *konbini* near the apartment and returned with sushi, fresh sandwiches, rice ball *onigiri*, chips, and soba noodles. He also bought many different kinds of Japanese bottled drinks. It was a feast! "If all Japanese food is this good, we'll be very happy here."

He laughed in a teasing way, knowing this was nothing compared to the culinary treasures we would find in our new home.

That first night we all stayed awake until 9:00 pm, pleased that even with the time difference from Minnesota, we were going to sleep at a normal Japanese bedtime. We put on pajamas, brushed our teeth, and fell soundly asleep in our new beds. The only problem was that small children don't know about jet lag or how to manage those first waking seconds when you need to slowly roll over in bed and fall back asleep. Emma stood next to my side of the bed. "Mommy, I'm awake."

I groggily said, "Can you try to go back to sleep?" I didn't look at the clock.

"No, Mommy, I'm awake."

I made myself glance and saw it was midnight. I rolled over to look at Fred. He was peacefully sleeping. I didn't disturb him, and I got my very pregnant body up and out of my warm and comfortable bed.

I hauled myself down the hallway to the television I had noticed the night before in the corner of the living room. I thought maybe I could turn on the equivalent of Sesame Street or some other children's show. I turned the knob, and on came sumo wrestling! I stood flabbergasted. Unexpectedly, a hiccup mixed with a chirp escaped from my mouth. I had heard of sumo wrestling but had never seen it in action. The humongous girth of the men, the long black hair pulled tightly on top of their heads, the revealing loin cloth, and the oversized feet were all striking. Then I remembered Emma was standing next to me. The look on her very adorable face was priceless, a mix of horror and fascination. At midnight on our first evening in Japan, I was not ready to tackle the topic of sumo wrestling. I turned off the television. It was only after a second in the dark room that I realized it was going to be a very long night.

I turned to Emma, gave her a wrapped present left over from the plane ride, and we began to play. It was a nice night together, but I was relieved to see Fred emerge from the bedroom at 6:00 am. "Did you guys sleep well?"

Chapter 7

We showered to get the short night behind us and went outside. It was a Tuesday morning. With Emma walking between us, we started to explore our new neighborhood, Daikanyama. There were people everywhere, walking on the sidewalks and driving in the streets. People were in pairs and alone and were all dressed up. Men had on dark suit jackets with ties, and women were in black skirts with heels. There were students easily identified because of their school uniforms and backpacks. Fred leaned over and said, "Everyone is expected to dress up when they are outside. They have to keep up appearances and blend in. There is a gardener at the apartment complex, Kamura-san. He arrives each morning in a suit jacket and then changes into his coveralls for work. The Japanese show respect for others by dressing their best when out in public."

Fred had heard about a bakery only a few doors down from the apartment building. He suggested we walk. As we approached the bakery, the smell of yeast and flour, and butter made my mouth water. Emma jumped up and down. "It smells great! Bread!"

The bakery was called the Daikanyama Pantry and was a little taste of heaven. The croissants were flaky on the outside and soft on the inside, and the baguette had a crunch that required your jaw to get involved in that first bite. We sampled one of each of the items we had purchased and decided to take the rest home with us, walking slowly back to the apartment feeling satisfied. We had experienced Japan. We were ready for the day to end, except it was only 9:00 in the morning.

Fred suggested we go to a shop he knew and buy pillows since he had not yet gotten regular-sized ones for our beds. We walked to *Ebisu* Station, purchased our train tickets, ascended the escalator to the tracks, and saw it was spotless. People were standing in straight lines and were waiting quietly to board. Inside the cars, everyone was sitting on immaculate upholstered seats. Some were reading the newspaper, having folded it meticulously so it wouldn't touch the person next to them. No one ate, no one drank, and people were quiet.

The train was full, yet the seats reserved for handicapped or expectant mothers were left open. A man near us indicated I should come and sit down. I smiled and used my only word, "*arigato*," loudly enunciating each syllable, a-ri-ga-to, through my gushing excitement. I think I scared him, but I was beaming. Fred and I celebrated with a smile and wink. I could officially now communicate in Japanese.

We got off the train at *Shibuya* Station. It is quintessential Tokyo. Upon exiting the station, there is a confusingly complicated crossing. One minute, cars rush by in seven different directions, all moving without incident. The next minute, there are literally thousands of people flooding the streets with no one bumping into each other. All around the crossing are skyscrapers with blaring video screens advertising things you could understand and lots of things you couldn't. I would never have imagined it then, but within months I'd be confidently driving through that crossing myself.

Over the noisy street sounds, I giddily shouted to Fred, "We are here in *Shibuya*. We are here with Emma!" We each grabbed her hand as we made our way across the gigantic street.

We were headed to Tokyu (You, not Tok-Yo) Hands. It was hidden in the back streets only a few minutes from the station. Fred already knew how to find it, which was critical because I couldn't see a single street name, and it felt like we were walking through a maze to get there. Tokyu Hands is the Japanese version of Target, Walmart, and Home Depot; all rolled into one. There are eight floors, with every numbered floor also having an A, B, and C level. In other words, there are twenty-four total floors twenty-four!

We had a very specific item to purchase, pillows. It seemed like it was going to be almost impossible to find, so we just started walking up the stairs. When we finally got to the eighth floor, level B, we found the bedding and the pillows. With Emma squishing each one, flattening them with her head, and loudly exclaiming, "This one is best!" we quickly picked out three.

A cashier stood attentively, waiting for us at the register. I realized *arigato* was not going to be enough to buy anything. I turned to Fred. He was our expert in Japanese since he knew several more words than my one. He waited while the clerk rang up the total and showed him the amount. Fred had cash and paid in yen.

The clerk spent the next five minutes painstakingly wrapping our three pillows. First he put in tissue paper, then wrapped them in a plastic bag, finally he used an oversized paper bag that fit all three. A cardboard holder was crimped over the bag handles so it could be comfortably carried all the way home. The clerk came around to our side of the cash register, bowed deeply, and gave us the gigantic bag. I then said, "*Arigato.*" Nailed it!

After completing our pillow-buying adventure, we were hungry. We decided this one time we could cement the American stereotype and disgrace ourselves by eating at McDonald's. We waited in line and ordered from the menu by pointing. I had actually not eaten at a McDonald's for years, and Emma had never been to one. We laughed at ourselves, hoping this would be our first and last meal at McDonald's in Japan. It wasn't.

After being out and exploring all day long, we were able to get a much better night of sleep which was important because we were going to see Dr. Fuji, the Japanese obstetrician, in the morning.

Chapter 8

We got up early, taking Emma to be with Colleen, a friend of Fred's from the Minnesota office of Northwest. She lives in Tokyo with her husband and new baby. She was one of the people Fred had spoken to about Dr. Fuji and his practice. I immediately felt a deep appreciation for her. She took sleepy Emma for the morning.

As we approached the doctor's office, my all too familiar chill of apprehension returned, this time with a vengeance. I tried to overpower it, and with each step toward the office, I told myself *this would be fine. This would be fine. This would be fine.*

The waiting room had English language magazines and comfortable chairs. We were immediately at ease. Fred found us seats, and I walked up to the window, "Hi, I'm Sarah Deschamps. I have an appointment with Dr. Fuji. I have all of my pregnancy records from my doctor in the U.S." I handed the bulky bag to the receptionist and sat down.

Four other women were in the waiting area, all of them at differing stages of pregnancy. As I looked at them, seeing relaxed women who appeared not to have a care in the world, I desperately wished I could finish my pregnancy looking like them. I sat, absolutely still, waiting for my name to be called. *This will be fine.*

Almost to the second of our appointed time, we heard, "Sa-rah Day-Shaun!" They got it right! It was a sign this was going to go well. I jumped up more enthusiastically than I intended. The nurse led us to the doctor's office.

In front of us was an oversized dark mahogany desk. As I glanced around the office, I saw wooden bookshelves filled with medical journals, all in English. Interspersed around the room hung framed medical degrees, awards, and honors that had obviously been bestowed upon this doctor. He clearly seemed to be qualified. Out the window, I could see the statuesque Tokyo Tower, which was a symbol of the price the doctor paid to be in such a prestigious location. All of this conveyed the status this doctor had in Tokyo. He wouldn't let us down.

The side door to his office opened, and he stepped in regally, head held high, white authoritative lab coat with his name stenciled above the pocket, fine black wool pants, and glistening wing-tipped shoes. He looked straight into our eyes and formally shook our hands. With an American accent, he said, "I am Doctor Fuji. I am so glad to meet you. I know you arrived in Tokyo a couple of days ago. Hope it was a good trip." I liked him. He gestured for us to sit in the two highbacked armchairs in front of his massive desk. He had all of my medical records spread out in front of him and my ultrasound images on his computer screen.

Fred sat up straight in his chair, and I watched as his fingers gripped the arms. We were both filled with a mix of worry and hope.

The doctor exhaled loudly, seemingly choosing his words carefully. "There seems to be something in the lower abdomen of the fetus. I have spent considerable time looking at it and trying to understand your records from Minnesota. I can't quite tell what the issue is. I have an ultrasound machine in the next room. I'd like to have a look myself."

After the high-risk doctor in Minneapolis refused to do anything, I was relieved Dr. Fuji wanted to see for himself. He motioned for us to come into the ultrasound room next to his office. I squeezed Fred's hand. Moving to Japan was the right thing to do. This doctor would take care of us. Maybe this time we'd get the news we wanted to hear.

The room was warm, and I felt comfortable. I climbed up on the table covered in fake green leather, with the paper crinkling underneath me. I lifted my shirt over my belly. He neatly put towels over my clothes, applied the warm jelly to my stomach, and touched the ultrasound wand to my skin.

The baby jumped into view. She had grown, so it was easier to make out her body in the images. Fred smiled. The doctor began to use the full capabilities of the ultrasound machine, and just as had been done in

Minnesota, we started to see the colorful patterns of blood flow in and out of the heart and brain and circulation throughout her tiny body. This time felt different. I had Fred with me, and he could ask questions if we didn't understand. We were a team. We would figure it out together.

Dr. Fuji looked and probed and had me roll from one side to the other. Photos spit out of the machine as he continued to type, measure, and move the wand over my stomach. He sighed, removed the wand, wiped the gel from my belly, and helped me sit up. "Please step down from the table, and let's go back into my office."

With no embellishment whatsoever, he said, "it looks to me like the brain and heart of the baby are not functioning properly. She is missing one kidney, and something is wrong with her abdomen. I have no medical training for these complexities, and my delivery hospital is not prepared to assist you if there are extreme interventions needed when the baby is born. I was holding my breath, not able to believe what he was saying.

"I cannot continue to see you," he went on. "I'm referring you to the best level three trauma hospital in Tokyo. It specializes in obstetrics. It is called *Joshi Idai Byoin*. They are exceptional, and you will be well cared for there."

He didn't look at me. I guess that bad news is hard to deliver in any country. "I'm going to write a letter of introduction for you to this hospital. You will need to present this piece of paper to the front desk when you arrive, and they will help you see a specialist who can understand the issues much better than I can." This was not fine, definitely not fine.

Fred and I looked at each other, and I could see my fear reflected on his face. The doctor pulled out a small blue piece of paper. It looked like an origami square. I desperately wanted to take the paper, fold it into a crane, and make a wish to have all of this fly away. I looked out his window, picturing it out there, far away from us.

He wrote Japanese characters in straight lines, top to bottom, right to left, across the page. It was a note I'd never be able to read. He didn't fold it or put it in an envelope. He stood behind his desk and gently grasped the corners of the paper. With extreme formality, he bowed as he handed it to Fred.

31

Somehow, my medical reports and ultrasound images wound up in a bag in my hand. He came around to our side of the desk and firmly shook our hands. We left the office with our heads hanging low, stunned and scared into silence.

We had been in Tokyo for less than 48 hours. I had not even unpacked our suitcases. As we left the building, I felt the air become thin. Suddenly, I stumbled. The birth I had been counting on, with a talented Japanese doctor at an American-style hospital, was gone. The enormity of our situation overwhelmed me. I had a baby inside me that could have complex brain, heart, and abdomen issues, and now I had no doctor who could manage this complicated pregnancy, neither in the U.S. nor in Japan.

I sat down on the steps of the office. "What just happened?" Fred grabbed and squeezed my hand in unity.

At that moment, the baby started to kick. Instinctively, I rubbed the place on my stomach, realizing she was alive and was with us. As I touched her, it dawned on me that no matter what we had learned, our only option was to go to a level three trauma hospital, and it was in Japan.

Chapter 9

The next morning, we took Emma again to Colleen's apartment. Our little girl was looking bedraggled and overwhelmed by the sights, sounds, and lack of her parents' attention. I had my medical records in a bag, and the blue origami note from Dr. Fuji held tightly in my hand. Fred put out his arm to hail a taxi.

I had written down the words for the name of the hospital that Dr. Fuji had told us and said them to the driver, "Jo-shi I-dai B-yo-in." Luckily, that was all the driver needed. I paid attention to the taxi meter going up and up until I lost count. There were so many zeros on display. We were far from our neighborhood, over 30 minutes away. Unlike our two days of walking in the city where I had seen bakeries and restaurants and storefronts that felt familiar, there was nothing familiar to hold onto the further we drove. Not only was everything foreign, but I was too.

As we stepped out of the taxi, my heart stopped. The hospital was an old rundown building. It looked like it was from the 1960s. It hadn't had a remodel, ever. After being in Dr. Fuji's office, the sight of the building shocked us. Our baby was going to be born in this hospital in the middle of nowhere.

We walked through what appeared to be the front door of the hospital, but there wasn't a welcome desk at the entrance and no one standing there to help. It was dark inside. The floors were dark green and black linoleum, and the walls were dark brown. We wandered down a hallway and found an open area with wooden tables placed around the perimeter. There were small pieces of paper strewn across the tables and pens with chains attaching them so they couldn't be removed. Everything was in Japanese, and there wasn't a clue to indicate what we were supposed to do. In the middle of the room, several people were sitting on metal folding chairs meticulously placed in rows. It was there that we saw two receptionists with their heads peeking over a very high counter.

Fred and I walked very closely together, taking small hesitant steps toward them. I looked down and noticed I had squeezed my hand so tightly that I had crumpled the blue piece of origami paper from Dr. Fuji. I bowed my head in shame and handed the paper to one of the ladies. She took it and pointed to a box in the middle of the counter with numbered pieces of paper. The receptionist was staring at me. I backed away from her and picked up a number. We were eighteen.

It occurred to me a moment too late that I no longer had Dr. Fuji's note. I thought of that piece of paper as our lifeline. It couldn't get lost. I panicked, but I had no Japanese words to explain. With wild eyes, I looked at Fred. He gently opened my clenched fist holding the bag full of my medical records. He lifted it onto the counter. The receptionist took it and motioned for us to go and sit down.

We sat. We were the only foreigners in the room, and it was silent. There weren't magazines, tables, or anything comfortable or reassuring about the space. The rusty chairs bumped and squeaked along the linoleum floor if you moved, so no one moved.

After ten minutes of this awkwardness, I saw someone with a lab coat appear. The receptionist spoke out loud, and someone stood up. I tried to understand exactly what had been said. The person walked up to the receptionist's desk and gave her the small numbered piece of paper. Ah ha! To see a doctor, they call your number. We had a number. So, you need someone in a white lab coat to appear before your number is called.

Then I remembered we don't speak any Japanese. We had no way of knowing how to say or hear the number eighteen, our lottery number for the day. We also didn't know which doctor we were waiting for. An hour went by and then another half hour. We sat in silence. Sometimes numbers were called, and people came forward. We determined it was completely random which number was called, so we couldn't rely on numbers being said in any kind of order.

34

Another person in a lab coat appeared out of nowhere. The receptionist called out a number. No one got up. We saw heads turning to look at us. I could feel the heat rushing up my neck. Were they waiting for us? After another second, Fred and I looked at each other, shrugged, and stood up. There was an audible sigh.

We went up to the counter, I tipped my number eighteen toward the receptionist, and she nodded. Fred and I hugged. We had crossed a cultural barrier, and without a single word of Japanese, we had figured it out. The only problem was all we were allowed to do was follow this man in a white lab coat. We didn't know who he was or what he did. He spoke no English.

We went up a flight of incredibly narrow stairs. After gingerly climbing up two steep flights, we reached a long hallway.

We entered an examination room. It was similar to any other, with a metal table in the corner, a small desk, and two chairs along the wall. There was a window that looked out on electrical wires with large gray birds perched on them. The man motioned for us to sit down and held out his hand for us to wait again. He bowed and left. This time it was Fred and me alone with the door closed. We tried to recalibrate where we were. Both of us started talking at the same time.

"Oh my god, this crazy place is our only option. We can't leave. There isn't another hospital that will accept us."

"This is ancient and backward and creepy." Then a woman in a white lab coat entered the room. She gently put out her hand for us to shake and said in English, "Welcome to Joshi Idai. I have read the letter of introduction from Dr. Fuji. You can be assured you will get excellent care in this hospital. The hospital looks old, especially since you have obviously come from the U.S., but we have the best equipment and can handle whatever needs your baby has. We'd like to proceed right away with some tests so we can be prepared for the birth of your child." I was shaking. I grabbed Fred's hand and squeezed. She was speaking in English. She was kind and spoke in a thoughtful and knowledgeable voice. He squeezed back. We had a new way of communicating.

35

She paused before continuing, "I have arranged for you to have a full ultrasound. Dr. Fuji wrote down that he thought there were brain and heart issues. We will scan them to know exactly what to expect. We understand it looks like there is a missing kidney and a problem in the lower abdomen. We will look at these as well." She then explained I should follow, and she told Fred to wait in the room. I desperately wanted him with me. I didn't want to be alone again, but it happened so fast that I got up and followed.

The doctor brought me down another long hall. I stopped and stared in disbelief. The ultrasound room was no room at all. There was a black tarp stapled to the ceiling. It draped down the walls of the hallway like my blanket forts did when I was a child. Awkwardly, off to the side, there was a jerry-rigged opening in the tarp. I could see someone in the space and what looked like an ultrasound machine next to a metal table.

The doctor smiled warmly, indicating I should enter the tarped area and lie down on the table. The ultrasound technician didn't speak English, but the doctor sat right next to me and reassuringly explained the now-familiar procedure. I tilted my head down to my chest and covered my eyes with my hand. I knew whether in English or Japanese, I wouldn't understand the images on the screen.

I replayed a conversation that had consumed me since we left Dr. Fuji's office. I heard my Minnesota obstetrician saying, "Sarah, no one would do this. I don't know of a single other expectant mother who would make an international move to a place where they don't speak English."

Then the high-risk doctor's voice came thundering at me, "the Japanese medical system is not capable of helping a woman with a high-risk pregnancy. You'd be making a mistake." We hadn't listened. We defiantly dismissed the doctors in Minnesota and threw aside their warnings. Instead, we thought we knew what was best. We had chosen Japan for the birth of our daughter. We believed that the doctors and medical system were exponentially better, yet here I was, alone, frightened, and lying in a makeshift ultrasound room, stuck in a dire situation. We had brought this on ourselves.

Then I remembered Fred was with me in the hospital, and he'd be with me for the birth. He'd protect the baby and me. We'd live through this together, hand in hand.

"Sarah-san, you are okay," said the doctor as she lightly touched my face. I was squeezing my eyes shut, gritting my teeth, and clenching the table so hard I had lost all feeling in my fingers.

"It's all right," she said softly. "We are going to figure this out together. We already have lots of information. I bet this feels so unusual, but you can trust us. The doctors and many of the nurses and technicians at this hospital are trained not only in Japan but abroad as well. All of the doctors speak English, and we are specialized in high-risk pregnancies."

I opened one eye, then the other. I saw her leaning over me, not with a cross or in a condescending way like the doctor in Minneapolis, but in a caring way. She wanted me to know I was in the right place. They knew exactly how to care for our baby and me.

The technician gently wiped the gel off of my stomach, and the doctor helped me to sit up. "Let's go back to the room where your husband is so I can tell you both what we found."

When we got to the room, Fred's relief was palpable. He smiled tentatively and mouthed, "are you okay?"

I hadn't spoken since I left him almost an hour before. I was surprised to hear words coming out of my mouth. "I'm scared." As I sat next to him, I remembered how gentle and reassuring the doctor had been and added in a shaking voice, "maybe they know what they are doing?"

He grabbed and squeezed my hand. "We saw absolutely no issues with the baby's brain." Relief. Something good. Finally. Something positive. "We also saw no issues in the baby's heart. There were no missed beats, no murmurs, and nothing to indicate that blood flow was not normal. I'm sorry Dr. Fuji made you worry, but it is always better to check. We have experts trained exclusively in ultrasound for high-risk pregnancies in this hospital. We trust this analysis."

We hugged each other. We couldn't believe it. Two of the most critical and worrisome issues were not problems at all. Maybe we would be fine after all?

The doctor had more to tell us. "Just as everyone else seems to have observed, there is a dark shadow in the baby's abdomen. We are a level three trauma hospital, and I have seen other babies that have had this same dark shadow. Some ended up having problems, and others had none. We have as much information as possible with all of your records and the extensive ultrasound we did today. The baby seems to be growing, and even though she is still breech, we'll manage when you give birth. I'll give you my phone number here at the hospital, and please call when you go into labor. We'll be ready for you when you arrive." She handed me a piece of paper with a phone number on it.

She paused a little too long and looked right at me. "Sarah-san, when you go into labor, you must come here alone, without Fred-san. We do not allow anyone other than medical staff in the delivery room. We keep it sterile. I think I understand you have a two-year-old daughter, and we don't allow small children in the maternity ward at all. It is hospital policy. You will have to come alone."

Fred wouldn't be with me for the birth. He couldn't protect the baby and me or care for us. We wouldn't live through this dreadful situation together, hand in hand, after all. The color drained from his face. He was as stunned as I was. It was clear that this hospital had rules, and we were to obey them.

I stood motionless on the sidewalk outside the hospital. I wanted to get out of this country and get away from this disaster. Even worse, I knew I couldn't. I was past the date in my pregnancy when an airline permitted me to travel, and with all of my risks, no doctor would write a letter to allow me to fly anyway. It was too late.

I saw Fred put out his hand for a taxi and say something to the driver after we got in, and the taxi drove further and further away. As I stared out the window, Fred gently spoke to me. "Sarah, what we learned about the baby was good news. There is nothing wrong with her brain and nothing wrong with her heart. Today, we didn't get any new information. This doctor, in a very kind way, said that she had seen other babies with this same dark shadow. She said some end up having problems, and others have none. We still might be in the category where there are no issues whatsoever. Our baby might be just fine." He softly massaged my belly.

"I'm going to say something that I know will be hard to hear. I'm wrestling with what they said about me not being able to be with you. I don't think there is any option here. Rules in Japan can't be broken; I've already learned that the hard way in the office." I didn't look at him.

He touched the side of my face to turn it away from the window and pulled both of my hands inside of his. "Sarah, you can do this. I don't just say it because that is what has to happen.

I say it because you are the strongest, most determined, and smartest person. No one I know could give birth alone in a Japanese hospital, but you can. I know you can." I remained silent, overwhelmed.

When we picked up Emma, I ran to her. She is very tall for her age, usually a head above the other children. She has dark brown curly hair and a face that radiates happiness. I was so happy to see her. She was right there in front of me. I lifted her up and squeezed her so tight she squealed. I whispered in her ear, "I love you so much." She beamed.

Chapter 10

Fred went back to work the next morning. I could feel both his reluctance and his relief as he kissed me goodbye. Emma and I were left alone to figure out our plan for the day. We kept it simple. We had some sugary Japanese cereal and milk, got dressed, and went out into the private Northwest Airlines garden. It was our first time exploring the space beyond the Ginkgo trees.

Emma ran off of our terrace and danced and twirled like Maria in the *Sound of Music* out into the vast yard. "Mommy, look at the swing set! We have one right here!" She pushed the swings and then ran through the yard. At the back of the grassy space, there were lots of very tall trees. They were so thick you couldn't see where they ended even though the loud city street was just beyond the trees. We found ourselves lost in a forest in our own backyard. There were big boulders, mounds of dirt, and even a bridge running over what was now a dry brook. There was a very high wall surrounding the entire complex, so no one from the bustling sidewalk and street a few feet away could see us playing inside. Emma created an imaginary world, and we disappeared into it, playing hide-and-seek, having a tea party below the bridge, and playing together for hours.

When we emerged from the forest, I looked at Emma's skin. It was covered in one-inchwide, red welts. Her entire body seemed to be swelling up with bumps as we walked across the yard. I looked down at myself. I didn't have a single bump. She wasn't bothered by them, but she could tell my anxiety was rising with each lump I counted. Trying to keep my voice calm, "Honey, I think we should see if we can find an ointment to stop those red bumps from getting bigger."

Having lived in Minnesota for a good portion of my life, I really hoped they were mosquitos. We got inside our apartment, and I put allergy cream on the bites. Over the next couple of hours, the bites disappeared. I was glad we weren't experiencing a medical emergency because aside from Joshi Idai Byoin Hospital and Dr. Fuji's office, I didn't yet know where or how to take Emma to a doctor. I put it on my list to figure out immediately.

Over the next few days, Emma and I started to venture beyond the walls of our apartment complex. She gleefully jumped into the small umbrella stroller we had brought with us, and she and I were off. We discovered the *Meguro* River not far from our home. "Look, Mommy, the water is going fast!" We sat on a bridge staring at the water and the people going by, taking in how different it was from St. Paul and how happy we were to be somewhere new and, most importantly, somewhere together.

After eating Japanese food from the *konbini* for almost a week, it was time to find a grocery store. I had been told by a neighbor in the Northwest Apartments that there was one along the *Meguro* River. I was intimidated by the idea of going into a grocery store. I wondered what I would find and how much it would cost. Fred had given me a stack of yen, and since I had not quite grasped the dollar-to-yen conversion rate, I hoped I had enough.

As we pushed our way through the grocery store's sliding glass doors, the employees, in unison, shouted out, "*Irasshaimase!*" I jumped, and my face turned red. I was certain they thought I had stolen something. I blocked the door for a second, ready to turn and run, and then saw they had all gone back to what they were doing. Looking to my right and left several times, I entered as if nothing had happened.

Straight ahead was the produce section. It was stunning, like a fruit and vegetable painting. There was an inviting rainbow of colors. The tomatoes were not just placed in the same area, like in the U.S., but one was flawlessly put on top of another. Every tomato stem was tilted to the left. I couldn't wait to taste the sweetness of the fruit. Emma and I grabbed a basket and slowly wound our way around the grocery store. "Emma, help me pick out the best items to make for our dinner tonight." She smiled and sat up in her stroller.

I didn't plan to replicate what we ate in the U.S. However, quite unexpectedly, I was able to purchase exactly what I was used to buying. They had pasta, some ground beef, which looked like the absolute best, some tomato sauce, and a thick-cut loaf of white bread that softened to the touch like Wonder Bread. There were many items I didn't recognize and some pungent smells coming from the seafood section, but the store was immaculate, and their offerings were of the highest quality.

As a treat, I let Emma choose an item from the candy section. She picked one that had Japanese characters were all over the package, but it clearly said Kit Kat at the top. The flavor, written in English, said Aloe Vera. "Hmmm," I said out loud to Emma. "I only know Aloe Vera as something you put on an ouchy to heal it, like the one we put on your mosquito bites."

Emma lifted her shirt and pointed to her belly button, "Mommy, let's try it. Maybe when I eat it; it can help my insides too."

As I approached the cashier, I was actually perspiring. I wanted to fit in and look like I knew what I was doing. There were several people standing behind me in line, watching as we checked out. When every item was tallied up, the cashier spoke to me. I understood nothing. *Arigato* was not going to help. She kindly turned the cash register screen around to show me the total. It was 10,150 yen, close to $100. I only had a few items, how could I possibly have spent so much? Clearly, I would need to adjust the kind of food I bought. I pulled out my thick stack of cash. My hands started shaking as I started counting the bills. I was relieved to see I had enough. Once outside, I precariously hung the groceries on the back of Emma's stroller, and we slowly walked home.

During those first days of exploring our new world, I tried not to let myself dwell on what might happen to the baby. There was nothing I could do anyway. I felt good. She was moving and kicking, and I told myself this meant she was turning her head down, getting ready for the birth. I had the phone number for the doctor placed on my bedside table and kept reassuring myself she was an outstanding doctor and would take good care of me.

I learned a few more words. *Onegaishimasu* (please). This was a good one. I finally knew how to say please and thank you. I had also mastered *sumimasen* (excuse me) and *gomenasai* (sorry), which came in handy when I clumsily bumped into people with my growing belly. We seemed to be given a lot of leeways, especially since Emma had learned to put her hands together and bow from her stroller at everyone as we passed by.

Fred called me from work a couple of weeks after we arrived, "I have great news. Our shipment from St. Paul arrived. All of our stuff is here." The large truck backed into the apartment complex. As each box was brought in, I got more and more excited. Emma's bed, our dining room table, our plates and pots, and books. Finally, they brought in our artwork. I saw the Belgian Matisse from our travels to Brussels and the small bronze statue we had purchased of a mother helping her baby to take her first step. The last thing we unpacked was the little white bassinet we would be using for the baby. I placed it on its stand next to our bed, anticipating her arrival into our lives.

We decided to celebrate our first night with all of our belongings in the apartment by ordering pizza. It turns out Domino's is in Tokyo. I passed the phone in the apartment to Fred, hoping he knew how to say cheese pizza in Japanese. He dialed the number he had gotten from a colleague and let it ring. Without any hesitation in his voice, Fred said in English, "I'd like to order a pizza to be delivered." On the other end of the phone, I heard, "Yes sir, what would you like?" I couldn't believe it! I burst out laughing. I had no idea anyone would speak English. Fred then said our address, again in English, "17-10 Sarugaku-cho #1A, Shibuya-ku, 150-0033." For as simple as that was, I could tell we would be having lots of Domino's pizza.

After putting everything away, Fred and I stood in the middle of the living room, disbelieving that our dream had come true. This was home. We lived in Tokyo, Japan. This was what we had been hoping for and dreaming of since we first met in college so many years before. No matter what happened with the baby, we couldn't believe we had made it come true.

Emma crawled into her very own bed from Minnesota and fell fast asleep. I checked on her several times and was so pleased to see how deeply she slept. At that moment, everything felt right.

Chapter 11

On June 6, 2000, at 2:00 in the morning, only a month after arriving in Tokyo, my water broke. I thought I'd wet the bed. I'd been asleep, so my first reaction through my grogginess was an extreme embarrassment. How could I have wet the bed? It didn't occur to me I was having the baby. My due date was still two weeks away. I didn't even want to wake Fred up. How awful to tell him I was incontinent. With Emma's pregnancy, the doctor had to break my water, so I didn't know the sensation. The severity of the situation gradually dawned on me.

The moment was here. I had to go back to that hospital. The week before, I had learned how to ask for a *ringo* (apple) in the grocery store, but I still couldn't tell the doctors or nurses my labor contractions were so powerfully painful that I could barely breathe. I wouldn't have someone there to advocate for me, no one to hold my hand, give me kisses, reassure me I'd be all right, and tell me we were going to have a beautiful baby girl.

I finally woke Fred up. He was immediately alert and focused. I got up and went to the bathroom. Fred handed me the phone and the piece of paper with the doctor's number. It was at that moment I realized it *only* had her number, not her name. I carefully dialed and waited.

Would that doctor even be at the hospital at 2:00 in the morning? Would she pick up the phone? I had to hope she would be there because if anyone other than a doctor who spoke English picked up the phone, I wouldn't know what to say.

The phone rang and rang. After about ten rings, the doctor, the one we had met, answered. I recognized her calming voice. "*Moshi-Moshi*" (Hello?) I hesitated. "This is Sarah Deschamps. I came to see you about two weeks ago. My baby was supposed to be born on June 21st, but my water just broke."

"Have you started having contractions?"

I had not. It was a rush of relief. Maybe I didn't have to go to the hospital in the middle of the night all by myself if I wasn't having any contractions. Maybe I could stay home until they started. "No. Nothing yet. Can I stay home until the contractions start?"

Her response was immediate and emphatic. "You must get to the hospital as quickly as possible. You cannot delay. Once the water is broken, infection can enter the birth canal. We don't want there to be any other complications with your birth."

The hope of avoiding the hospital was eliminated. I had to go. She told me to come to the emergency room entrance, and she hung up. I called my parents in Minnesota. It was late afternoon, and luckily my dad picked up the phone. I blurted out, "I'm headed to the hospital. My water broke. I don't have any contractions. The concern is about infection, so they want me there." My dad understood and could hear the panic in my voice. My parents knew there was the potential for medical issues with the baby, and they also knew I was going to the hospital alone. I hesitated; my voice cracked, betraying my stoic resignation. "Goodbye." He told me he loved me, and I quickly hung up.

Fred helped me pack. I was in the bathroom desperately trying to remember what we had brought to the hospital for Emma's birth. "Stick in that yellow nursing shirt. Can you find the black maternity pants?" I knew he didn't know where I had placed any of these things, but he looked. He hastily pulled out a toothbrush, toothpaste, and a hairbrush. At the last minute, I remembered to ask him to pack the new baby outfit I had bought before we left Minnesota. I had a matching one for Emma. Fred and I were planning on taking lots of photos of the girls together on the day the baby came home from the hospital. With his fingers fumbling, he put everything in a small bag.

I took a warm shower and got myself dressed. I walked down the hall, stopping in Emma's room. I gave her a kiss and watched her sleep. She would be a big sister soon, and I was already looking forward to further exploring Tokyo together.

Throughout those early morning preparations, I wasn't afraid or panicked. Fred told me I could do this, so I would. I had created a scenario in my head. I'd take a taxi, get to the hospital, have the baby, and see Fred in a few hours. I could do that.

Fred gave me another pile of yen, enough to pay for the ride to the hospital. As I grabbed the money, it dawned on me that I didn't have a cell phone. I had used the landline in the apartment to make calls. We wouldn't have a way to contact each other.

It hit me. I truly would be alone. With the front door only steps away, I gasped, my knees folded under me, and I dropped to the floor, sobbing. Fred got on his knees and held me, quietly letting me cry.

He gently pulled me back up to my feet, giving me the longest hug and kiss. He was trying. There weren't words. How do you say goodbye knowing you won't be together for the monumental experience of giving birth to your child? Choking back tears, "Sarah, you can do this. I know you can. I love you."

I walked out the door, down the stairs, and through the front gate to the sidewalk. I didn't look back at him standing in our doorway. I knew I wouldn't leave if I did. Taxis drive at all hours of the day and night, so I just had to hold out my arm for one, and then I descended into the Japanese medical world, not knowing how I'd find my way out.

Chapter 12

The taxi driver was an older gentleman. I said, "*Jo-shi 1-dai B-yo-in, o-ne-gai-shi-masu.*" (Joshi Idai Hospital, please.) Then I paused because I knew the next word was not going to be in Japanese, "Emergency Room, *onegaishimasu.* As I spoke, I could tell he was taking a closer look in the rearview mirror at the passenger he had picked up. He saw my bag and my belly. Through the dim lights of the city, I could faintly see he was smiling. It was reassuring that someone thought this was all going as it should, even if it was a taxi driver.

After the thirty-minute drive, he went right past the front of the hospital where we had gotten out only two weeks before. He pulled around to the back. I thought he was making a joke and had brought me to the trash area. There were massive black metal garbage containers all lined up along the red brick wall in front of us, and there was a foul smell seeping into the taxi. I plugged my nose. He could see my hesitation, and through the windshield, he pointed to the small letters above what appeared to be an afterthought of a hospital back door. "EMERGENCY" was written in English. "Holy Shit."

I forced myself to get out of the car. Through my disbelief, I handed the driver all of the money Fred had given me. Thankfully, he pulled out what he needed. He got out of his taxi and spoke in Japanese in a way that sounded very kind and gentle, and then he bowed deeply. I bowed back, hoping I was not insulting him. I said, *onegaishimasu,* the only word that came to me, and I walked up the steps toward the strange Emergency entrance near the trash area into Joshi Idai Byoin, where I would be giving birth to our daughter.

I yanked at the heavy door and walked down a dark hallway. There was no check-in desk or doctor or nurse there to greet me. If this was the emergency entrance, there were no emergencies happening. No one was there. Ahead on the left, there was what looked like a small clinic behind an open window. I approached it and stood still, hoping someone would notice the pregnant foreigner. No one did. I cleared my throat. I stood still, bewildered about what I was supposed to do.

Finally, someone came to the window and glanced at me. He clearly was not going to speak any English. I realized the situation I had put myself in by forgetting to ask the doctor for her name before I hung up. Sweat started dripping down my face, and I could feel it sliding down my back. *What was I doing?*

I stuck the crumpled piece of paper with the doctor's phone number through the open hole in the window. I said, "Doctor. Phone Number. Giving Birth." I pointed to my stomach and made a contorted facial expression like I was having a contraction. I still wasn't having any, so I was completely faking it for the purpose of over-dramatizing my situation, hoping this man would find the mysterious doctor connected to the phone number. He glanced down at the paper and said many words in Japanese, not one of which I knew. He moved his mouth but made no hand gestures to help me. I didn't hear him say even once *onegaishimasu, arigato, gomenasai, sumimasen,* or *ringo.* I pointed helplessly to the tiny piece of paper and put my thumb and pinky finger up to my ear and mouth, indicating he might give the phone number a call. He disappeared.

I started to rapidly go through the conversation I had incoherently had with the female doctor at 2:00 in the morning. What had she said about where I was supposed to go? Who was I supposed to see? Except for the green linoleum and dark walls, I couldn't see anything resembling the waiting area where Fred and I had been only two weeks before. Maybe I was at the wrong hospital?

I didn't move a muscle from the window. There weren't any places to sit anyway. I had my small bag precariously hanging off my arm. I was actually thinking about turning around and leaving. Maybe I had imagined everything, and this was all a mistake?

The man had been gone a good ten minutes, and I was feeling faint. I hadn't thought to eat or bring any food with me, so I was thirsty and hungry. He finally returned with the female doctor. She spoke to the man in Japanese, and he went back behind the window. She turned to me, "I'm glad you are here. It must have been a few scary hours. You weren't expecting to go into labor for a couple more weeks."

I was so relieved to see her, tears started coming down my cheeks. I felt like she understood. I was alone, not only in this hospital because my husband couldn't be with me, but in my new life in Japan.

She had me follow her up two flights of stairs to the third floor of the hospital. It was 4:45 in the morning and still dark outside. The third floor was absolutely silent. She walked me down to a bathroom, and a nurse met us. The nurse said something in Japanese. I understood nothing. The doctor translated, "Please put on this hospital gown and Japanese slippers. When you are done changing, the nurse will take your personal items and will put them safely in a locker until you need them." I grabbed the gown and slippers from her and disappeared into the bathroom to change.

I did what I was told. It was the best plan. They had rules. I was going to follow them, and I'd quickly get this over with, have our baby, and be done. That was my plan.

They were both waiting for me when I emerged. After I handed the small bag of my personal items over to them, all that remained was me. I glanced down and noticed the hospital gown was really short. I'm 5'9", and most Japanese women are shorter than me. I tugged at the bottom to no avail. I was now wearing a hospital gown that looked like a mini dress with my bulging belly, making it even shorter. I'd put on their Japanese slippers, and they were two sizes too small with my heels falling off the back. I was cold, awkward, and embarrassed.

I lowered my head and followed the nurse and doctor down another long and dark hallway. We stood outside a room. It was pitch black, with its door closed. "You have been assigned to one of the beds in here. There are many other women in the room, all waiting to go into labor. You will join them." She motioned that I should enter the room. "I'll do an exam to see if you are dilated or not. I want to know how far along you are in the birthing process." She opened the door, and with the dim light from the hallway, I could see there were ten beds all lined up along the wall with thin curtains pulled along only the sides of the bed. The windows were covered, so you couldn't see

49

outside. The beds were packed so tightly in the room that there was barely any space between them.

I froze. I couldn't move. I couldn't believe I was going to be simply a number in a lineup of women all waiting to go into labor. The doctor sensed my hesitation. She gently touched my back, coaxing me into the room. She whispered as we entered, "You'll be all right. It is safe here, and we can monitor the activity of the baby. You need some sleep."

The doctor pointed to the one open bed. I would have five women on my right and four on my left. I was directly in front of the door to the room. Each time someone would enter or exit, I'd see them, and they would see me. All I wanted to do was run away, but I did as I was told.

I stood at the end of the bed, and the doctor and nurse stood next to me. I could see I was supposed to get in. At seven months pregnant, I wasn't sure I could do it. I shuffled my feet along the side and bumped into the bed of the woman next to me. I hoisted one leg up and pushed off the floor, and flipped onto the bed with my mini hospital gown twisted around my body. I landed with a loud grunt, and my head flopped on the plastic pillow, making a loud crinkling sound. I felt huge and stupid and ugly and so very out of place. It was the exact opposite of what Fred had told me I was. I wanted to go home.

A tiny light turned on over my bed, and another nurse appeared with a tray filled with medical instruments. She set it on the bed at my feet. The doctor said, "I'm going to do an exam to see how far along you are in labor. Since your water broke, we need to monitor you and your baby very carefully." She was whispering because everyone was sleeping. It made me feel uncomfortable, like I was doing something wrong.

To be clear, the "exam" is embarrassing. The doctor sticks her hand into your cervix to see if your uterus is dilating. Since I was in front of the door, people coming and going from the room could see me. It was humiliating, but I just let her do it. "You aren't leaking amniotic fluid; this is a good sign. We are going to try to keep the baby inside of you for at least another day. We want her to grow a bit more since you are still two weeks before your due date."

50

I blurted out, "is the baby protected?" "Yes, she is safe." She clarified, "You aren't dilated, so you aren't in labor yet." The doctor listened to the heartbeat of the baby. "She doesn't seem to be in distress."

Learning this news, I became desperate to get out. "Can I go home and wait until I go into labor?"

"You have to remain in the hospital until you give birth. We will monitor you, and if there are any changes or concerns, we will immediately deliver the baby. You should try to rest."

The clock on the wall said 5:30 in the morning. How long would I be here? I wanted to be in labor. I wanted to get this over with. As the doctor and nurse went out the door, I realized I had never learned the doctor's name.

I was alone with nine strangers in the deathly silent room. I had been so caught up in the frenzy of activity and my own emotions I hadn't asked to use a phone to call Fred. I wasn't sure they would give it to me anyway since it was silent in there. I hoped Fred would be able to explain to Emma where I was and why I left in the middle of the night. Still shivering from the cold, I tucked my legs beneath the thin blankets. The clock ticked a minute after. I sat, immobile, and watched it go around and around.

At 7:00, the hospital food service arrived. I was starving. They brought the tray and placed it on the tiny table that had been at the foot of my bed. When they removed the silver cover, I gagged. There was an entire fish, head, tail, including skin, with a rather large eyeball staring up at me. There was white rice, a pickled thing in a separate dish, miso soup with tofu floating in it, and some sticky bean dish that had a very pungent odor. I was an adventurous eater, but this time I wanted something I knew. I had been dreaming of a croissant and baguette from the Daikanyama Pantry.

They didn't provide a fork or spoon, so with the chopsticks and my stomach growling, I ripped at the fish's flaky skin, trying to get to the meat. I put the fish in my mouth. It was cold and smokey and salty. I only ate a couple of bites but was instantly proud of myself for trying it. I inhaled the rice and drank the miso soup straight from the bowl. I told myself I didn't have to eat the pickled thing. I poked at the smelly beans. The more I touched them, the more they stuck to my chopsticks. I decided that was enough food and set down the sticky mess. I sipped the hot green tea. The food service employees came by again and removed the tray. I was glad I had moved the food around, like a kid who was trying to make it look like I had eaten.

I needed to use the bathroom, but I didn't even know where the bathroom was. I just crossed my legs and held it, which is almost impossible when you are seven months pregnant. I knew everyone was awake, yet there continued to not be a sound in the room. There weren't televisions, not even a communal one. A pin could be heard dropping on the floor.

At 9:00 am, a male doctor appeared at my bed. I was so desperate to go to the bathroom at that point I blurted out, "How do people go to the bathroom here?" He laughed, but I didn't care.

I didn't even know if he spoke English. I started to get up and wobbled off of the bed. I careened into the bed next to mine with the curtain being dragged with me. He opened the door of the room for me and pointed to the end of the hall. I almost ran, not caring who saw my gown flapping behind me or about the fact that I had forgotten my slippers next to the bed. I'm sure I looked like a crazy lady fleeing the hospital. I got to the bathroom door, swung it open, and was absolutely thankful I had a minute to myself.

I wanted to be anywhere but here. I wished I could run down the stairs and have Fred come and get me. I felt so out of place and so unable to understand. I wanted out.

When I reappeared, the doctor was standing outside of the bathroom waiting for me as if he knew I was about to leave. I remembered that I'd made quite a spectacle of myself. I smiled and shoved my hand in his direction, "Hi, I'm Sarah."

"I know who you are. You made quite an impression on us when you arrived so early this morning." I wasn't sure if that was a good thing or not, but it felt like he was singing to me when he spoke in English. Another person who spoke my language. Halleujah! He gestured I should walk with him. We were headed back to that room, to that bed. "I'll do another exam on you to see if labor has started." He asked if there had been any changes since last night.

"No, I've felt nothing." I did a less humiliating job of hauling myself onto the bed this time, and he examined me and found there was no change. I was sure my body should've gone into labor because I had gulped down the eyeballed fish.

He checked the baby, listening to her heart and to see if there was any distress. "I don't hear any problems." He jotted information on a notepad. "We will monitor you all day long. We want your baby to come as naturally as possible. So long as she is safe, we will wait and see." I asked him for a telephone to call Fred. I had seen that they had wireless ones and hoped they could bring one to me since I knew they wouldn't let me out again anytime soon. The doctor moved away from my bed and switched to Japanese to speak to the nurse next to him.

Fred came on the phone, and I started to cry. I went from tears to sobs. I couldn't get words out. He tried so hard to sound composed and strong. "Sarah, what is happening? Is the baby born? Where are you?" Just hearing his voice was making me hysterical. I couldn't speak. Fred was so far behind in understanding where I was now; how would I catch him up on everything that had happened? What could I possibly say? Everyone in that room, including the doctor, could hear me. Trying to get ahold of myself, I searched for a tissue, but not finding one, I finally blew my nose on the bed sheets.

I swallowed, took a long pause, and whispered, "I'm fine. No baby yet. How is Emma? Tell her I love her."

Fred said he would. He asked again, "Is the baby safe since your water broke? What's going to happen?"

As he asked, I realized I didn't know the plan they had for getting the baby out of me. "I don't know what's going on. They want the baby to stay inside. *This is impossible!*" I was shouting. I wished he was there with me. Finally, words tumbled out with no logical sequence, "I can feel the baby kicking and moving. They keep checking the baby and me and don't seem alarmed. I'm lying in a hospital bed, staring at a clock, desperately wishing my body would make the contractions start. I'll call when I can, but I have no phone. Doctors don't come often, and the nurses don't speak English."

"I love you. I'm anxious to see the baby, and Emma is looking forward to seeing you and to meeting her new sister." His voice sounded sing-songy and high-pitched, not like his normal strong deep voice. We hung up with an awkwardness between us. I didn't realize it then, but we wouldn't speak again until after the baby was born.

I sat there all day long, watching as the minutes ticked by. I wanted a book or music or anything to distract my mind. I had nothing but the clock. The nurses and various doctors came and went from the room, fanning out to take care of the ten of us one by one down the line. I wondered about the other women. They remained silent, so I could make up stories. Maybe they were all high-risk pregnancies. Maybe they missed their partners as much as I did. Maybe they felt awful and hated the rules and wanted to run with their slippers and gowns and leave, just like me. If it wasn't that, then I stumbled upon the idea that they were silent because a foreigner was there, and I was making such a spectacle of myself that they were embarrassed into silence.

Lunch came and went, another whole fish and other strange items which I couldn't stomach. I ate the bowl of rice and nothing else. I didn't even push the food around on the plate this time. I just didn't eat.

The same doctor I had seen in the morning checked me again later in the afternoon. I told him I felt nothing different, and he confirmed there was no change. I was tired of hearing that. I wanted this to end.

Dinner was another fish. This time it was pink on the outside, and it was accompanied by more sticky rice and miso soup. I ate the tofu in the soup, convincing myself it was enough protein to keep the baby and me going. A different doctor came in after dinner. I was desperate. I told him, "Pitocin was used to induce labor with my first daughter; could we try that?"

He said, "The doctors are in agreement we will induce labor tomorrow if it doesn't start on its own tonight." He walked away.

That was it. One more night of not sleeping. One more night without Fred and Emma and one more night of worry about what the day would bring. With all of this painfully cycling through my head, I finally fell asleep.

When I woke up on the morning of June 7 at 6:00, I desperately needed to go to the bathroom again and didn't even ask this time. I stumbled into the lady's bed next to mine, luckily never seeing her because of the gauzy curtain that separated us. I ran down the hall to the bathroom. There was someone in there. I stood, dancing in my bare feet, doing what I could to keep from peeing on the floor. A woman appeared, seemingly surprised to have kept the foreigner out of the bathroom. I raced inside.

I went slowly back to my bed this time. The reality of what was about to happen electrified my body. I went back into the room and took a moment to stare at the ladies in a row, forcing myself to take a mental image of this room. I went to my bed and obediently got back in.

The doctor appeared. "Let's do an exam before you have breakfast. If there isn't any progress, then after you eat, we will take you to another room and will induce labor." I couldn't believe what I had heard. I was going to have our baby. This was going to end.

Chapter 13

After a delicious breakfast of eel, which I didn't touch, they asked me to get up and out of that bed for the last time. I wanted to run up and down the room and say I was going to be leaving them and I was going to get to have my baby. Instead, I put on my tiny slippers and quietly shuffled along the floor and out of the room.

I followed the doctor down the hall. He was a shorter man, with black hair slicked back with gel to keep every strand in place. He had black shoes that looked a bit worn, probably from too much walking along this hallway. We went down a narrow flight of stairs and then another long hallway. I wondered why there weren't any elevators in this hospital. How big was it with all of these strange corridors? It couldn't be only me who found all this walking uncomfortable. I clenched the back of my gown to try to close it and give myself a tiny bit of dignity while grabbing the railing to steady myself in the too-small slippers.

We ended up in front of a room that had three beds in a row, with much more space between them this time. In front of the beds, there was a nurse's station with two computers and three nurses furiously watching what happened in the room.

At the end of the space, I could see two operating rooms. They were separated from the labor room with large glass windows. The space looked ancient. I could see a stark metal table in the middle, an overhead fluorescent light, and white-washed concrete block walls. I shuddered. I could see exactly where our baby would be born, and it wasn't what I wanted for us. It wasn't warm or intimate, or comforting. I turned away and told myself not to look.

The doctor pointed to the bed nearest the bathroom. It was open. My heart skipped a beat.

I had a bathroom right next to me. No more hallways to run down. It felt like a taste of freedom. There were thicker curtains between us this time, with two women already occupying the other beds. In addition to more space for each person, there were monitors and machines placed near each of the beds. It should have felt reassuring to see all of this equipment, but it didn't.

It was 8:00 in the morning on June 7th. It seemed like time had finally sped up. I had been in the hospital for two nights, and aside from my water breaking at home, nothing medically had occurred. The doctor who had brought me to this room told me that he was going back to see the women on the other floor, and I would be seeing different doctors for the rest of the day. "Please lie down, try to get comfortable, and another doctor should be here soon."

I got into bed much more gracefully this time. At 9:00, another male doctor arrived. I thought there would be one specific doctor who would be with me from now on, but that wasn't the case. They approached me one after another, sometimes with a nurse, other times alone. They all started to look the same. White lab coats, black shoes, black hair, and perfunctory ways of speaking to me. The doctors all spoke English, but the nurses didn't, so we had a harder time. They mostly came to look at the monitors, trying not to look me in the eye. I didn't ask anyone's name, and they didn't introduce themselves. I did what they said, hoping it would speed up the delivery.

A doctor finally said in English, "We are going to induce your labor now, and I hope to have the baby out by noon. I would like to put an IV in and use a medication that will start your contractions." I felt emboldened. He was talking about something I understood.

I sat up tall, "Pitocin is the medication that was used when I gave birth to my daughter almost three years ago." As if it mattered, I said, "I'd like to use Pitocin. Also, at my daughter's birth in the U.S., the doctor was able to put in an epidural block so I didn't feel any painful contractions during labor. I would like to have an epidural again."

The doctor came back about ten minutes later with an IV needle and a drip bag. He pointed, "Pitocin." I smiled, reassured I knew how this would go. A nurse put the needle in my arm, and then the Pitocin started to flow. I

57

reminded the doctor that I wanted to have an epidural to block the pain from the contractions. "Yes, the procedure has been ordered and will be administered shortly." I was worried the contractions would start, and I knew they would hurt.

With the epidural I had for Emma's birth, I experienced almost no pain. It had been peaceful. For this birth, I also wanted to avoid pain. I didn't want to be exhausted after the birth.

A few minutes later, another doctor and nurse team arrived. They said they would put in the epidural. With my legs hanging over the side of the bed, the doctor asked me to lean as far over as I possibly could, which was not very far with my protruding belly. I could feel the needle penetrating my spine as I had when I was in labor with Emma. The injection didn't hurt, it was over in a couple of minutes, and they left.

I was alone again, lying on my back, waiting for the contractions to start. There was much more activity in this room. Doctors and nurses were coming and going and speaking with the two other laboring women. There were always nurses at the nursing station. There was an urgency I could feel.

By 10:30, I started to feel a tightening, gripping in my belly. It started low and finished high. At first, the contractions came every ten minutes, so I had lots of time to recover. A doctor came to check on me at 10:45. He measured my cervix, and I was finally dilated. I was relieved. It was finally happening. I would give birth today. "I'm starting to feel the contractions, and they hurt. With the epidural, I didn't have any pain last time."

With a straight face, he said, "At this hospital, we only give epidurals that numb the patient below the uterus. We need you to feel the contractions so you can work with us through the entire labor."

I sputtered, "Well, that seems pointless. What is the epidural you gave me supposed to do?"

"We use it in case you need to have an emergency cesarean section. If that happens, when we take you into the operating room, you will already be numb below the uterus. We can quickly make the cut to get the baby out." As he was saying this, I felt another contraction, and this time it was strong.

The doctor left, presumably to attend to another patient, but most likely to avoid my anguish as it was beginning to dawn on me that I was going to have a fully natural birth with all of the pain included, and I would experience this all by myself.

The contractions came closer and closer together, first eight minutes, then seven minutes, then six. I could see that a nurse was monitoring me from the desk. When the contractions were coming about every five minutes, she came over to my bed. I felt a sense of relief that someone, anyone, was focusing on me. Up until that moment, I felt like I was just one more laboring woman in a room full of them.

By the time she got to me, I was on my back, loudly gasping for relief. We had no words in common, but I sensed that she wanted to say something. I desperately wanted to tell her how lonely and sad and overcome with exhaustion I was, but nothing came out of either of our mouths.

Another excruciating contraction gripped my body. She stood over me. She said what sounded like soothing words in Japanese, but I understood none of them. She patted my arm and motioned for me to watch her. She started to pantomime, rolling her arms one over another. She placed her hands on the bed and arched her back like a cat. I did what she said. I rolled over on all fours and let my large belly hang down. It didn't feel natural or even safe on that bed, but she was trying to help. I couldn't catch my breath. I was in so much agony. I began swaying on my hands and knees, hoping I wouldn't fall off the bed. The nurse walked away, seemingly satisfied that I was managing labor correctly.

Another doctor appeared and checked to see my progress. "You are fully dilated. We are gathering the medical team, and we are going to bring you into the operating room so we can deliver your baby."

I was terrified. Contraction after contraction came now, each one stronger than the last. The bright lights above and my strange position on the bed, combined with other women hearing me at my most vulnerable moment, were overpowering. I had no familiarity, no matter where I looked. The raw exposure to an overload of emotions and extreme pain were swirling in my head. I felt a rush of fear and doubt, and dread about what I had allowed to happen.

I held my breath and gripped the edges of the bed. I squeezed my eyes shut and made my world stop, just for a second. I don't know how, but I blocked everything; all of my feelings, sorrow, and loneliness. I had to concentrate because nothing else mattered but delivering our baby. I opened my eyes and saw the doctors and nurses standing around the bed. I nodded to them. I was ready.

They put me on my back again and wheeled the bed into the sterile operating room. I was lifted onto another table. The cold of the metal on my back sent a shiver through my body and made me hyper-alert. They shoved several pillows behind my back that crinkled as they touched me. Someone moved my feet into the stirrups at the end of the operating table. It was an uncomfortable position, and it felt humiliating to be this exposed in such a strange place.

A doctor, who I didn't recognize at all, sat off to my right. He spoke calmly in English. "I can see the baby, and she is ready to come out. So long as you continue to work with me, I am certain this can go smoothly."

I was intensely focused on the baby. Without further direction from anyone, I sat up and started to push. I saw beyond my feet several male doctors assembling at the end of the operating table. There must have been six of them standing there, all straight and still. The doctor near my feet said, "The baby is breech; her feet are coming first." She hadn't turned after all. "I'm going to do an episiotomy on you to cut enough skin to make it easier to maneuver the baby without hurting her." I could see her feet start to appear.

The doctor spoke softly to me, and I focused on pushing. It didn't take long. He gently, expertly pulled the baby out. I could see she had the umbilical cord wrapped around her neck. I watched him slowly remove the cord and saw him turn her upright; just then, she cried. The doctor smiled. He unceremoniously cut the umbilical cord, something Fred should have been there to do, another reminder I was alone. The baby was then passed to one of the doctors at the foot of the table, who was taller and looked authoritative and in charge. He had a blanket in his outstretched arms, took the baby, turned, and the row of doctors all filed out one by one.

My immediate reaction was not about my baby. It wasn't about holding or nurturing or desiring that first touch of new life. I was overwhelmed with a feeling of relief. It started in my numbed toes and shivered through every part of my body up to the top of my head. I did it. I had given birth. The baby was out. She breathed. She cried. She was in one piece. There were no dark shadows, no holes in her brain or her heart or her lower abdomen. Nothing that had been pounded into me these last many months was true. None of it was real. Fred and I were right to believe the baby would be healthy, and all of those doctors were wrong.

I glanced away from everything that was happening. The clock on the wall said 12:15. I remembered it was June 7, 2000, and our daughter had been born in Tokyo, Japan. Our dream had come true. I looked back down and saw the doctor still there, stitching me up. "I made a very small incision, and it will easily heal."

I was still numb below my belly, so I didn't think I needed to pay attention to him anymore. I rested my head and back on the crinkly pillows. I said to no one in particular that I'd like a phone to call my husband. As a nurse arrived with one, the doctor who had taken my baby from the operating room came to see me. "The baby is fine; she has something called 'imperforate anus.' It will require one surgery, but she will recover. You can see the baby soon. Your husband can come now." As if he had said everything there was to say on the subject, he walked out.

I already knew the baby was fine. I had seen her. The drama was over.

I dialed Fred's number quickly, I was desperate to talk to him. "Hi." I didn't give him a chance to react or speak. "Our baby's been born, but I haven't held her. I survived, and so did she." As I caught my breath, the doctor motioned that he was done stitching me up. I nodded in his direction and continued with Fred. "She is with a lot of doctors. They said you could come now. Finally, you can be here." The urgency in my voice quickened, "Please come to the hospital. Please come right now." I hung up.

61

I was lifted off of the operating table and put back onto a bed that was wheeled into the room I had left only a short time before. Moments later, a nurse brought me the bag that was filled with my personal belongings, the one that Fred had packed for me several days ago. I dumped them out on the bed, anxious to see again what had been packed. The room and bed were the same, and my personal items were the same, but I felt different. Giving birth here, in this hospital, in this way, would haunt me forever.

I wasn't woozy, wasn't numb anymore, and didn't even feel as if I had given birth. I stood up, untied their gown, and let it fall to the floor. It didn't fit. I wanted to get dressed in my own clothes. I pulled each item on slowly, thinking to myself, no more tiny gowns, no more plastic slippers. Just me. I sat on the edge of the bed, waiting for Fred, so we could see our baby together.

Chapter 14

He ran into the room, out of breath, as if he had run instead of driven. I'm not entirely certain how he found me in the maze of the hospital. Its endless dark hallways and steep staircases that appeared out of nowhere didn't intuitively lead anyone to where I was.

He lifted me off of the bed, wrapped me in his arms, and wouldn't let go. It was his way of saying all the things that couldn't be said, all the emotions that we both had experienced over the last two days. Words didn't seem like they would be enough to span the river that separated us.

A gasp, like a last breath, escaped me. Gut-wrenching sobs came next. He was here. We were together. I was done being alone. We were parents of a newborn baby girl, and the doctor said she was healthy. This was finally behind us. I had done it, so we could continue our lives in our new foreign home.

Over my shoulder, I meekly pointed to the operating room where our baby had been born. It was Fred who broke down this time. Overcome with what he had missed, with what I had gone through, with what separated our lives as parents now. He managed to get out, "I'm so sorry."

Seemingly out of nowhere, a female doctor stood before us. I hadn't seen a woman doctor during the whirlwind of medical staff traipsing through my anguish. "Sarah-San," she said, and I shuddered to attention. I was back in Japan, in this hospital, being addressed in formal Japanese again. "I'm doctor Kato." She reached over and firmly shook our hands. In spite of her formal manner, she looked more approachable than the other doctors. She wasn't as tall, had a huge, glowing smile, and, surprisingly for a doctor, had perfectly formed ponytails with red ribbons placed evenly on either side of her head.

"Please follow me." We followed. We descended a staircase or two, losing track of how many. She walked quickly, so we almost lost her in the long dark hallway. She rounded a corner and then stopped, so we stopped. We stood in front of a locked sliding glass door.

To our right were several shelves with meticulously arranged fake leather slippers like the ones I had just left behind. Next to them were several cardboard boxes. She put her hand in each of the boxes, pulling out paper hospital gowns and puffy blue hairnets. "Please put these on." She bent down and pointed to the shoe rack. "Please remove your shoes and put on these slippers." I already knew they didn't fit. I watched as Fred struggled to put them on and make them stay. As she helped us, her ponytails bounced up and down. It was surprisingly playful.

We were not expecting all of these extra precautions to see our baby. In the operating room, the doctor had told me that aside from a small medical issue, there wasn't anything wrong.

It seemed strange there were so many barriers in place to enter the nursery.

We waited while the secure glass door was opened from the inside. As it slid open, we were struck by the powerful stench of bleach. This place was definitely clean. We followed the doctor and turned into the room where presumably the babies were being cared for. I halted in the doorway. This was definitely not a normal hospital nursery. We were entering the neonatal intensive care unit, the NICU, for this Japanese hospital, and our baby was inside.

The room was lined with what looked like fifteen bassinets, all resting on metal legs. There were tubes and wires coming out from under each baby's blanket like the legs of an octopus. Machines beeped, and tiny infants cried. There were no other noises. The nurses appeared to be so focused on what they were doing they didn't stop to interact.

I was baffled because the room had no parents, no comfortable chairs, no curtains to pull for privacy, and no lighting except for the harsh fluorescent bulbs on the ceiling. The all-too-familiar shock and panic rose up inside me again. *What kind of a place was this? Why were these babies alone? Where was our baby?* To steady me, Fred grabbed my hand. The doctor led us around the room to a corner where she pointed to our daughter.

I rushed to her bassinet and put my face right up to hers. She had the most exquisite face I had ever seen. It was petite and cherubic. It simply drew me in by its beauty. I could not imagine why this magnificent child would be in such a bleak place. She seemed flawless to me.

It was when I allowed myself to slowly pull back from her face that I began to notice the rest of her. Through the blankets, I could tell she was tiny, truly dainty, smaller than most babies. I started to look fully at her head. From underneath her little pink hat, I was startled when I saw her right ear was missing. In its place was a small piece of folded skin. I was stunned. I stared into the bassinet expecting to see her ear. I thought if I looked long enough, it would appear.

As I pulled my head further away, I began to notice all of the wires and machines and nurses and now doctors around her bassinet. Fred was standing off to the side. He was shaking, too, and looked ashen as if he might pass out. There were obviously more complications than a missing ear. The Japanese doctors looked despondent as they saw me begin to grasp the overwhelming enormity of the medical issues facing our daughter.

Two chairs appeared behind us and were placed right next to the baby's bassinet. The nurses motioned for us to sit. They gingerly reached into the bassinet and attempted to pick her up, tugging gently on one wire just to tangle another. Finally, they put her in my arms. I couldn't believe it; after all these months of waiting, all this time filled with dread and worry, and hope, we finally were able to hold our baby. I clenched her tight to my body, setting off a cacophony of machines. I tuned them out and just held on. Fred leaned in and hugged both of us.

Cradling her head in my hand, I gently brought her down to rest in my lap. She weighed almost nothing. I glanced and saw that there was a pink tag on the front of her bassinet. It said 2570 grams and 32 centimeters. I had no idea what that meant, but I did know she felt a lot smaller than Emma was when she was born. The doctors all stepped away, allowing us to see her for the first time. "We love you." I gently placed the baby in Fred's arms, so he could feel her weight and hold her too.

After a few minutes, I said to the female doctor who had reappeared, "I'd like to nurse the baby." She didn't respond. I nursed Emma only a few minutes after giving birth. The doctor translated to the nurses, and there was a look of surprise on their faces. I couldn't tell what the issue was, but it didn't look like babies could be nursed in this large room. I read before we came to Japan that nursing in public was frowned upon. It seemed strange to me that this same restriction might be placed on mothers with newborns in the hospital.

I didn't move, and neither did Fred. We were clearly not going to allow the baby to be taken out of our arms. There were more perplexed faces, deep breaths, long pauses, and a back-and-forth exchange in Japanese between the nurses and the doctor. They finally decided to allow us to go into a separate space with the baby. They motioned to a small room with a door. I smiled, showing that this was what I wanted. They wheeled the bassinet with all of the wires and beeping machines into the room. I took tiny steps in my too-small slippers holding the baby gently in my arms. They closed the curtains and the door and allowed us to be alone.

With the baby asleep on my lap, we disappeared into a conversation we needed to have. "The entire time you were gone, I was so worried. I sat on the couch in our living room, waiting for my phone to ring. I tried to keep Emma entertained, tried to feed her, and be with her, but all I could think about was you." I had never seen Fred this distraught. He spoke quickly, feeling them watching us, wondering when they would make him leave again. "I tried to imagine anything that might be similar to where you were, what you were doing. I pictured that strange entry hall at the hospital, where we hoped for our magic number to be called. I thought about the small room where I sat when you had the ultrasound a month ago, but I didn't know what anything else looked like in this bizarre place. The worst images came to my head. I didn't know what to do."

I was not prepared to be emotional, but I started to cry. "During the actual labor, I was in excruciating pain." As I remembered it, I clenched my fist so hard it turned bright red.

Fred didn't know what to say. What could be said? If he had been there, it would have been different. All that came out was, "I'm sorry."

"Not only was the baby breech, but the umbilical cord was wrapped around her neck. It was really uncomfortable. There were doctors standing in a line at the end of the operating table, staring at me. They did nothing but watch. When she came out, they whisked the baby away. They didn't seem to think I wasn't necessary anymore." I stopped speaking. I couldn't catch my breath as I remembered what had happened and realized how much I needed him there. Words that didn't make sense tumbled out of my mouth. "This doesn't even explain it. I don't know how to. There isn't anything familiar. I'm not sure you could ever understand." I wanted him to. I wanted to say every word to make him see it, but how do you explain the most distressing moment in your life?

"What did you do for those two days while you sat in the hospital?"

"I was placed in a room with nine other women all in a row." I paused. "Every meal was fish. Eyeballs. Scales. It was the entire fish." I quietly added, "I haven't eaten much of anything since I arrived."

"What? Oh my god!" With remorse in his voice, "I wish I was there."

I turned to our baby and tried to nurse her. She latched right on, and instantly I had a rush of adrenaline. This was a feeling I knew. Out of nowhere, my face brightened and I uttered, "This is going to work. See, she looks and acts like Emma did. We can manage even this. It will be fine after all." Fred didn't say a word.

Just then, we started to hear beeping and buzzing from the machines. The monitors started to flash red lights. The door to our private space flung open, and a nurse entered. Knowing we would not understand Japanese, she pointed to the bassinet. We had to put our baby back.

The little room was now reverberating with discordant sounds, high-pitched, low-toned, constant, and short staccato ones. It was as if Fred, I, and the baby were all screaming at once. Dr. Kato stood rigid in the doorway as if nothing was happening. She was no longer sweet in her ponytails. She was brusque and authoritative. "You have to leave now. There are certain visiting hours for parents in the NICU, and they are done for the day. You have to leave and let the doctors do their work."

I stood up a bit too fast and became dizzy, so my words came out as a desperate shout, "What? Wait! How will I nurse her if I can only see her during your visiting hours?" Rules. There were more rules.

"This is our policy. We cannot change it. The doctors and nurses know exactly how to care for your daughter. You do not need to concern yourself about that. For nursing, you will have to start pumping your breast milk and store it in a freezer. We will feed your baby when it is not visiting hours." I could tell this was nonnegotiable. Fred put his arm around me, and we turned to exit the room. The doctor pointed the way out of the NICU. We wouldn't be allowed to see our newborn until the next day. We didn't even know when.

I continued to hear the beeping as I watched the nurses wheel our baby into the main room. I turned and looked at the bassinet that held our child. I wanted to run to her, to scoop her up and take her with me. Fred felt it and wrapped his arm around me more firmly, guiding me further and further away.

Her no-nonsense manner continued, obviously changing the subject, "We will head to your own room, Sarah-san; you will spend the night so we can monitor you after giving birth." I heard her words and registered that this was something that made sense to me. I had spent a night at the hospital for Emma's birth in Minnesota. At least this time, I understood where we were going.

We passed through the locked door of the NICU. We removed our sterile hats and gowns and placed our Japanese slippers on the rack. We easily found our shoes, the ones hanging far over the side of the shelf.

Fred and I obediently followed the doctor up more flights of stairs. This time, we ended up on a floor with a reception desk and lots of rooms along the hallway. A nurse stepped out from behind the desk to greet us. She bowed, and we stood still, not knowing what to do. She led the doctor and us down the hall.

On the doorframe outside of one of the rooms, the doctor pointed to a small pink piece of paper slipped inside a plastic holder. It had typed Japanese characters on it. The doctor pointed and said phonetically as she ran her finger along the characters, "That is your name. *SA-RAH DAY-SHE-YA-N*." This simple tag was something I understood. A name, my name, was on the door, indicating it was my room.

The doctor gestured for us to go in, and without saying anything, she turned and left. The hospital room looked like one I would have expected in the U.S. It was a single-person room with an attached toilet and sink. I wouldn't have to share. I didn't have to feel self-conscious about my tall body or about how loud I was compared to the Japanese women.

In addition to the private toilet and sink, the room had a hospital bed with a visible remote control to make it go up and down, a side table, and a large chair next to the bed. The dark and stark theme of the hospital continued into this room. The light overhead was fluorescent, and the floors were dark green linoleum. There was a faint smell of bleach, which added to the somber feeling.

Fred gently closed the door behind us, trying to shut out what we had just experienced. Not our baby, but everything else.

I climbed onto the bed, and Fred sat in the chair next to me. "Hey, look, you have a phone in your room!" We burst out laughing. Even in the most difficult moments, he found a way to make us laugh. The "phone" didn't really resemble one. It was definitely from the 1960s. It was huge, clunky, and bright yellow with a large rotating plastic dial for making calls. I couldn't even imagine how Fred would reach me if he needed to, but after all, I had been through, it seemed decadent to have a phone in my room.

A food service person delivered a hot meal. She put it on the small table between the two of us. After she left, Fred ceremoniously lifted off the metal lid. "Ta-da!" I couldn't believe it, another whole fish. This time it was with a dark scaly outside and a big black eye. "Welcome to the delicious and very, very nutritious hospital food of Japan!" I motioned to the tray, "*Dozo*" (go ahead). It was a new word I learned when the foodservice ladies dropped off my meal.

69

"Enjoy your meal," I said, "and I want you to eat every bite, even the scales, because they are a delicacy and will give you the nutrients you need to recover from your childbirth."

Fred chuckled and ate it, all of it with only the eyeball remaining glaring at him from the plate. I picked up the rice, sipped the miso soup from the bowl, and drank some of the *ocha* green tea. I knew not only had I lost a lot of weight with the birth, but I definitely had lost weight because of my aversion to eating fish eyeballs.

In my pregnancy with Emma, I gained 50 pounds, and it took a year before I got back to my pre-pregnancy weight. This time, I hadn't gained as much, to begin with, and I knew I was probably entering a bit of a danger zone by not eating. "I'm going to go and find you something you *can* eat," Fred said with conviction. "Maybe there is a *konbini* that would have soba noodles or a ham sandwich?" I started to salivate. Emphatically he added, "There *has* to be a store nearby."

A half-hour later, Fred returned, grinning. "Well, I was able to find you food." He laughed, "Or at least something you will eat." There was a long pause, "there are *Konbini* on every single corner throughout the miles and miles of the city of Tokyo, but there is not a single one within a two-block radius of this hospital." He set down a bag. "I managed to find a very small pharmacy attached to the hospital. It was dark and had cardboard boxes filled with dusty medical supplies, so I wasn't sure it had any food at all, but in the back, along a low shelf, I found these!" He pulled out four different candy bars. A coconut Bounty Bar, a Snickers, and two Milky Ways. I grabbed them, noisily tore off the wrappers, and started to inhale the chocolate. I ripped, peeled, bit, and swallowed. I don't think I even tasted them.

Fred stood next to the bed, watching me. "Wow! You WERE hungry!" Then we laughed about the fact that, most likely, all of the food groups were not equally represented in my meal.

After my delicious dinner, we called my parents on Fred's work cell phone. I braced myself. "Mom and Dad, it's Sarah." It was the middle of their night, but they were wide awake, waiting to hear from us. "The baby was born at 12:15 PM Tokyo time. Fred was able to bring Emma to Colleen's apartment, and he is here with me at the hospital. We saw the baby a couple of hours ago. She is in the neonatal intensive care unit here at the hospital. We don't know everything yet, but there are obviously a number of issues. I'm not sure when we will learn more, but it is very confusing. We did get to see her. I got to nurse her, and we both got to hold her."

Without a second of hesitation, my mom said, "I'll come to Tokyo. I can help with Emma, and you can begin to figure out what you need to do with the baby." I hadn't admitted to myself the gravity of our situation. I was glad someone seemed to see the bigger picture.

My mom definitely didn't have time to come to Tokyo, let alone stay for an extended period of time. She was a professor at the University of Minnesota. She had graduate students who depended on her for their dissertations, and she had classes to prepare. Coming to Tokyo was the last thing she needed, but she knew more than we did that we couldn't do it without her.

My mom is a strong-willed woman who has courageous convictions and always speaks her mind. She is full of energy, involved in her church, and has multiple causes she champions. She embraces her life-long friends and dedicates her time to her work and students, but the thing she cherishes most, aside from my father, is her children. She keeps a watchful eye, is protective beyond words, and believes nothing should get in the way of their plans, hopes, or dreams. She is committed to her children's needs, no matter if she has the time or not.

I put Fred on the phone, "Hi Marty, thank you for understanding what is happening here. I'll get you on a Northwest plane. I'll have my office organize it." He choked up, lacking the words needed to convey what we were experiencing. He whispered, "Thank you," and hung up.

The nurses came in and told us it was time for Fred to leave. Another rule. He needed to go anyway because it was late. It was important for him to be with Emma. Before he left, a doctor I didn't recognize came into my room. "We need to meet with both of you in the morning to discuss the issues with your daughter. Can you be here at 7:00?" Fred nodded.

I whispered to Fred as he left, "I'm so worried about Emma. I miss her so much."

"She is doing surprisingly well." I knew my disappearance for so long must have been confusing for her, but I was glad Fred didn't add that to my growing list of concerns. He hugged me tight, "I'll see you in the morning. Get some sleep. I love you."

I said goodbye, and right after he closed the door, my mind started spinning out of control. I had given birth but didn't have our baby. I was making breast milk but couldn't feed her. Who was feeding her? Who would tell us the medical issues? They went around and around in my head and would not stop.

After tossing and turning for hours, I finally fell asleep. I tried to hold the image of her spectacular face, of me nursing her, and of Fred sitting by my side. It was all I could do.

Sometime in the middle of the night, my door opened. Someone walked in and abruptly turned on the light. It was a doctor in a white lab coat, and he was waving an X-ray. He approached my bed and stood next to me. Without waiting for me to wake up enough to understand him, he said, "We found multiple issues with your baby." Oh no, not again. "We did an X-ray. We were not expecting this, but we will need to speak with you and your husband extensively in the morning about what we have found. It is much, much more than we originally thought. In order for the baby to live, she will need to have an operation right away in the morning after we meet. We will need you to sign the paperwork for the surgery. I, and a team of doctors, will see you in the morning." He turned, shut out the lights, and left.

It was so disorienting to have him in my room that by the time I was somewhat coherent, he was gone. I didn't catch most of what he said, but I clearly understood our baby would have her first surgery less than 24 hours after her birth. How could this be happening?

Finally, at 5:00 in the morning on June 8, after lying in bed staring at the ceiling and crying, I looked out the window and saw it was raining. The entire month Emma and I had played together, the weather in Tokyo had been glorious, with sun and warmth each day. June, I had heard, was a rainy month, and it had obviously decided today was the day to start.

I was tired and felt awful. I wanted a shower, and there wasn't one in my room. It seemed like a simple enough task, but this was a Japanese maternity ward, and not a single one of the nurses spoke English. I resolved to find a way. Over my pajamas, I slowly put on the too-small robe and slippers provided by the hospital and shuffled down the hall to the reception desk.

There was a nurse standing there. I wanted a shower. Simple. I walked up to her knowing she would not speak English. I had thought a bit about the pantomime I could do to show what I wanted. Without saying a word, I stood there and put one hand on my head, and started swirling my hair in circles. I put my other hand under my armpit and started rubbing it. I hoped I was communicating I wanted to take a shower. It was either that or I had turned into a monkey.

The front desk nurse nodded. I smiled. She also probably wanted me to stop looking like a fool at her desk. She didn't point me in the direction of a shower, though. There were obviously rules. She pointed to a yellow pad of paper she had placed on top of the reception desk. There were two separate columns going down the page. She moved her pen slowly from line to line as if that was going to help. One column contained Japanese characters, and the second one had numbers. What did all of it mean? I exasperatingly let out a deep breath. At the very top of the page, there were more Japanese characters, this time in big block letters. Clearly, seeing I had no idea what to do, the woman wrote phonetically in English across the top, SHAH-WAH. I slowly and loudly said it out loud. I got it. This was some kind of a list about taking a shower.

The nurse pointed her pen at me and then pointed to a blank line on the yellow paper. I was desperate. What was she doing? Since I was not going to figure it out, she walked around the desk and down the hall to my room. I followed. She pointed to the pink slip with my name on it at my door and then to the room number in the middle. She went back to the yellow paper and wrote the same characters that were my name. Then in the column next to it, she wrote my room number. Ah ha! This was a list of names and room numbers. Got it!

The problem was I still had no idea about how I got to take a shower or even where it was. The nurse pointed to the line above my name and then used two fingers to walk them across the desk. She paused and, with a fist, knocked on the desk. She said, "SHAH-WAH," trying to get through my thick foreign head. I'd know when it was my turn because the person on the line above me would read my name and room number on the list. Then she would knock on my door. I decided speaking Japanese was exhausting.

I went back to my room, sat on my bed, stared at my closed door, and anxiously waited, hoping I had understood the rules of the shower game. At 5:30, someone knocked. "*SHAHWAH.*"

I said, "*Arigato,*" realizing 'thank you' in fact, was the right thing to say. The next little problem was I had no towel, shampoo, or soap. I didn't know where the *SHAH-WAH* was. I walked out of my room with what must have been a bewildered look on my face. The same nurse was ready for me. She pulled out a tiny towel the size of a washcloth and then motioned for me to follow her down the hall. She pointed to a small room, not bigger than a broom closet. Not knowing what else to do, I awkwardly bowed to the woman saying over and over, *arigato.*

Still bowing to the nurse, I backed into the closet and locked the door. I was safe. I saw a silver shower handle on the wall and a showerhead above. It was something familiar. I didn't need to ask for any more directions. Much to my relief, there was even a minuscule bar of soap and a small bottle of shampoo.

I stepped into the warm water and let it fall over me as if it was shielding me from what was just beyond that door. I cried for me; I cried for Fred and Emma and the baby. I let it wash over me in waves and then let my sadness go down the drain. After many minutes under the very hot water, I awoke as if out of a trance and thought it must be way past my time in the communal *SHAH-WAH,* and someone must be waiting for me to get out and knock on their door. I reluctantly shut off the water, dried off a bit with the tiny towel, put back on my robe and the too-small Japanese slippers, and dripped all down the hallway to the front desk. I dutifully crossed off my name, smiling at the nurse, showing my understanding of the rules. I could not possibly read the Japanese characters of the next lady's name on the *SHAH-WAH* list, but I could see the room number.

The nurse could tell I was about to wander up and down the hallways to find room 326, and she definitely was not going to allow me to do that. She brought me to the room and pointed. In front of 326, I cleared my throat, and in my best Japanese accent, which meant I sounded like a Minnesotan, I said, "*SHAH-WAH*," and ran down the hall in case the woman said something to me other than *ringo, sumimasen, onegaishimasu, dozo, shah-wah,* or *arigato.* Unfortunately, my ever-growing vocabulary of Japanese words still would not get me food other than fish for breakfast, which was waiting for me when I returned to my room.

I rolled the fish over to make sure it had both eyes still intact. This time though, there was a small glass of orange juice accompanying the cup of hot green tea. I eagerly drank them both. Fred arrived as I was pushing the food around on my tray. He had gotten home late the night before, but he and Emma had bought me a ham and cheese sandwich and *onigiri* rice balls with salmon inside.

"A doctor came into my room last night and woke me up," I said, taking a huge bite of my sandwich. I swallowed hard, wishing I had more orange juice. "They need to do surgery on the baby this morning."

Fred stopped and looked down at the floor. He switched topics as if he didn't hear, "Your mom is on the flight from Minneapolis to Tokyo. The office arranged it." How could it only be a few weeks since we'd made that same flight from Minnesota ourselves?

Chapter 15

On the dot of 7:00 am, another doctor appeared at my door. I think it was the one from the middle of the night, but it was all really blurry in my mind. He asked us to come with him. The hallway we walked down had the same menacing dark green and black linoleum. We turned and entered a room with four large white linoleum tables, all pushed together, almost filling the space. Strangely, the lights were off, and with the rain pouring outside, our eyes had to adjust to the darkness. There were three other doctors already seated in a row on the other side of the table.

They stood when we entered and bowed after introducing themselves in English. I didn't pay attention to any of their names; I didn't want to know more doctors.

We were ushered to seats across from them. The formality and lack of light in the room made for an austere feeling. The doctor who came to get us stood at the front of the room and introduced himself. "My name is Dr. Fujikawa. I am a pediatric surgeon here at Joshi Idai Hospital." He spoke in English with a slight British accent. "We know this hospital looks different from what you are used to, but it is important for you to know your daughter is very well-cared for here." Realizing I had been holding my breath, I exhaled a little louder than I intended.

"During the night, we thoroughly examined your baby girl, taking X-rays, and did other tests of her abdomen, brain, and heart." He went to the whiteboard at the front of the room and started to draw. "Before I begin, I want you to know her brain and heart are normal." This was obviously a relief, but he said it as almost an afterthought, so we didn't react.

He picked up a marker and started to draw. On the left-side of the board, he drew an outline of a small baby with a head, body, legs, and arms. Then he filled in what was recognizable as the parts of the digestive system. On the right side of the board, he drew another outline of a baby, but instead of a digestive system, the drawing had a circle in place of the abdomen with squiggly lines through it. Fred and I sat silently.

The doctor spoke slowly. "Here, on the left side, you see the normal formation of a lower abdomen." He explained what we had learned in high school biology. "You eat food; it goes into your stomach so food can be digested. It then moves to the small intestine, then the large intestine, and it exits as waste out through your rectum." As he was saying this, he was moving his pen down through the drawing on the left. This all made logical sense. We both nodded our heads.

The doctor then moved to the right side of the whiteboard to the drawing with the big circle with lines through it where the abdomen should be. "Based on the tests and X-rays that were done during the night, this is what your baby's lower abdomen looks like." The doctor paused. There wasn't anything recognizable there. How could that be her digestive system? I looked from the drawing on the left to the one on the right, hoping desperately to make the pictures the same. I didn't understand what he was talking about. I glanced at Fred. He had tightened his face and was squinting at the board, clearly confused too.

The doctor continued, "It looks like your baby has something called 'Cloacal Anomalies or Cloacal Malformation.'" He scribbled it on the board and then turned around to face us. He stood silently. A minute went by. The room was quiet except for the cheap clock ticking on the wall reminding me of the long hours I'd already spent in this hospital. The three doctors looked stiff in a row and were now staring at us too. They were keenly observing us as we came to terms with the fact that our daughter's digestive system was missing.

Under the table, I was squeezing my hands so tightly I lost all feeling in my fingers. I looked down, not wanting to meet their gaze. "In babies born with Cloacal Anomalies, there is some abnormality of the bladder and bowel. As you can see in the drawing on the right, instead of being separated and each body part having a separate function, in your daughter's body, they are all formed in a single common channel. This is one of the most challenging pediatric problems that can occur. Right now, your baby cannot release stool because she has something called an imperforate anus. She will die if we don't operate immediately."

Die?! The doctor continued talking, but I could feel myself drifting. I heard him say words about Cloacal Malformation occurring in girls and boys and in about 1 out of 5,000 births. Babies with this condition most likely have issues with controlling their bladder and bowel for their entire lives. He also said there can also be problems with menstruation and pregnancy later in life.

What? What? What is he talking about? I had seen her. She was the sweetest baby. She was cute and petite and alive. She drank and slept and looked like every other baby. How could this be true? I wanted to stand and yell and tell them this must be someone else's baby. This could not be happening to us.

Dr. Fujikawa must have heard the shouting in my head. "The reason you cannot see any of these issues is because it is all inside her body. You have obviously noticed she is missing an ear. Sometimes Cloacal Anomalies come with a constellation of other complications in babies. Her ear is a part of this. Many babies have brain and heart problems, but thankfully we don't see any of that."

This time he did not pause nor hesitate to deliver the knockout punch. "The immediate issue is that she has no hole for stool to exit her body. Sarah-san," he addressed me formally, "I spoke to you after you delivered the baby and told you she had an imperforate anus and would need surgery."

Suddenly I snapped, shouting, "YES! But you said she would need only one small surgery, and she would be able to live a normal life. How could you have said that? You lied! When we got to the NICU, the first thing we saw was her ear was missing." I stood up, leaned forward, gripping the tabletop, and screamed. Why-Didn't-You-Tell-Me!?" Fred didn't stop me.

The doctors across the table looked horrified. Japanese rules obviously didn't allow parents to yell at doctors.

Dr. Fujikawa smiled a paternalistic smile. He walked toward us, and that made me shrink back down into my chair. "Sarah-san, I thought you had been through enough just by giving birth; telling you about her ear would only have added to your worry. Also, we hadn't done any tests at that point except to examine the baby visually." He said again, what I could not hear, "It is critical we operate on her today. If we don't, she will not live." Then he sat down at the table across from us, along with the other doctors.

"We are not entirely certain what we will find when we operate this morning, but our goal is to do this small surgery so her body can function at a basic level."

"There is no hole for stool to exit her body," a different doctor said. "The surgery we are going to perform today is to create a colostomy. It is a small incision or stoma. It is made below the ribcage on the right-hand side. The surgery brings a piece of the large intestine through the incision and sutures it in place so the bowel can still empty successfully through that hole."

One of the doctors pulled out a manila file folder and put it on the table. Dr. Fujikawa opened it and pulled out a piece of paper. The ink on the paper was green, and there were several boxes going down the sides. It looked like something that needed to be filled out, but everything was in Japanese, so we had no way of knowing.

"This is the form you need to sign before we can proceed with today's surgery." He reached across the table with the document facing us and pointed to each line. It stated we would not hold the hospital accountable if the surgery did not go as intended. There was information about the payment, which made me think for less than a second that I had absolutely no notion what all of this was costing. When he finished, he pointed to a small box at the bottom of the paper. He translated, "It says baby's name."

That jolted us both back into the room. It had not even crossed our minds we would be discussing our baby's name before she would have surgery. This felt wrong. How could we officially name our daughter in front of these strange doctors moments before she was whisked off to have an operation where she might die?

Many months before, we had talked happily, joyfully, and endlessly about names for this baby. Before Fred left for Japan, we had used the same baby name book we had used for Emma. We knew we wanted a first name that would sound the same in every language, as we had done with Emma. We hoped our girls would travel the world, so we wanted names that were easily pronounceable in all languages. We had settled on Lily. Her Belgian last name, Deschamps, means 'of the fields,' which we thought was beautiful with the name Lily. All of this was in place before Fred left Minnesota so many months ago.

What was left was choosing a middle name. We needed one that united the first and last. We had not had time to finalize our decision, but here we were with doctors staring at us and the empty green box almost blinking to force a decision. One of the doctors checked his watch. Tick tock, we felt rushed and stressed. Fred and I turned toward each other. I whispered, "Before Emma and I left Minnesota, I looked at a book with a few Japanese names. There was one that caught my eye. It is 'Mai, M-A-I' pronounced 'My.' The book said it meant 'dancing' in Japanese. I don't know if that is actually true; I think it would make a powerful name." Our baby would be 'Dancing Lily of the Fields.'

We both looked up. We didn't ask the doctors if 'Mai' was a Japanese name or if it meant dancing. From that second on, it meant dancing to us. Fred wrote the name carefully in the small green box, 'Lily Mai Deschamps.' We both smiled and grabbed each other's hands under the table. Our baby's name incorporated the cultures she would always carry with her in life, American, Belgian, and Japanese. It felt right.

The difference was that this form wasn't a celebration of her name being placed on her birth certificate; this name in this box allowed the doctors to cut a hole in our baby's belly. She could then have waste exit her body, which she couldn't now do on her own. Fred signed the paper and reluctantly shoved it back across the table. Dr. Fujikawa said they would get Lily within the hour so they could do the surgery.

I said, "Stop! We need our daughter Emma, who is almost three, to meet her sister before you do this operation." I looked at Fred frantically, and he nodded. "We can have Emma here in about an hour and a half. You need to wait." There was hushed murmuring across the table. I was guessing they didn't get many parents making demands with respect to surgery, but we were not going to budge. Simultaneously, Fred and I got up and walked out of the room. Fred left and said he would return with Emma as quickly as possible. I went back to my hospital room to wait.

As I arrived, a nurse came in. She brought me a breast pump. I knew it well because I had used one to express milk for an entire year for Emma. I hooked myself up, realizing this meant I would not be nursing my baby except during the strict visiting hours. Someone I didn't know would be feeding her with a bottle.

After only an hour, Emma ran into my room with Fred smiling behind her. She flew through the air and landed on my bed. I hugged her and kissed her, and in a rush of words, said, "I'm so excited to see you! You have a new, beautiful baby sister. We named her Lily."

Emma stopped moving for a second. She said it slowly, "LI...LY." She smiled and said, "I like that name." The nurse must have been watching for Emma and Fred to arrive because, within minutes, Dr. Fujikawa was knocking at the door. He said we should come out into the hallway.

I held Emma's hand, and we walked together. There she was. Emma ran over. Lily was in a small clear plastic bassinet with wheels. It was only a few feet off the floor, right at Emma's height. Unbelievably, there were no machines or wires attached to her. She looked like any other baby who was only a day old. Emma leaned in to see her sister. Right there, in the middle of the hallway, in front of the nurse at the front desk and Dr. Fujikawa, Emma grasped her sister's head. She pulled her face close to her own and said, "Hi. I'm your big sister Emma. I love you, Lily." It was the first time Lily had heard her name. It was a moment that took my breath away.

Hovering near us, Dr. Fujikawa moved closer. I could tell he was ready to take Lily for surgery. Fred and I moved forward. We leaned into the bassinet and gave Lily a kiss on the forehead. "Be a strong little baby. We love you."

On June 8th at 10:30 in the morning, we watched our less than one-day-old daughter be taken away for surgery. The three of us stood silently in the hallway. Emma didn't ask where Lily was going, and we didn't offer any explanation.

My mind started racing. Lily's beautiful, smooth belly would be gone. It was too brutal to imagine. She was tiny; how would they find the colon? How big an incision would they need to make? What was her life going to be like? How were we going to care for her?

I wanted everything to stop. We had our baby. She was in front of us. She looked perfect. She completed our family. I needed the ever-growing worry to end. We had already experienced months of all-consuming stress; how could we possibly tolerate more?

The nurse was now leaning over her desk, staring at us. Without words, she was clearly indicating Fred and Emma had to go. More rules; this time it meant no spouses and no children. I lowered my head, realizing I was again going to be alone to deal with the results of this surgery. Why did they have all of these rules? Why couldn't I just have my family with me? They caused no harm to anyone. I needed Fred there to soothe my endless worries and soften the tragedy unfolding before us.

The reality was it didn't matter what we needed because we didn't have a choice. The baby was born in this hospital, and they had just taken her for a surgery that would save her life. There were no other options, this was where we had to be, and now we had to wait.

I forced a smile on my face. I picked Emma up and twirled her around. She laughed, and I laughed, and for a second, right there, right then, we were together, just the two of us. It was cleansing to feel her joy and her innocence. "Mommy, are you coming home with us? I miss you, and I want to go and play with the mosquitos again. I think Lily will love the forest. I can carry her and show her the trees and the hiding places. Can we go to the grocery store again? I love those funny Kit Kats. I can't wait for you to be with me at home again." Hearing her growing vocabulary, and full sentences, surprised me. I had only been away from her for a couple of days, but she spoke with more confidence. It seemed that moving to Japan had already been good for her. I turned my face away, set her down, and looked at Fred.

"I'll be with Emma, and I'll keep my phone nearby. If you can figure out how to make the ancient phone in your room work, please call me once you see Lily." We hugged tight, said we loved each other, and he and Emma left the hospital.

The hours went by slowly. I sat on my bed waiting. At 3:30 in the afternoon, Dr. Kato, who had led us into the NICU the day before, came to my room.

She repeated as if I hadn't seen her the day before, "I'm Doctor Kato. I came to tell you the surgery is done, and your baby is recovering in the NICU. In about thirty minutes, I'll come and get you, and you can see her." She didn't even say if the surgery had been successful or not before she left. I wondered why they did that. Why did doctors leave before you could ask anything? It was dizzying to have so many questions flying around in my head and not be able to ask.

I again sat on my bed and waited as the endless minutes ticked by. At about 4:00, she reappeared in my doorway. She didn't say anything, so I got off the bed and followed her down to the NICU. Shoes off, plastic Japanese slippers on, followed by the paper-thin blue hairnet and gown. The sealed glass door opened, and the smell of bleach wafted in my nose.

Chapter 16

As I entered the room, the nurses all stopped what they were doing. Visiting hours must be over for the day because no parents were there. My presence was interrupting their work. I frantically looked and couldn't see Lily where she had been the day before. I scanned the room desperately, trying to find her. I couldn't. As I stared into the fifteen bassinets, I saw the tiny babies covered in blankets. Their diminutive heads had a hat perched on them. There were different machines for each infant, most of them with flashing lights or beeping incessantly, begging for the attention of the nurses in the room. It made it real; these were babies, too, like mine. They were in this room for a tragic reason as well. It was the only way a newborn would be in here. My daughter was like them. She, too, needed this room and those machines and all that attention just to live.

We rounded the corner into the next room. This space was much quieter. There were only three babies in here; instead, every wall was lined with bassinets. There was a large window looking into the other room. That was the only light in the space.

Lily was the very first baby on the left. Instead of running to her this time, I held back, my heart pounding. I wasn't sure what I would find. I wouldn't admit it to myself, but I was afraid of my own baby. She would have a large cut in her, one that created a hole in her belly, a hole that should not be there, but one that made it so she could live. I couldn't believe it. I didn't want any of this, not for her, nor for me.

Dr. Kato stood close to me, calmly waiting for me to focus. When I finally peered into the bassinet, I saw the most beautiful shining face looking up at me. Lily was breathtaking. She had a sweet pink rosebud mouth, eyes that seemed to sparkle, a head with long cheekbones, and a nice round chin. I smiled. Like the day before, when we saw her for the first time, she grabbed my heart and would not let go. Since she looked so perfect to me, I wondered how the news could be so bad.

"Lily," she began, and I was so glad to hear her use Lily's name, "had to have surgery that was more complex than we originally thought. It involved more than simply creating a colostomy for her bowel to function. She had to have a vesicostomy as well."

A what? How do you say that?

"A vesicostomy is created in babies who are born with Cloacal Anomalies when the urinary tract is completely malformed. In other words, she doesn't have a clear outlet for either her stool or her urine. The clinical term is a high vesical-vaginal fistula. It is a bladder dysfunction. It occurs in 65% of the Cloacal Anomaly patients."

I wasn't tracking and wished Fred was here. I was still back on the beautiful baby part. "Without the surgery," Dr. Kato continued, "Lily would have had massive amounts of urine and stool collect inside of her, and it would have led to toxic bacteria accumulating, which would have caused irreparable damage and, ultimately, death."

Death. I nodded my head, pretending I understood what she was saying, but I didn't understand a thing.

In my professional life as a Spanish teacher, I had attended many seminars and conferences on the three different types of learners. There were Auditory, Visual and Kinesthetic. In my classroom, I taught all three types. For my auditory learners, I spoke clearly in Spanish. For my visual learners, I drew those same concepts up on the board, and then for my kinesthetic learners, I used the same material in games or skits so they could move and touch the material. I covered every learning style almost every day, so each of my students could grasp the material. In all those years of teaching, I had never stopped to consider how I learned.

Standing there, I realized grasping intricate medical terms and descriptions was exactly like learning a foreign language. Nothing was recognizable. That morning in the conference room, I tried to no avail to visually learn from the drawing on the white board, and now I was standing looking at Lily and trying to hear what I was being told to me. I couldn't understand this new medical language from what I was seeing or hearing.

Much to my own detriment, I discovered right then that I'm a kinesthetic learner. If the thoughtful and intelligent Dr. Kato had drawn on her own lower abdomen or even used my stomach as an example, I would have had a much better chance of understanding what she was saying. With her talking at me, no matter how much I tried, I wasn't going to understand.

She was now pointing to Lily, and her words kept coming, "this is called hydronephrosis; usually, it is accompanied by an elongated urogenital sinus, and there is usually a problem with the vagina as well." I heard the word "vagina," and whatever she had said was clearly not something you wanted for your baby. After that, my ability to pay attention ended.

I tried looking intently into the bassinet as if I was taking it all in and hanging on her every word. In fact, I was not listening at all. If Lily had to stay for a while in the hospital, then maybe I could decorate her bassinet with pictures of Emma, Fred, and me. Since we couldn't be with her all the time, she would still see her family and know we loved her.

Dr. Kato stopped talking. Feeling completely lost and unable to ask a single coherent question about our daughter's extremely complex medical issues, I said, "You speak English well. Where did you go to medical school?" She looked aghast. I didn't care. Lily seemed happy and calm, so the surgery must have gone well. I could stay in denial for another minute or two.

"I studied in England, but I'm finishing my training here at this hospital." Her English was perfect, which helped me even if I didn't understand the medical terms.

We both looked at the baby, and that was when I realized that Lily's body could teach me. By touching her, I could understand. My kinesthetic learning might actually help me, not hurt me. I could love her, hold her, and learn about her medical needs by taking care of her. With a bit more confidence, I refocused my attention.

"Could you please show me what you did during the surgery?"

"Of course."

Finding a safe and easy place to start, I looked away from her and saw two machines, both with monitors attached to her little body. "What are these?"

"One of them monitors her vital signs, which are her blood pressure, heart rate, pulse, and temperature." She pointed to each of the specific measurements. "If there are changes from the normal range, the machines will beep, indicating there is an issue. The second machine has this bag on it," she pointed, "which contains an antibiotic to make certain she has no infection from the operation."

I understood those machines now, but unfortunately, I knew what was coming next would break my heart before I could even begin to understand. Dr. Kato gingerly began to remove Lily's blankets. Her belly was covered with a hospital gown, but I could see enough of her that I started to do a thorough inventory of her body parts. I counted ten fingers and ten toes. I saw legs and arms, and apart from a tiny IV needle sticking out of the middle of her right arm, I saw nothing was any different than any other baby. I already knew about her ear, and she still had such a cute pink hat on her head; I didn't need to focus on that.

Then Dr. Kato removed the hospital gown. I gasped. I closed my eyes for a second, inhaled deeply, and blew it out. I forced myself to look. Lily had two large incisions on her tiny belly. At first glance, they looked like they covered every inch. One was on the right side, above her belly button, the other in the middle, just below it. Each one had a strange object sticking out of it. The lower one had a clear tube the diameter of a straw. The one higher on her belly had a bright red squishy object the size of a quarter poking out through her skin. These were her insides, and now they were on the outside. I was looking at parts of her that should never see the light of day.

"This," the doctor said, pointing to the red squishy thing, "is a colostomy. Since Lily has an imperforate anus, which means she has no hole for stool to exit through her bottom, this colostomy will serve that purpose." Dr. Kato continued, "What you see here, this red thing, is her colon. The surgery we performed brought it to the surface. Through this hole, all of her stool will exit her body." Poop was going to exit our baby through a hole in her stomach. I couldn't even fathom how that worked.

"On top of the red stoma, a plastic colostomy bag will be glued in place and regularly changed. The bag will hold all of the stool." It sounded disgusting. In my mind, I was pleading with her, no more, that is enough, but she continued anyway.

"This is the vesicostomy," she said as she pointed to the straw-like tube poking through Lily's skin below her still-healing belly button. "This tube will serve as the drain for Lily's bladder. It will constantly flow with urine and will keep her kidney and bladder healthy."

The tube was the diameter of a pencil and extremely long. I could see it awkwardly protruding from inside her belly, but I couldn't see where it went because it plunged over the side of the bassinet fastened to it by a metal hook shaped like the letter S. A foot below the bassinet was a thick plastic bag. In the bottom of the bag, far, far away from Lily's sweet body, there was a tiny amount of yellow liquid. That was her urine.

I crouched down, staring at the bag of pee, taking a moment away from the sight of her butchered body. Our daughter had two holes in her belly, both of which were created during surgery when she was less than one day old. If she had not had the surgery, she would have died from the toxicity of the waste made by her own body. I plopped down on the floor with my knee hitting the pee bag as I landed. I closed my eyes and mumbled to myself, "We're fucked."

The doctor wasn't tall, but she was now towering over me. I looked up at her and could see she was waiting for me to get up. These medical issues were not going to go away because I didn't think I could deal with them. In fact, the longer I sat, the more likely it would be that I would be labeled as a mother who couldn't cope.

I got up, careful not to touch the tube or the bag, and nodded for the doctor to continue.

She didn't have many more words to say, but they were just as gut-wrenching. "We want Lily to stay in the hospital for the foreseeable future. The possibility of infection it too great to have her go home now."

Not take her home?

"As you may recall," Dr. Kato continued, "there are visiting hours here in the NICU. That is why you never see other parents. They are only allowed in the room from 1: 00 pm – 3:00 pm each day. Outside of these hours, we will be caring for Lily. You will bring your pumped breast milk with you when you come each day. We will feed Lily when you are not here. Do you have any questions?"

A doctor finally took the time to ask if I had questions, but I didn't know where to start. *How can I possibly move her with that snaking tube? How do I put clothes on her without poop going everywhere? Will those awful holes be with her for the rest of her life? How can I get to know her if she is locked in here?* I shook my head.

Since it was way past 5:00 pm, I could tell I was expected to leave, those were the rules.

While I was standing there in disbelief, the doctor, now aided by a nurse, was starting to put Lily's hospital gown and blankets back in place. Instinctively, I reached in to touch her. The doctor and nurse backed away. I leaned in and kissed her, and I whispered, "I love you. I'm going to take care of you." I was overcome, my tears dripping onto her fragile body as I pulled away.

I knew the routine. NICU door closed, gown off, hairnet off, slippers off, and placed on the shoe rack. Shoes on, and then I walked back to my hospital room with the doctor. When we reached the room, she told me that Dr. Fujikawa, who was the lead surgeon, wanted to meet both of us at 10:00 the next morning. "You will be discharged from the hospital tomorrow. After the meeting, you can go home."

I closed the door to my room, ran to the phone, and was determined to make a call so I could hear Fred's voice. I picked up the cumbersome handset and heard a strong beep, beep, beep. I couldn't make a call.

I opened the door, walked to the reception desk, and stood in front of the nurse who had helped me get a *SHAH-WAH*. I placed my thumb to my ear and my pinky finger to my mouth and started saying, "*onegaishmasu, arigato, ringo*," and desperately hoped she understood I wanted to use the phone. In case my Japanese didn't work, I said, "number?" I said it slowly, "NU-M-BER?" I thought my slowness would make it possible for me to be understood. I added, "HUS-BAN-D, CAA-LLL." She picked up the phone on the desk and showed me I needed to dial "9" first to get an outside line. I ran back to my room, dialed 9, and then Fred's number. It rang only once before he answered.

Words tumbled out of my mouth, "She has two holes, and one of them has a red squishy thing coming out of it. She will poop through that thing. Below her belly button, there is a H-UG-E tube, like a snake. It comes straight out of her belly, and then it goes all around her bassinet. It ends up almost on the floor in a bag that collects her pee. She can't pee or poop without all of this stuff."

I was shouting and most likely incoherent, saying all the things I couldn't ask the doctor. "How do we pick up a baby with tubes and bags? How will we hold her and carry her? What is her life going to be like? What is our life going to be like?" Tears started streaming down my face. "She is so cute. She has the sweetest face and the tiniest lips. As an afterthought, I added, "She has all of her toes and all of her fingers and hands and legs; I counted."

Fred quickly added, "Well, thank goodness for that."

"They won't let her leave the hospital. She is hooked up to machines and has drugs going into her. They have to put some bag over her red squishy thing. It will catch poop. It sounds disgusting. They have visiting hours; we can only see her from 1:00 – 3:00. I can't figure out how you will possibly see Lily in the middle of your workday."

When I finally ran out of things to say, Fred's words were more measured, much more so than I'm certain he felt. "It doesn't sound like what we were told this morning or like what the doctors were predicting. Emma and I are in a taxi picking up your mom at the Westin Hotel. Her bus from Narita

Airport arrives soon. I'm going to need to focus on helping her to get acclimated to our apartment, getting dinner, and getting Emma to bed."

I was shocked back into reality. My mom arrived! I was so glad to know she was about to join us. I quickly said, "You and I need to meet Dr. Fujikawa in the morning. Can you all be here at 10:00?"

"Yes, see you in the morning." He paused, "I love you. We'll figure this out," and the line went dead.

I sat on the bed and blinked, staring out at the rainy gray sky outside my window. I needed something I could do, something I could control. If I was in pain from giving birth, it didn't even register. I jumped up off the bed and raced around the room. I gathered all of my personal things and stuffed them frantically into the bag I had brought as if my life depended on it. I wanted to be ready when Fred and my mom came in the morning. I placed my bag next to me and sat back down on the bed with my legs folded, staring at the door. It never occurred to me that I had given birth and should be tired or in pain. That didn't matter. Only Lily mattered.

Packing took 30 seconds, I still had fifteen hours to wait.

Chapter 17

Fred, Emma, and my mom walked through the door of my hospital room at 9:30 the next morning. It was raining outside, but it was like the sun had come out, and a rainbow was over my room. My mom was here. She didn't look as if she had unexpectedly jumped on a plane for twelve hours traveling to a strange place. She had her usual bright and warm smile and was dressed impeccably in pleated pants, an ironed shirt, and a suit jacket. "Hello, sweetheart. You look wonderful. I'm so glad to see you in person instead of worrying about you from home. Dad is worried sick about you. He is glad I'm here too." She started to take a step toward me when I jumped off the bed, and just like Emma had done the day before, I flung myself in my own mother's arms. Her being there brought an immediate sense of relief and familiarity, and warmth. We had help, someone we all loved and could rely on in this ever-growing catastrophe.

Dr. Fujikawa came to get us at exactly 10:00. Emma and my mom stayed behind in my room. Emma joyfully played on my hospital bed, making it go up and down, squealing in delight, most certainly breaking multiple rules. Fred and I followed the doctor down to the NICU. I was so glad Fred would get to see Lily and ask a doctor his own questions.

Fred sat on one side of Lily's bassinet, and Dr. Fujikawa sat on the other. I was behind them listening, but I wanted Fred to have a chance to see and hear everything up close. Lucky for us, I already knew that Fred was an auditory learner, so he would grasp easily what was being told to him.

In his measured and scholarly manner, Dr. Fujikawa spoke. "Lily's situation is much worse than we anticipated. The surgeries we performed have made it so Lily can live. Her waste now has a way to exit her body, so there is no more risk of death." As Dr. Fujikawa talked, I saw the color on Fred's face leave. It was one thing to hear about our daughter on the phone from me; it was something else to be sitting next to your baby and absorbing it on your own.

"All of her body parts are still mixed up and intertwined, as I showed you in the drawing."

Oh no, not the drawing again.

"This includes her bladder, bowel, and uterus. It can all be fixed. We are extremely lucky there are surgical procedures that can be performed to reconstruct all of these organs, so they function properly. Even a few years ago, this particular surgery could not be done. Babies like

Lily did not have a good prognosis for a full life."

I looked at Fred, who was now listening to talk of stomas, vesicostomies, colostomies, infections, bags of urine, and tubes. He was staring out the NICU window, appearing not to listen anymore. All of a sudden, his hand shot up in the air as if he had a question in a classroom. The doctor paused. Fred enunciated clearly, "chotto matte kudasai." I didn't know that phrase, but the doctor understood. He stopped talking. Fred gulped and then blew out air, looking as if he was trying to keep his composure while absorbing our terrible new truth.

The hopes and dreams, and wishes we had for our future as a family were disappearing. Our life would now be exclusively caring for and worrying about our newborn baby. Our world would be here in this Japanese NICU, and there was no known date when it would end.

Not acknowledging Fred's obvious anguish, after a minute, he began again. "There is a doctor named Hardy Hendren who pioneered the surgeries that will reconstruct Lily's tiny body. He is currently practicing in Boston. The first surgery she will need is the single most complicated procedure for babies that is non-life threatening."

I was struggling as I listened. I still couldn't understand how this tiny beautiful creature in front of us could be in so much trouble. The doctor kept saying words like death and life-threatening; I didn't think it looked like those things could be possible. She was living and nursing, and sleeping. Then I reminded myself that in order to go to the bathroom, she had to have her colon sticking out of her belly and a tube the size of a long snake coming out of her lower abdomen. I wanted to doubt what they were saying, I wanted it to not be true, but as I looked at her, I realized this time there was no room for doubt.

Dr. Fujikawa pushed forward. "Dr. Hendren once spent seventeen hours in the operating room with one patient doing a cloacal repair like Lily's." He looked down at the notebook he was carrying and read from it. "A book has been written about Dr. Hendren called, The Work of Human Hands: Hardy Hendren and Surgical Wonder at Children's Hospital. You should get the book right away so you have a better understanding of what to expect."

Fred scribbled the name on the back of a receipt he pulled from his pocket.

"I can tell you now she will need multiple surgeries over the next several years. She will need the reconstructive surgery first, then surgery to close the colostomy, and then she will need the vesicostomy closed." I was tabulating in my head the number of surgeries he was talking about. We were up to four, counting the one he had just done.

"Most likely, Lily has other issues," Dr. Fujikawa added. "Cloacal babies typically have many different problems as a result of the malformation. As I think you already know, Lily has only one kidney, and this might cause her trouble in the future. This will be carefully examined during the reconstructive surgery." No one had actually confirmed that with us, but now we knew for certain. Dr. Fujikawa ended with, "As you have already seen, she only has one ear, which is definitely a part of her cloacal anomalies. My specialty is pediatric internal surgery, so I don't know about the reconstruction of ears. We did a quick test on her hearing, and she has 100 percent hearing in her fully formed ear, so hearing is not an issue." It hadn't occurred to me that she might be deaf. I gasped, thinking about what this could have meant for all of us.

What Dr. Fujikawa said next surprised me. "I have done a couple of these reconstructive surgeries myself. Instead of going all the way to Boston, you could stay right here in Tokyo, and I can work with you. Unfortunately, I will not be at Joshi Idai hospital anymore. I am trying to find a new hospital

94

in Tokyo. Once Lily stabilizes here and goes home, you can see me in the clinic where I will be working."

At that moment, staying in Japan with Dr. Fujikawa felt like a good idea. After so many months away from Fred, I didn't want to add more, and I liked the doctor. He seemed kind and knew how to explain the medical information so at least Fred could understand it. I was impressed that he knew how to do the complicated reconstructive surgery for Lily. I started thinking maybe we were lucky to be at this hospital in Tokyo, with its antiquated building and infuriating rules. Dr. Fujikawa had saved Lily's life. We were fortunate, I thought, to be here. He said, "Do you have any questions?"

From behind him, I blurted out, "When can she go home?" After watching Dr. Kato show me Lily's stomach, I came to the conclusion I could change a colostomy bag and empty a pee bag too. I didn't know what that entailed, yet I was certain I could do it. After all, I was her mom.

He craned his neck to look at me. "She can't go home anytime soon. The problem isn't the colostomy and vesicostomy; the issue is there is a tremendous risk of infection. We have opened Lily's tiny body and exposed parts of her that are extremely susceptible to bacteria. Infection, if it comes, will be quick and forceful. The hospital is the best place to monitor her. We don't know when she will be stable enough to go home, but she certainly needs to grow to get ready for the major surgery."

I couldn't imagine Lily growing up in the NICU until all of those surgeries were done. "When can she have the reconstructive surgery?"

"It will be a while. She is a very small baby, and the larger she is, the better the chances are of having a completely successful surgical outcome. It will be at least a year." Oh, my, God, Lily will live here for a year? An entire year! I felt like I was being punched, and the wind was knocked out of me. I looked around the room, trying to find an exit, one where we could take Lily. It felt like we were in the most impossible situation. How were we going to get to know our child? Fred could not possibly take off from work for two hours in the middle of each day to see our daughter. My mother was here to help us, but she was only staying for a few weeks. I knew I couldn't manage to live for an entire year with our baby locked behind a door with doctors standing on guard.

Dr. Fujikawa didn't even flinch, as if my panic was normal. He tried to change the subject now that we had all of the information that he was going to provide for us. "The nurses will show you how to lift Lily out of the bassinet with all of her tubes. Until Lily can go home, however, the hospital staff will take care of all of her medical issues. You are to be her mother, and we will take care of everything else."

The words came tumbling out, "We are ready to care for her; we don't need the hospital staff to do that for us. I can change a colostomy bag if you show me how. I can empty a pee bag. I will bring her back to the hospital if there is an infection. I can manage all of these issues at home."

He looked past me. "She will remain here until she grows." And that was that. Our newborn baby was destined to remain in the NICU. It felt like he was saying she would be here forever.

As if he knew I could not possibly tolerate any more difficult news, he reached into Lily's bassinet and pulled out a very small wooden box that had been placed above her head. "I almost forgot, there is a Japanese custom that we keep a piece of the umbilical cord. We place it in this special box, and it symbolizes the giving of life. This is for you to keep."

I was very touched that they extended the Japanese tradition to our family. I put out my hands, and he gently placed the box in them. I opened it and indeed saw a piece of shriveled skin. I didn't let my face move an inch. I didn't want him to see that I thought it looked disgusting. It was, in fact, precious because it was the only part of our baby that we could take home. I put the lid back on the box and bowed, "Arigato."

Doctor Fujikawa stood up and motioned for a nurse to come over. He spoke to her in Japanese, then translated to tell us that we could now hold Lily, also indicting that he would be leaving. We both stood up next to him and firmly shook his hand, a sign of greeting in our own culture. He then bowed to us, and I followed Fred's lead, and we bowed even lower. We wanted to show him respect in his own culture. With our heads down, Fred said, "Thank you. You saved our child. Thank you."

"It is my pleasure, she is a beautiful baby. I think you will see she will become a stunning young woman." I couldn't believe he said that. He just gave us a sliver of hope in the middle of these dark days. Maybe after all of these surgeries, Lily would be fine. I shut my eyes and took a picture in my head of this moment. I wanted to remember what Dr. Fujikawa said.

He handed Fred a piece of paper with the address of his new temporary clinic, and then he left the NICU. It would be several months before I would see him again.

The nurse stayed and helped us hold Lily showing us how to move the tubes and wires out of the way so she could be in our laps. She was sound asleep, so I woke her up, and without asking for permission in case I was breaking a rule, I nursed her. She easily latched on as if nothing was wrong. Fred and I sat together, touching her and finally feeling joy, the kind parents get with their newborn.

My mom and Emma were waiting for us. We picked up my little bag and walked out of my hospital room. On the way out, I grabbed the pink paper off of the door where my name had been written in Japanese. Aside from Lily's umbilical cord in its tiny box, this was my one souvenir from giving birth in a Japanese hospital. We walked past the nurse at the front desk, and I bowed low, once again trying to show respect. She had helped me even though we had no common language. As I bowed, I said, "Arigato."

Emma pushed the elevator button, and I picked her up. "Emma," I said, "Lily has to stay in the hospital for a while." I twisted my head away from her, then inhaled and held my breath for a second so I wouldn't cry. "She needs to have the doctor check on her a bit longer." Emma nodded her head and held onto me tightly, and I hugged her back just as hard. No matter what, it was good to be going home.

I stepped outside for the first time in three and a half days. It felt like an eternity had passed. I looked the same but felt very different. I had given birth. We had a new baby, but we had to leave her behind.

Fred hailed a taxi. The four of us all crammed in the back with Emma on my lap. After telling the taxi driver our address, Fred said, "I paid the bill for your hospital stay before coming up to your room. Do you know how you pay a hospital bill in Japan?" I didn't. "You pay in cash! My office helped me get the thousands of dollars in yen from our bank account. I had a big backpack with me stuffed with the bills." He patted the now deflated bag he had put on the floor of the taxi. "I felt like a bank robber. They sat and counted each yen bill in the business office. What a strange way to do business."

Chapter 18

The next morning, I jolted upright, sweating and hyperventilating as our bedroom slowly came into focus. It wasn't a nightmare. It was real. The image of that rundown hospital. The incomprehensible Japanese language and medical words. The drawings we saw on the white board in the dark room. The beautiful baby had tubes, holes, and a red intestine oozing out of her skin. It was all real.

I threw off the covers and put my feet on the ground steadying myself. I was in our apartment with all of our belongings. I got up and went to Emma's room to make sure she was here. I walked to my Mom's room and slid open the door a crack to see that she was here too.

Fred had left early that morning, relieved to be back at work, doing what he had come here to do. There were no massive phones, no fish eyeballs on my breakfast plate, and no need for running down the hall shouting *SHAH-WAH*. For a second, a rush of relief spread over me. I was home.

Then I remembered I had to go back. I had to again say to a taxi driver those words, 'Joshi Idai Byoin.' I had to walk back through the doors and into that NICU. They had my baby, so they had me too.

At noon, I reluctantly opened our heavy apartment door and let it bang behind me. I forced myself to leave, holding in my head the image of Emma and my mom drawing on our terrace. A part of our family was happy and at peace. That felt reassuring. I had pumped milk for Lily and put it on ice in my bag. I stuck my arm out for a taxi and whispered, "*Joshi Idai Byoin, onegaishimasu.*"

The stress and worry were oppressive enough, but it was dawning on us that because this hospital was so far away, it would be over six hundred dollars a week to take a taxi there and back. We couldn't afford that, especially since Lily wouldn't be leaving the hospital anytime soon. Fred and I agreed we had to buy a car. We needed the independence and flexibility it would provide, but the idea frightened me. Tokyo was gargantuan, sprawling for miles and miles. I barely knew how to walk around our neighborhood, let alone how to drive to the hospital.

To convince myself I could get to Joshi Idai on my own, I took out a pen and paper and started to write down everything I could see as the taxi sped through the city. There are very few street names in Tokyo, so I wrote down whatever I saw. 'Tall green building on the right, a smaller statue of a man on the left, a wide street being crossed called Aoyamadori, large underpass with train tracks above, a round building on the right,' and so it went for four pages. As the taxi pulled up to the hospital, I looked back at my notes. They were full of what could only be described as scribbles and gibberish. There was no way I would ever return here on my own.

I found my way up to the NICU. There was a line of women, mothers like me, standing silently outside the locked door. They already had on their blue gowns, hairnets, and slippers. I ran my eyes up and down the line. I was the only white person. I was a foreigner. I knew I would be, but I hadn't thought about how it would feel. We had all been at this hospital to give birth, but there had always been a thin curtain or a thick door separating us. This time there was nothing. It was me in front of them. Below their billowing blue hairnets, I saw a few of them lift their heads and look at me. I bowed deeply, put on my gown and slippers, and went to the back of the line.

At exactly 1:00, the door unlocked. Since I was new, and these women understood the routine, I looked down at the floor and followed the path to where I hoped Lily would be. She was still in the smaller room.

There was a metal stool next to each of the bassinets, so mothers, there were no fathers, could sit uncomfortably next to their babies. Aside from the stools, the room hadn't changed at all. There were no curtains to provide even a tiny bit of privacy.

Not knowing what else to do, I pulled up the stool next to Lily's bassinet. It made a loud screeching sound, like fingernails on a chalkboard. A wave of heat shot up my spine. I once again felt like I was making too much noise.

I looked in Lily's bassinet and forced myself to forget about everyone else. Lily was awake. Her eyes were bright, and her lips were rosy. She pulled my heart right into the bassinet. I easily picked her up, holding the tube and wires to the side. I didn't make a single machine beep and wanted to scream out to the nurses and doctors, 'Hey, I can do this; let my baby come home.' Instead, I held her close. I tucked her nicely in my lap and pulled out the photos I'd brought with me. I placed them around her bassinet.

My favorite photo was of Fred and Emma. She was on his shoulders. They both had their heads thrown back and mouths wide open, laughing hysterically. Another one was of Emma on a swing with her feet up high and her cheeks red from the cold. I could hear her saying, "weeeeee," as she flew through the air. The last one was taken only a couple of weeks before. It was of the three of us after we had arrived in Tokyo. We were sitting on our apartment's terrace, having dinner together. In the photo, my belly is big with Lily safely inside. I hoped these photos would bring her as much comfort as they brought me. I needed to know she could see her family even if we weren't with her.

Unlike the clocks in the rest of the hospital that never seemed to allow a minute to pass, those two hours went by in an instant. I ached for time to stop. I just wanted to be with my baby. I wanted to feel her, bathe her, dress her, and have her baby scent with me. I couldn't believe I had to leave her behind.

The nurses said nothing at 3:00 but slowly fanned out around the room, clearly indicating that time with our babies was over. The other mothers obediently set down their children and, without any words, started to walk out of the room. I didn't do that. I held onto Lily for a few more minutes, obviously a few more minutes longer than I was allowed. This time, I couldn't follow the rules.

I didn't actually know very many Japanese rules. I should have studied them before I moved to a country so foreign to my own, but I didn't. I thought I could easily figure them out. I couldn't imagine it would be that different from my own. I was wrong.

I broke almost every rule all the time. I didn't intentionally harm anyone, and I always tried to show the utmost respect, but it was hard. I put my hand out to shake when I was supposed to bow. I walked into a room with my shoes on when I was supposed to take them off. I went to the park with Emma in jeans and tennis shoes, when the Japanese mothers wore Gucci.

If you didn't follow the rules, you disturbed the *Wa*, the peace of the people. In the NICU of this very formal level three trauma hospital, not only did I not understand the rules, I didn't want to follow them. It went against everything I knew and held dear. In that NICU, just by my existence, I felt like I disturbed the *Wa*.

Fred, Emma, and my mom were all outside our apartment, enthusiastically greeting me when I returned from the hospital. In the driveway was a dark green, slightly used Toyota Estima minivan. Fred gleefully said, "Look! My colleagues helped me get it today! It is ours!

Cool, huh? I got it for $5,000! A total bargain from another ex-patriot who was leaving Japan. He just dropped it off." I stood motionless, blinking. The minivan was a monster for the streets of Tokyo. It was literally three times the size of any other car on the road. How was I going to learn to drive such a beast? I burst out laughing; yet again, I had to adjust to something I hadn't expected. I should be used to it by now.

"Well, okay then, good choice."

With the excitement of the unveiling behind us, Fred and I stood next to the car, almost daring the other to open it. I had driven since I was sixteen in the U.S., and I had gotten an International Driver's License before we left, so legally, I was able to drive in Japan, but that didn't mean I could. Neither of us wanted to figure out how to drive this machine. It was Emma who said, "Yay! Let's go!"

With trepidation, I opened the sliding door and peeked inside. It looked like any other minivan in the U.S.; the only problem was the steering wheel was on the other side. In fact, everything was on the other side, including all of the cars on the road.

Deciding to go for it, I shouted, "Get in; I'll drive." I sat for a minute, adjusting to the very strange sensation of having the steering wheel on the right side. Fred sat in the passenger seat, and my mom sat in the back. Emma was in her car seat. Everyone was ready to go. We sat in the driveway.

I hoped I looked like I was concentrating on all of the technical parts of the car, like how to operate the windshield wipers and open the windows. I could tell I wasn't going to be able to stall much longer. By the time I finally got us in reverse to back out of the driveway, it was rush hour. I was certain this was absolutely terrible, but it turned out to be the best. With the roads bursting with traffic, cars moved slowly, very slowly, so I could easily get my bearings. I decided to try and shift lanes. I found the turn signal and pushed it up, which was the wrong direction, but I made it to the next lane without harming anyone.

We drove along in a straight line for about 15 minutes. I was so excited I was driving beautifully; I hadn't paid attention to where we were. We were now far from home, and the only way back involved turning around and going the other way. This was not good. U-turns don't exist in Japan, and the entire idea of turning, any kind of turning, struck me with fear. What if I went into oncoming traffic? Was the flimsy International Driver's License actually valid? How do you get cars repaired in Japan? Do the police come if there is an accident? Did we even have insurance?

We had now driven 20 minutes in the same direction. I glanced back and saw my mother clutching the sliding door for dear life. She had a very awkward smile on her face, like a mother with her teenage daughter learning how to drive. *Great job, Sarah, but could you please take us back now?* Emma, on the other hand, had her feet swinging and her arms above her head like she was on the best carnival ride ever. "Go, Mommy, this is fun!"

Fred sat next to me, giving me "advice" about what to do, "NO, NO, don't do that," with his hands bracing against the dashboard in front of him and his feet slamming into the floor. I was going to be a great driver in Tokyo.

After an hour, we all calmed down and relaxed. I did figure it out, and it became exciting to see Tokyo above ground instead of in the subway or from the window of a taxi. With Fred's help, we drove to the hospital, and I was glad to figure out I didn't have to make any turns – it was a straight shot. We safely arrived back home and ordered Domino's to celebrate our accomplishment.

The next afternoon, I got back in that minivan to go to the hospital. I convinced myself I could make it. For the duration of the trip, I had to slam on the breaks only once, didn't go through a single red light, and arrived in one piece.

The elation and relief were short-lived because I realized I had to find a place to park my enormous car. The hospital didn't have a parking lot, and I was not about to learn how to parallel park, going backward on the wrong side of the street into oncoming traffic.

I spotted an open parking spot directly across the street from the hospital entrance. It was in between two cars, and it was tiny. While I sat contemplating what to do, a line of unhappy drivers started to form behind me. No one honked—that would disturb the *Wa*—but I could feel their annoyance mounting. I put on my blinker, signaling the wrong direction, and gunned it straight into the spot. I hit nothing.

After parking, I realized I was so close to the other cars that not a single door on either side, not even the sliding door, would have space to open. After what I had just gone through to drive there, my emotions boiled over. I became hysterical, shouting, screaming, and pounding on the steering wheel. *I'm entombed in my car! I'll never get out!* Through my fury, I flipped my head around and realized there was a way I could climb out of the trunk. I shook off the anger, got up, turned around, and began to bang my body like a pinball on the seats of the minivan, trying not to think about the impact on my recovering body. It was when I was crouched in the small trunk area that I realized that in order for it to work, I was going to have to quickly open the trunk door, roll out onto the sidewalk and land right in front of the hospital. Definitely, I was disturbing the *Wa*.

I entered the hospital feeling triumphant, having conquered the driving and parking demons. I almost had a swagger. I felt like a champion. It was a strange feeling, one I didn't recognize. I had driven and parked a million times, but here, it was different. Here, to me, it felt like a monumental feat worth celebrating.

I observed how the nurses treated other babies when I was there. I saw the kindness and care that they showered upon them. Lily was growing and responding well to the urine tube and colostomy bag. I convinced myself they gave that same kind of attention to Lily. I had to believe and accept it. That was my only choice.

When I got home each evening, Emma, my mother, and I would play. We'd run into the yard and have time on the swings, then wander into the forest and sit on the terrace having fun with stickers and paper and puzzles. At night, there was story time, bath time, and bedtime, which she loved, especially with grandma. We kept Emma's life as close to a routine as possible. I told Emma every afternoon when I got back that I had seen Lily. I said there were photos of our family in her bassinet and explained how Lily couldn't wait to come home from the hospital to be with her sister.

Emma always said, "Tell Lily I love her."

It was on the weekends that the misery of our situation was placed directly in front of us. It wasn't the rules at the hospital that caused our sorrow; it was the interruption to our life. Fred wanted to have time with Emma, but it was hard to make that happen when we had to leave at noon for the hospital. At the hospital, Fred found it awkward and frustrating to be stuck in a tiny room sitting on a rickety stool in front of so many other parents for two hours. "The stools make my back hurt." It was then that I touched my own back and felt the riveting pain knotted into it because of so many hours of sitting. For me, it was a relief to have him there. Even though we felt trapped, I wasn't alone. I had someone to talk to, to gaze at Lily with, to share my feelings and sadness and worry.

We agreed that Lily seemed to be getting excellent care, but we spoke softly both to her and to ourselves that we wanted her to come home, we wanted to care for her, we wanted to love her all day, not just for two hours.

Before my mom left Japan, the hospital broke the rules in the NICU and let my mom visit Lily. We had to wait until all of the other mothers had left for the day so they wouldn't see someone other than Fred or me entering. My mom had to wear the hairnet, the slippers, and the gown and stand at that dreaded door until they unlocked it. She held Lily, tubes and bag and all. "Sarah, she is beautiful. You made a perfect baby." Then she looked down at Lily. "You are going to be okay. You have parents who will care for you and give you the best life possible." After three special weeks with my mom, she had to go back to her Ph.D. candidates and to her more than full life in Minnesota. I can't image what we would have done without her there.

Fred called his family often. They knew the details about Lily, and even though they were far away in Belgium, we felt close to them. They understood our situation, especially his mother.

She was working as a project manager for a huge multinational company in Brussels. Denise's English was better than mine. She also spoke Flemish in addition to her native language, French.

When I moved to Belgium after graduate school, she kindly welcomed me into her home and showered me with kindness. At Fred's and my engagement party in St. Paul, Denise flew all the way from Brussels just to be there. After Emma's birth, she came to Minnesota and showed us what all new parents need to know. She and I had established a relationship bound in love and friendship.

When my mother was getting ready to leave Tokyo, I panicked. There was no way we could possibly manage our life. Once again, Denise said she would help. Her arrival brightened our lives and provided a sense of relief. She is a petit woman who quietly observes everything. Emma adores her, so when she and Fred arrived at the airport, Emma ran to the door and flung herself at Grand-maman. She gently bent down and wrapped her arms around Emma, "My, look at you! You live in Japan! What a big girl you are." Emma grabbed her hand and brought her outside to the terrace.

"Grand-maman! Look at the forest way over there! I love to play there, and right here at this table, I draw and paint. Will you paint with me? I want to read you a book." Emma walked back into her room to find her favorite one. Denise, like my mother, did not look like she had taken a twelve-hour flight. She was joyful and relaxed and ready to step in right where my mother

106

had left off. I hugged her deeply and told her how relieved I was to see her and to have her here with us.

"No, Sarah, it is me who is glad to come and help."

After five weeks in the hospital, I was well-aware there had been no change in Lily for a long time. They had removed all of the machines, so she had not been getting antibiotics regularly for weeks. She was lying in her bassinet, smiling sweetly at the world.

On July 10, when I arrived at the NICU, there were several doctors waiting for me. I recognized Dr. Kato with her kind and gracious smile, but none of the others. I hadn't seen a doctor with Lily for a long time. Without fanfare or explanation, they announced, "Lily will be going home in a few days." I had no idea what precipitated it. They didn't say, and I didn't ask.

I jumped into action. "Tell me exactly what I need to do to care for her." For the entire time she had been in the hospital, I had not performed a single one of her medical needs. In the Japanese way, I was expected to only be a mom. I was to feed and love her for two hours a day. I had to leave the rest up to the qualified medical team. Now I had to learn, and they had to teach me.

I turned to Dr. Kato, "Where do I get all of those medical things? How do I care for her? Can you please show me?" Dr. Kato walked away from me and into the NICU office. When she returned, she handed me a list, written in Japanese, of all of the things I needed to buy and told me to go to the hospital's pharmacy.

The pharmacy was dark inside, so as I entered, I had to squint. I immediately recognized it as the place where Fred had gone so long ago to get me chocolate bars. The green linoleum, brown walls, and ancient feeling of the hospital continued in this space. It wasn't at all like the meticulous, precise Tokyo culture I had gotten to know beyond the hospital walls.

The flimsy metal shelves were dusty and rusting from lack of attention. There were boxes and boxes full of items all stacked on the shelves in no particular order. In the back of the room was one overhead light. Under it, there was a man with reading glasses perched crookedly on his nose. His head was down. He seemed to be working hard not to pay attention to me. I approached him. I couldn't find anything on my list from Dr. Kato without him. I started with confidence using my Japanese words, "*Ohio, sumimasen, arigato.*" Then I moved into English, slow and loud with lots of enunciation, "Ugh, sorry, ME-DI-CAL, DAU-GH-TER." He had a blank stare. I was only making a fool of myself, so I handed him the list. He disappeared.

After several minutes, the man came back with an overflowing garbage-sized plastic bag. He spoke in Japanese. I had no idea what he said, but I nodded with a large smile on my face. I knew I had to pay, so I pulled out all my yen. He had a manual calculator. He punched in numbers and showed me the total. I counted out the bills, proud to have the right amount. I bowed because that seemed appropriate, grabbed the bag, and raced back to be with Lily for the last few minutes I had with her that day.

I sat on the floor in front of her bassinet and dumped out the contents of the bag, with everything spilling all over the floor. Dr. Kato saw me come in and quickly walked over with her ponytails and pink ribbons bouncing all the way. I asked much too loudly, "What are all these things?"

She surprised me by sitting next to me on the floor with her starched white lab coat crinkling. I was thankful she joined me. Dr. Kato could tell I was eager to begin the lesson.

Sifting through the pile, she picked out one item from the mess.

"This is a special pair of scissors you will use to cut the colostomy bag to size." They were rounded scissors, so you could easily cut the bag to fit the part of Lily's little red colon that stuck out of her belly. Next, she pulled out a box the size of a pair of shoes and opened it. This had what looked like hundreds of colostomy bags. They were thick, flat pieces of malleable plastic, the diameter of my fist. These were the bags that collected Lily's stool. She showed me where the scissors would be used to cut the hole in the plastic. The next box contained very thin clear square pieces of plastic the size of a Post-it Note. I plucked one out of the box and flipped it over. They were called "Tegaderm." It was written in English, and they were made by 3M in Minnesota. The irony of coming all the way to Japan, buying my medical

108

supplies in a dusty old pharmacy, and having them come from my hometown struck me. In some bizarre way, it was reassuring.

"You will put this Tegaderm adhesive on her body to hold the plastic urine tube in place." The next item she picked up was a box of plastic urine bags. On the floor was one of those large metal S-shaped hooks that held the urine tube securely to her bassinet. I asked the doctor what it was called. She said, "It is an S hook." I burst out laughing. I wasn't so stupid after all. Among the pile were cloth tape, sticky tape, gauze, an entire box of plastic gloves, baby wipes, and a full shoebox of alcohol swabs. "When your husband is here this weekend, I'll show you what you will need to do. Then you can take Lily home." She picked it all up and put it back in the bag; then she walked away.

On July fifteenth, almost exactly five weeks after Lily came into the world, and after I had visited her for 35 days straight, she was discharged from the hospital. We were told to come in the morning before the visiting hours. We thought maybe they were doing this to give us time and privacy to learn how to care for our baby.

Denise, Emma, Fred, and I all went to the hospital together. This time, we didn't have to park our car in the insane parking lot across the street. Dr. Kato had told me they would clear a place for us right near the emergency room entrance where I had come into the hospital all those weeks ago. To bring us full circle, the hospital garbage containers were overflowing and toxically smelly.

Fred and I were brought into the NICU and taken to a special office where only the doctors and nurses were permitted. They had Lily in there, and she was naked, without a colostomy bag, but with the long snaking urine tube sticking out as it always did from her belly. It was attached to the side of the table with the trusty S hook. Fred and I both gave her a kiss and knew it was time for us to learn how to medically care for our daughter.

"Let's get started," I said to no one in particular. Dr. Kato came forward and began. She held up a colostomy bag. She picked up the special round-tipped scissors, flipped the bag over, and showed us that on the back, where Lily's skin would be touching the bag, there was a dotted circle around the center. We had to create a hole and make it the size of the red colon sticking

109

out of her belly. She handed it to me. I cut, following the dots, and it seemed to be about the size of Lily's colon.

"You need to clean Lily's skin with the alcohol swabs." She gave me one. I opened it, with the strong smell getting caught in my nose. "She doesn't have any feeling in the colon, so you can touch it, and she will feel nothing. The skin around the colostomy bag can easily get irritated; that is why you always need to clean it with alcohol when you change the bag. The next thing you will do is peel off the sticker on the back of the bag and attach it to her skin over her colon."

I gave the bag to Fred, so he could do it. He hesitantly placed the bag over her colon and stuck it to her belly. Ta-da! The bag was on, and it only took us thirty minutes. We were already pros. I had been dreaming of this moment since I first saw our baby so long ago. I was overcome with joy. This was it. We were taking Lily home, just like every other baby. We now could experience that happiness too. I twirled in the middle of the NICU floor.

Dr. Kato snapped me back into reality by reminding us, "Be careful." With a stern face, she said, "If you do not do this properly, then stool will come out onto Lily's clothes, you will have a fairly awful mess, and she will get a rash." Party over.

The next thing she showed us was how to empty the pee bag. That was easier. You go to a bathroom, pull up the end of the long snaking tube, twist off the green rubber cap on the end of the bag, and pour out the pee into a toilet. You could use a new bag each time or keep the same one; it didn't matter.

Once we had all of the medical pieces in place, it dawned on me that Lily didn't need a diaper. Her stool would be caught in the colostomy bag, and her urine would be emptied through the tube. No waste touched her bottom. This one was hard. She already would have an unusual bulge on her belly and a long cumbersome tube coming out from under her clothes, but without that padding on her bottom, she would look even more different. It was another reality that hurt.

Maybe to be kind, or because the colostomy bag might burst, the doctor put on a diaper. "Just in case." I smiled at her thoughtfulness. The doctor assured us the tube would remain in place on its own.

Dr. Kato continued. "Lily is healthy and safe now. She will need to grow and become stronger with you at home. Sometime in the next six to twelve months, she will have to have major reconstructive surgery. For now, you can relax and enjoy your beautiful baby girl."

With great fanfare in my head, I pulled out the outfit I had bought for Lily to wear when she came home from the hospital. I had saved it and held it and loved it at home, hoping and waiting for this day. It was a purple dress. It came with a little white sweater, a cute purple hat, and little panties. It was when I tried to put them on that I had to stop. How do we get the tube through her pants? The doctor gently pulled the tube over the diaper and through the leg of the pants, then pulled the pants on. Another thing to manage. I picked her up, Fred grabbed the tube, and we were ready to walk out of the NICU.

I paused a moment, standing in the middle of the room. I wanted to make certain I remembered what the NICU looked like where Lily had spent the first five weeks of her life. I saw all of the babies in rows along the walls, the stern lights above, the lack of privacy, and the stools, always the stools. I removed the photos from Lily's bassinet. I wanted to keep them as a reminder of how I tried to help our baby know her family even when we couldn't be with her. I felt numb.

This emotion resembled the one I had when I looked one last time at the operating room where I had given birth to Lily. What I had been through left a scar, a wound that would never heal, on my soul.

We started to say our goodbyes, and a nurse ran up to us with a black garbage bag. We already had all of the medical supplies at home. I had no idea what it could be. The nurse said in English, "Breast milk, your breast milk. We had too much." The giant bag was filled with the frozen packages of milk I had been bringing for weeks. I tried not to think about what they had been feeding Lily. Dr. Kato handed Fred a box the size of a filing cabinet drawer. "These are all of Lily's medical records." It was another sign of what she had been through.

With Lily and the urine tube and bag in my arms, we bowed deeply to Dr. Kato. I knew a bow was not going to be enough for me. For as strange and unsettling as this NICU had been, Dr. Kato was my medical and English-speaking connection to our baby for those five long weeks. I would never have survived if not for her. I gave her a non-Japanese hug. She lightly hugged me back.

We turned to the nurses, who were all lined up at the exit in their meticulous white hospital uniforms. We bowed to each one. They were medical in their interactions with us, and we were unable to communicate in a common language, but they all played a part in the cross-cultural experience of saving our baby. Fred and I turned around and faced everyone. We bowed very deeply and said, "Domo arigato gozaimasu."

As we approached the locked door, my numbness changed. I felt a sudden rush of joy. For the first time, Lily was going out with us. We would care for her, and no one would tell us what to do or how to do it. I thought I'd be nervous, but the anticipation of this moment and the fierce feeling of needing to care for our baby overtook any anxiety. Her future was now ours. As if by magic, the NICU door opened for us for the very last time. We removed our gowns, hairnets, and slippers and left it all behind.

Denise and Emma were waiting at the end of the hallway and ran up to us. It was an extraordinary feeling. Emma wanted instantly to hug her sister. I knelt down with Lily in my arms and the snaking tube in my hand. Emma wrapped herself around the baby. Emma said, "I love you, Lily," as she had the first time she saw her and every day of the five weeks she had been in the NICU. Denise stood back, marveling at this powerful moment in our lives. We were all crying as we walked out of the hospital. We got in our minivan, and our whole family went home together.

Chapter 19

I had brought a white wicker bassinet with me from Minnesota that had been used for me as a baby and then for Emma. After making a large hole in the bottom big enough for the tube and urine bag to pass through, that bassinet would be Lily's too. From the shelves in our bedroom, I carefully removed all of the trinkets and souvenirs we had collected and filled them with all of Lily's medical devices.

Emma was thrilled to have her baby sister at home. She constantly talked to her and even had the great pleasure of having a built-in audience whenever she wanted. I would gently strap Lily in her bouncy seat on the floor, and Emma would open and read book after book showing Lily the pictures on each page.

On other occasions, she would announce, "Lily, we are going to the forest. Would you like to come?" There was no response, just a peacefully sleeping baby, followed by, "Mommy, Lily said she'd like to come with us to the forest." As we walked through the yard, Lily got an explanation of all of the fun things to do. "We play ball here in the open part of the yard. I swing on that swing set, and you will watch me." Then, as we reached the forest, "Mommy, could Lily play hide-and-seek with me? I'll hide first."

Even at Emma's bedtime, she wanted Lily there, sound asleep in her bassinet or not. Emma would narrate to Lily her nightly routine. "I'm putting on my pajamas. I can't button the buttons, but Mommy helps me with that. I brush my teeth, see?" Inches from Lily's face, Emma made a big toothy grin to show her success. After she got in bed, Emma told Lily, "Now we are reading, *If You Give a Mouse a Cookie*. I laugh and laugh at the silly mouse." Lily had started to laugh by then, and hers was a gleeful, joyful laugh. Emma could not get enough of trying to say or do something funny just to hear her giggle.

Emma didn't ask about Lily's tubes and bags, yet she closely watched as we changed or emptied them. Maybe she thought that was how babies were. Maybe she just knew that Lily was different. It wasn't that we didn't want to explain it all to Emma; she was curious and smart enough, but somehow in those first precious days of being a new family of four, Lily didn't feel different to us; no explanation was needed. Plus, with all of the belly issues stable, Lily was healthy, or so I told myself 100 times a day.

After a week of enjoying being a family and learning how to care for Lily's tubes and bags at home, we all decided to venture out into the world. For outings, I knew I had to pack a very different kind of baby backpack than the one I had created for Emma when she was little. This time, the backpack was filled with round-tipped scissors, colostomy bags, plastic urine collection bags, and multiple changes of clothes in case the bag leaked stool all over her tummy.

We hadn't had this happen yet, but we were certain the mess was coming our way.

I also had medical tape, diapers, and diaper rash cream, not for her bottom, but for her belly. I always had an extra tiny hat for Lily, so I didn't need to explain her ear. Denise had made the best creation of all. She had sewn two washcloths together and put a shoelace at the top to make a drawstring. We placed this "cover" over the urine collection bag, so we could fool ourselves into thinking we were hiding it when we went out.

Our first trip was to the Tokyo American Club. It was a gathering place for ex-patriots from all over the world and Japanese families too. It had some of the comforts of life in America, including restaurants with French fries and hamburgers, a library with books in English, a large swimming pool, and a bowling alley. The family-friendly Garden Café restaurant was our choice for our first outing for dinner.

We had been to the Garden Café many times with Emma when we first arrived in Tokyo and then with my mom and Denise while Lily was in the hospital. We had gotten to know other ex-patriot families through these dinners and afternoons at the swimming pool, and we were certain we would see them at the Garden Café.

Our biggest worry was how we were going to explain Lily. We didn't yet have the words, the confidence, or even the will to say what had happened. When we arrived, we asked for a booth in the back of the restaurant, but people saw us anyway. In passing, we were asked, "Where have you been? I thought you had a baby a long time ago; is she alright?" We mumbled and said the baby was fine, and luckily Emma waved and smiled. Another friend held out her arms toward Lily, saying, "She is so beautiful; I love to hold tiny babies." I said something about Emma being hungry, so we should get to our table.

We were uncomfortable. We weren't used to having to explain ourselves or try to hide Lily's complex body. Hoping not to experience that awkwardness again, Fred and I came up with what we wanted to say. It was a statement that was truthful. It would give a little insight into what had happened yet would protect both Lily and us from having to explain over and over what we didn't want to talk about. 'Our baby has some medical issues, so she comes with lots of extra stuff. It is hard to hold her, but you can see how incredibly sweet she is.'

After our uneasy beginning in the Garden Café, I started using the statement. The more I said it, the more confident I felt. People would peer into her baby carrier and see her shining eyes. They would smile at her, and she usually smiled too. Then the conversation would turn away from Lily.

When I look back on our first timid steps out into the world, I'm proud of our family. Unlike in the NICU, we found a way to fit in, use the appropriate words to explain our situation and start over. Lily could be Lily with a tube, a missing ear, and a colostomy bag. None of her issues stopped us from living freely. We could not believe, after all, we had been through, that both of our girls were with us and both were healthy enough. We embraced life again.

Chapter 20

Our time with Denise had been easy and comfortable. She was accepting of us as we were, which meant exhausted, confused, and anxious. Lily was a newborn, and she woke up during the night; she cried during the day. She needed to be fed around the clock, and now that was all on me. Denise took over the house, as she had done when Emma was born. She was up early, fixed Emma breakfast, played with Emma all day, and cooked us dinner each night. She provided an adult friend for me, someone I could talk to, worry with, and even find moments of joy.

She made life better, so at the beginning of August, when she had to leave, we were devastated. I wasn't sure how I would manage without her. "Fred, what are we going to do? I can't manage, not even for a day, without Denise. She takes care of everything, and I love being with her. We don't have any help if even one thing goes wrong. There isn't any backup. I'm so worried."

"I'm going to try to work less. I'll be available, and I'll check in with you during the day. Lily is fine now. We have a good routine. It is going to work." Fred was optimistic about our situation and passionate about spending his weekends with us. He created adventures and planned fun places to visit, but his job at Northwest came with enormous responsibility. For as much as I wanted to believe he could drop everything and help, I was pretty certain that wouldn't be the case. I had to find a way to make it work on my own, and I did…until Lily got sick.

On August twelfth, it was unbearably hot in Tokyo. The four of us tried to go on an ambitious outing, one that would be fun for Emma. We took the subway to an amusement park for the day. Emma went on a few kiddy rides with Fred watching the sheer elation on her face as she went high into the air. "Weeee, look, Daddy!!" Fred had the biggest grin on his face. We were all happy.

After being at the park for a couple of hours, I picked Lily up to nurse her and noticed she was really hot, more than from the heat of the sun. I said to Fred, "Feel her. She is burning up."

He was as surprised as I was. "Let's go." Much to Emma's disappointment, we left the park abruptly and hurried home.

In July, when Lily was discharged from the hospital, no one in the NICU mentioned any issues we might encounter. We were supposed to change the colostomy bag and empty the urine tube; that was it. However, as a precaution, they gave us the hospital's pediatric emergency room phone number. We planned to never use it. Aside from the occasional "blowout" of the bag on her belly, which was pretty yucky, we had no medical issues with her at all.

When we got home, I reluctantly dialed the emergency room number at Joshi Idai. As I waited for them to pick up, I tried to reassure myself the care we had received in the NICU had been outstanding and that they would help Lily. Instead of being positive, I couldn't shake the feeling of dread. The weight of that hospital and of those rules. It was closing in on me again.

I didn't even try a word of Japanese this time, "Is this the emergency room? I need someone who speaks English, please." There was a pause, and I could hear the phone being put down. When a person at the hospital came back on the line, I told him, "My daughter Lily

Deschamps was born at Joshi Idai Byoin two months ago. She was in the NICU for five weeks.

She has a very high fever, and I'm not certain what to do."

"She needs to immediately come in to be treated at the hospital." I quickly hung up.

Fred heard the voice at the other end of the line telling me to bring Lily back to the hospital. Not in character at all, he exploded, "Shit! Not again! I can't do this. I have to keep a job and keep healthcare for our family. I run the Pacific Division. It is a lot of work. I can't stop and start. I love you three.

I need to be here for you, but I can't be in two places at once. I can't mess this up."

He was right; it was such an erratic life we couldn't count on anything. We grabbed each other tight, and silence took up the space. I tried to think of anything that might help. Then it occurred to me that it was Sunday, and it was the afternoon. If I could get Lily in and out of the hospital in a couple of hours, Fred would be back at work on Monday morning and not miss a thing.

I bent down to Emma and said, "I'm so sorry, sweetheart. Lily is sick. Like you had fevers when you were little, she has a fever too. I am going to find out what's going on, and I'll be back as quickly as I possibly can. I love you dearly." I squeezed her tight and gave her a kiss.

I grabbed my backpack filled with Lily's things from our trip to the park. I didn't double-check what was in it; I wanted to figure this out and get her back home. I cautiously put Lily in her car seat, got into the green minivan, and drove back to Joshi Idai.

Luckily our van knew how to drive itself to the hospital because I cried all the way. The feeling of uncertainty was overwhelming. This time, I knew where the emergency room was. I didn't bat an eye, held my breath, and took the one parking spot next to the stinky garbage cans.

We were emergency room patients. We could park there.

In contrast to when I entered the hospital as a pregnant patient and had to find my own way with no one knowing who I was or what I was doing there. This time, there was a doctor standing at the entrance waiting for us. I immediately felt the chill return of the Japanese paternalistic attitude that I had experienced for so many weeks in the NICU. Without a word to me, he moved us down a long hallway where there were three small cot-like beds in a row. I was told to sit on the first one. There was no curtain, and we were in a public area, exposed and vulnerable. He had that paternalistic, I know what is best for your baby, look on his face that I now knew well. The way he spoke felt raw and like he was blaming me for letting my baby get sick.

118

The doctor removed Lily from my arms, placed her in a nurse's, and took her temperature. He looked at me, nodding his head. Pointedly he said, "She has a fever of 39.5 (Celsius)." I knew it was high, around 103 Fahrenheit.

Without any hesitation, a needle appeared, and he attempted to put an IV into Lily's arm. It didn't work. She started to cry. He removed it, and with the nurse still holding Lily, they tried to find a vein in her hand; it didn't work. Poke and remove. Next, her other arm. Failure. By that time, Lily was wailing, and I was forced to stand several feet away, just watching. I started sobbing. I had been holding her at an amusement park with Emma joyfully screaming on the rides only hours before. How could this have happened to us once again? How could we lose control of our baby and our lives in the blink of an eye?

The doctor finally found a good vein in her foot, so the snaking tube from her belly was now accompanied by one on the side of her foot. To this day, Lily has a scar from that IV.

I was overwhelmed by the thought of what might come next. Out of nowhere, some type of medical IV drip was being put into Lily through the needle, now securely in her foot. I didn't know what liquid they were putting in her. Next, the nurse pulled on the cover Denise had made for Lily's urine bag and yanked it off. She emptied the urine into a small plastic cup and left the area.

The next thing the doctor said scared me even more. "The baby is so sick. It could be so many things. We are going to admit her to the hospital. When a child is admitted, the parent must remain in the hospital every minute the child is here."

Oh! My! God! I thought I was coming for some medicine, like Tylenol and an antibiotic, and would be sent on my way. I had no change of clothes and no way to contact Fred. The world was closing in on me. Would we have to be here for another five weeks?

The doctor said nothing else to me. The nurse reappeared, placed Lily in the same type of bassinet we had left behind only a few weeks before, and started to wheel her and the IV pole down the hallway and into the elevator.

I trailed behind, like an afterthought in this hospital, completely paralyzed with fear.

We exited the elevator on the third floor into a tiny area with the ominous green and dark linoleum. Straight in front of us was a long hallway, but in order to access it, we had to step down two very large concrete stairs. It was absurd. How could there be stairs? The nurse and doctor awkwardly lifted the IV pole and bassinet, jiggling my screaming baby the whole time as they carried her down the steps one at a time.

It was a narrow hallway with stark white cinderblocks that looked exactly like the operating room where I had given birth to Lily. It was cold. I shivered. I didn't have a jacket since we had been out in the hot sunshine and humid air at the park. As we walked down the hall, Lily's tiny bassinet wheels spun on the floor, creating a whirring noise. Aside from the nurse's heels clicking on the floor, it was the only sound we heard.

I peered into the rooms as we passed. They had the same white-washed concrete walls as the hallway, and there were white bed sheets and thin white blankets on the beds. The ceilings were high, maybe twenty feet, with fluorescent bulbs buzzing on the ceiling. The only natural light in the room came from windows that were far up near the ceiling. Strangely, they were covered with bars. We were being locked into a prison cell.

I wanted to grab Lily and run to the NICU, where I at least understood the rules. This was completely different. After we walked halfway down the hall, we were brought into a room for Lily. The powerful odor made me gag. It smelled like an entire bucket of bleach had been dumped on the floor. The doctor said, "You will be taken care of by the doctors and nurses here. To be clear, you may not leave your baby alone." *Did he think I was going to stroll away and leave Lily behind?* The nurse and doctor left, presumably heading back to the emergency area. A few minutes later, another doctor appeared. He was shorter than me, and his black hair was slicked back on his head.

He said in English, without introducing himself, "This is the children's wing of the hospital. Your daughter has been admitted here and will remain until we find out what is causing her fever. With the IV drip in, we will simply monitor her." He walked out. My impulse was not to let him escape, so after a minute of hesitation, almost hysterical about leaving Lily behind in that awful room, I followed him down the hall.

I was trying to decide exactly what I was going to say. My mind was exploding with the feeling this children's wing was straight out of a horror movie. It was eerily silent. There was no parent lounge, no food, no place to be outside of your child's room, no TV, no shower, not even a visible bathroom. Nothing.

Up to that point, I hadn't pushed back on the paternalistic 'we know all,' but this was too much. I had allowed Lily to be in the NICU far beyond what seemed necessary because the doctors always appeared to know what was best. Maybe they did, but they had been rough and amateurish when they were putting in the IV, and then they put us in this horrid room with no plan.

I jogged down the hall and caught up with the doctor. He was already hovering over a computer at the far end of the hallway near the cinderblock stairs. I cleared my throat, "Excuse me, can you please tell me the plan for getting Lily out of the hospital? She has a terrible fever, which would seem to mean an infection. Is there an antibiotic you could use to fight it?"

He responded in a matter-of-fact way, "*O-ka-san* (mother), from her urine sample, we believe the baby has a urinary tract infection. It was most likely caused by the vesicostomy tube in her belly allowing bacteria to enter her bladder. We have started an antibiotic through the IV in her foot. We hope it will attack the infection and bring her fever down. We are now running tests to see if the bacteria in her urine is resistant to the medicine. We need her body to accept the antibiotic and to fight the infection."

I was exasperated, beyond holding in my feelings inside or behaving in a responsible way. I spit out, "How long is it going to take for you to figure this out?"

He remained calm. "Her temperature has to be normal before we will consider allowing her to leave. In addition, it will take us a couple of days to get the results from the urine culture. Once we know for certain if we are using the correct antibiotic, we will monitor your baby here at the hospital for at least a week."

I stood before the doctor with my mouth open wide, willing any words other than angry ones to come out. Nothing did. I turned around and stomped back down the prison hallway, peering into each room, hoping I could remember exactly which one was Lily's. I sat on the bed next to her bassinet, running my fingers along Lily's hot cheek. Instead of crying as I did so many times during those five long weeks in the NICU, I was fuming. I was stuck again in the Japanese medical system that didn't allow me to be an equal participant in my daughter's care. I couldn't leave with a sick child, but I was terrified to stay.

I didn't understand why it would take so long to figure out the problem. When I had a urinary tract infection, the doctor tested my urine, said I had an infection, gave me some antibiotics, and sent me on my way. I felt better in a day, finished the entire prescribed medicine, and that was that. I knew Lily's body was astronomically more complicated than mine, but it sounded like the process to treat her was exactly the same, only they were going to keep her here until she was completely cured. I couldn't wait.

I sat very still. I stared at the walls and the bars covering the windows up high. The bed was uncomfortable, the plastic bassinet was a reminder of our already endless time in this hospital, and the doctor's manner was beyond my comprehension.

For hours no one came into Lily's room. She was not hooked up to a monitor, and her IV drip went so slowly that the bag seemed like it would last forever. I sat and sat. Through my rage, I came up with a plan. It was a risk and could put Lily in danger of further infection, but I was certain I knew her and her body well enough by now. If I could eliminate her fever, and get the hospital to give me the antibiotic in a form other than an IV drip, then I could treat her on my own. I knew what was best for my daughter. I knew how to help her, and I was going to get us out of there.

I peered into her bassinet and spoke to her, "Honey, it is miserable here. I can treat you better at home, but I don't have the medicine yet to get you well. This will not feel good, but it will get us both out, so you can get fully better at home." She was a two-month-old baby, but somehow, I felt like we had become partners in getting out of this growing nightmare. She would bear the brunt of the pain, but I would be the mastermind to find our way out. Lily's little rosebud mouth had become more dazzling over the weeks, and right then, she gave me a glowing smile. I calmed down for the first time since we left the amusement park.

Since it was now late in the evening, I knew I would be there all night, and the earliest I could get out would be the next day, Monday, assuming my plan worked. I went back down the hallway and found a nurse standing by the lone computer. I asked to use the phone. She had a portable one, so I walked back to the room.

I was hesitant to call Fred. I knew he desperately needed to go to work on Monday. I took a deep breath and dialed. "Hi. I'm stuck in the hospital. They admitted us because they needed to find out the cause of the fever. They think it is a urinary tract infection, but they have to do some tests that take days to give results. In the meantime, they have put her on an antibiotic drip through an IV which they put in her foot, hoping that this medication is the one that will work against the infection."

I paused, for a split second, not long enough for Fred to speak. "They won't let me leave or move from her room. I have no clothes, no food, nothing. I only have a few colostomy and pee bags and changes of clothes for Lily. I have been nursing her, but I'm starving and have no way of getting any food since I can't leave the room." I realized at that moment that, unlike the NICU, there would be no locked door but also no way out.

Fred's nerves, anxiety, and anger all boiled over. "Sarah, I'm so sorry for what this has done to you. I can't believe how this gets worse and worse, especially for you. It is so much to manage. But I have to get back to work. I have tons of meetings scheduled for tomorrow, and I have to get to them. Emma can't come to work; there are Japanese rules. My colleague who took care of her when we first arrived is at her own job, and so is everyone in the apartment building. With our mothers gone, we have no one who can help with Emma."

"I don't know what to say, and Lily can't leave, so neither can I. I have a plan to get us out, but I can't start it until much later tonight." I paused, not knowing what else to say, "I love you." I couldn't hear another word, so I hung up.

Fred is an even-tempered person and is always in control. We were a good team at figuring out things together, but this time, with Lily and me stuck in the hospital and Emma with no care at home, we were stuck. There was nothing I could do to help him, so I focused on getting Lily out of the hospital. Her fever had to go down. My risky idea had to work.

I had heard if a child has a high fever, you could put them on an ice bath, and it would break the fever. I was counting on the fact that the doctor had chosen the right antibiotic. My plan wouldn't work if he hadn't. I believed with twelve hours of the medicine dripping into her, the infection would start to go away. The ice bath would eliminate the fever. My plan also included the hospital giving me a powder or liquid form of the antibiotic to take home to administer to Lily. Once they had the urine culture results, they could call me at home and let me know what to do.

I hoped I could pull this off. It energized me to think I could do something, anything. I was desperate to get home, to help Fred get back to the office, but mostly to be with Emma and have Lily healthy again.

I sat back on the bed and waited. We seemed to be the only patients, and no one had come into the room to check on us. There was always someone standing at the computer at the end of the hall, so I kept peering out, willing them to walk away.

While I was waiting, I carefully pulled the large sheet off of the bed next to Lily where I was supposed to sleep and rolled it up into as small a ball as possible. Around midnight, I finally saw no one at the computer and dashed down the hall. Strangely, there was no food of any kind or even a microwave, yet there was an ice machine about halfway down to the computer. It looked like the kind I knew from the U.S. I lifted the metal lid, found a large plastic scoop inside, placed the sheet on the floor at my feet, and started to pour scoop after scoop of ice on the sheet as quietly as I could. I gently closed the lid, hoping not to make any more noise, and bundled up the sheet. I started to tiptoe down the hall like Santa. I had a bag on my back, which was now starting to melt freezing water onto my shirt and pants, making me shiver even more.

Back in the room, I got to work. I put the sheet down on the floor next to Lily's bassinet, with the ice crackling on the floor as it hit. I carefully lifted Lily out of her bassinet and put her on my bed. I was a master at moving her with tubes and bags, so I knew nothing would get stuck.

She still felt burning hot to my touch. She was very sick. I hoped this would work.

With an eye on Lily, so she didn't move off the big bed, I pulled out the thin mattress that had been under her. I carefully held the sheet up over the bassinet and dropped the ice into it. It crashed loudly, hitting the bottom of the bassinet, crackling against the sides. I didn't stop. I arranged the ice so it would evenly cover the bottom and placed the mattress back on top. I wanted Lily to rest on the ice as if she had a very cool cloth touching her body. I didn't want her in the freezing water.

I was pretty sure if the nurses checked on Lily during the night, they wouldn't figure out what I had done. It was too dark in the room, deathly silent in the hospital, and we were simply waiting for the results of the urine test, so there shouldn't be a reason to bother her during the night. Besides that, I figured if I got caught, we were already imprisoned in this hospital, so we couldn't sink any lower.

I gave Lily a kiss on the forehead and whispered, "Help your fever go down so you can feel better, and we can go home." I lightly placed her back in the bassinet, where I could feel the chill of the ice below the mattress, and then I sat next to her on the bed, waiting and watching. I think I dozed for an hour or two, still sitting up, but not more than that. Mostly, I was watching to make certain Lily was safe, but also for the light of day to peek through the bars high above.

Lily didn't whimper or cry all night long. To this day, I believe sleeping on that ice actually felt good. Her sweaty, sick body was soothed by the coolness and was getting better by the drip, drip, drip of the antibiotic. While I waited, I planned what I was going to say to the doctor to get Lily out. The only problem was I had been so fixated on those words and on her fever dropping that I forgot I needed to remove the ice before anyone saw what I had done.

Unexpectedly, without the tiniest bit of noise or warning, the doctor from the night before entered our room. It was too late. Lily was sleeping on the ice. I was going to be labeled a terrible mother, they were going to keep Lily in their care, and we would never get out. I stood still, with my eyes looking away from Lily, and focused on the doctor in the doorway. Then, I moved between Lily and the doctor blocking him from seeing her. Madly trying to remember what I wanted to say, I blurted out, "*Sensei* (doctor), I think her fever is gone. I think the antibiotic has worked, and she is better. If that is the case, I would like to take her home."

He looked surprised, taken aback. His eyes got bigger, and he took a step backward, closer to the door, as if I was attacking him with my words. He was not expecting a parent to speak to him that way. I asked him to please take her temperature. He looked around the room and noticed Lily didn't have a vital sign monitor, so he turned and left to find a thermometer.

I leaped at Lily, removed her from the bassinet, and again put her on the twin bed with the tiny mattress next to her. I spread the wet sheet on the floor and ripped the bassinet off of its metal holder. I dumped the ice onto the sheet, making a terrible crashing and splashing noise. I didn't care. I flipped the bassinet back over, yanked a dry blanket off the foot of my bed, wiped the bassinet dry, threw the small mattress back in the bassinet, and put Lily on top. I shoved the ice-filled sheet under the twin bed. I used the now wet blanket to mop up the floor and, just in time, threw the blanket under the bed too. The entire process took less than 30 seconds. I finished as the doctor entered the door, holding a thermometer.

I was sweating, and my shoes and pants were soaked. I hoped he didn't notice. He took Lily's temperature, and sure enough, she was 37 degrees Celsius, normal. "She is better," he proclaimed.

"*Sensei*," I calmed myself down and continued. "You had said if her temperature was normal, we could leave. Could we please go home this morning? It seems this antibiotic is working. Isn't there a liquid or powder form I could give to her at home like adults take pills?" Our freezer at home was overflowing with breast milk. "I could easily mix the antibiotic into milk. Please let us go home," I implored. "She has spent enough time in the hospital. I can care for her at home. Please let us go home." I put my hands together and started bowing, bending as far down as I possibly could, showing the highest respect. As I bent over, I said in English, "please, please, please." I was begging. I knew he didn't want to let us go, so I said, "Please, *sensei*, I watched the doctors here in this hospital take such good care of her in the NICU for five weeks. I know what to do. Please let us go home. I will bring her back if she becomes sick again. Please let us go home." I held back my tears; I didn't want to let them fall this time. I wanted to get out. I wanted to be free to treat my baby by myself at our home.

The doctor bowed his head. "You may go. What we have used to treat her is called Bactrim. I have a powdered form of this antibiotic. You will need to give it to her through a bottle filled with your breast milk three times a day; she has to have it for three weeks. I'll be back soon with the medication and the discharge papers. If there is any follow-up or changes needed, you can come to the hospital as an outpatient." He turned and walked out.

From my bowed position, I fell to the concrete floor, curled into the fetal position, and started to weep uncontrollably. I had done it. I had gotten us out.

On the drive home, with Lily safely tucked in her car seat in the back, I was reeling from what had just happened. We had to escape from this hospital again. This time, being stuck there felt like a knife shoved in my gut. Through the intensity of the pain, I couldn't catch my breath.

I shook my head as the hospital got further in my rearview mirror. I tried to be logical. We lived here. We were still very committed to being in Japan. We still wanted it, craved it, and hoped to explore it as if it was our true home, but with Lily's precarious medical issues, we just couldn't be sure we could make that life happen. No matter what the doctor said about only going to the outpatient clinic if Lily got sick again, the possibility of being admitted was too great. I couldn't guarantee that we wouldn't be right back here in this impossible situation again.

With the weight of our family and our new life on my shoulders, I allowed myself to think of the impossible. We could break this cycle if we left Japan. We could break it if we went back to Minnesota. I finally admitted I couldn't see another way out. Emma, Lily, and I had to go.

When I got to the apartment, Fred looked frantic. His stress was as great as mine. He hugged me, "I can't do this."

"Neither can I. Emma, Lily and I have to go to Minnesota. We have to figure this out without the perpetual fear of having the floor fall out from under us." I started to cry. "I don't want to lose hope. I want to make it work here. I don't want you to leave this job. I want a life for all of us in Japan. We had wanted this dream for too long. Let's see if we can get some help in Minnesota, and maybe we can come back."

He nodded. We didn't discuss the separation that was coming our way; we both knew we were out of options.

"I'll figure out the flights and get you three there by the end of the week." I could tell from the quickness of his response that he had thought of this too. We had to leave him behind.

Fred gave me and the girls kisses and walked out the door to work.

Emma, Lily, and I went outside to play. I grabbed Emma's hand, so glad to have it in mine again. On the way to the forest, I let my mind wander. Our life had become overrun with insurmountable obstacles constantly blocking us, yet we always seemed to find a way around them. Five weeks in the NICU, be there. Driving in Tokyo, go. Replacing colostomy bags and emptying urine bags, get it done. Stuck in a prison hospital, get out. As we walked, I said out loud what I had been thinking about a lot. "We are moving mountains."

Emma was tugging on my hand as we entered the canopy of the forest. "Mommy, let's have a tea party!" Emma found the biggest boulder she could find and decided it needed to be moved to a better spot for the party. It was big, coming up to her chin, and definitely weighed much more than she did. I had Lily strapped in her car seat and set her down. Emma moved next to me, and we pushed. Nothing happened. Grunting, I said, "Dig in with your feet," as if a three-year-old knows how to move a boulder. Lifting and heaving, we somehow got it to move a couple of feet without anyone getting injured. Standing up, I declared, "this is the perfect place for our tea party!" Luckily, Emma didn't protest. I was still panting and sweating, so she went and grabbed the picnic basket she had carried out with us.

We sat down on the boulder to enjoy our now beloved aloe-flavored Kit Kat bars.

"Mommy, you said we are moving mountains. I think we are moving mountains like Ming Lo." She remembered! Of course, she remembered the children's story we had read a million times called *Ming Lo Moves the Mountain*. I hugged her and smiled, "Emma, tell me the story."

As she took a bite of the Kit-Kat, she started. "Ming Lo was very, very upset. He hated the mountain over his house. He had no sun, and it dropped rocks." She jumped off of the boulder and picked up little pebbles, dropping them one by one on top of the rock, plink, plank plunk. "Ming Lo's wife told him, 'Move this mountain!'" Pretending to be the wife, Emma stood and shook her finger up and down vigorously. She paused and looked a little bit lost. "Mommy, you say the rest."

"Ming Lo talked to the wise man in their village."

Emma burst in, "Oh yeah! The wise man said to put their tiny house on Ming Lo's back!" She bent over and pretended to put heavy things on her back and take big steps. "Then Ming Lo walked and walked. Then he stopped."

I joined in, "When they stopped, they weren't in the shadow of the mountain anymore. They put their house back together right there where they stood, and they had sunshine and a beautiful garden and no more rocks on their roof."

"Mommy, they moved a mountain." She paused. "We moved mountains for our family." "Yes," I sighed, "I think we did."

Chapter 21

Two days later, Emma, Lily, and I were on the twelve-hour plane ride headed back to Minnesota. I didn't know how long we were going to stay in the U.S., and we didn't book a return flight. By the time we got on the plane, the antibiotics had worked. Lily was much better. My parents were expecting us. I called and asked them to make an appointment with a pediatric urologist in Minneapolis as soon as possible. We had an appointment for the morning after we arrived.

Standing before the immigration officer in Minnesota, I proudly handed over three American passports. Lily had arrived only days before we left. It had a gleaming blue cover with the eagle on it, and her place of birth, Tokyo, Japan, was etched on the inside. Allowing myself a moment of happiness in spite of the circumstances, I smiled, thinking our baby was traveling internationally for the first time at five weeks old.

We saw my parents smiling and waving in the international waiting area. Relief spread throughout my body. They were there. We were here. We were safe with them. Emma ran and jumped in my mom's arms. My dad bent down and kissed Lily on the head. "I'm so glad to meet you, beautiful Lily."

They got on either side of Emma, grabbed her hands, and started to talk about all they would do together with her jumping and talking about her new life all the way. Walking behind them gave me a minute to catch my breath. We were here. No more craziness. We were back with my parents in a familiar place. Relief washed over me. Lily would get medical help, and I would gain the knowledge I needed to care for her. We walked out of the terminal into the warm sunshine of the Minnesota summer.

The next morning, I was completely jet-lagged. I pulled Lily out of a deep sleep, and we stumbled out the door to the urology appointment. We easily found the urology clinic with its ample parking lot. The second we entered,

I relaxed. There was a clean waiting area with bright lights, colorful animal decals on the walls, and a welcoming reception desk. The room smelled like summer flowers, not sterile bleach. I was certain we were going to get the help we needed.

According to my parents' research, we were about to see the best pediatric urologist in Minneapolis. He had a stellar reputation and knew all about complex urological issues. I was looking forward to meeting him. I came armed with a majority of Lily's medical records, at least the ones in English, and my long list of questions. I was feeling confident when we went back into the examination room.

"Hello, I'm Dr. Anderson." He was tall and thin with a bright smile. "I hear you have come from Japan. Please tell me exactly what is going on." He spoke calmly and easily, and I felt welcome in his office.

"Lily was born in Tokyo, Japan, on June 7, at Joshi Idai Byoin Hospital. She has Cloacal Anomalies. She had a colostomy and vesicostomy made when she was twelve hours old. She was in the hospital for five weeks. You can see the urine tube here and the colostomy bag under her clothes when we undress her." I continued with a summary of all that had happened in her short life. "She got sick a few days ago with a urinary tract infection. She is taking powdered Bactrim for the infection." I told him as much as I knew about the reconstructive surgery and that we had not yet decided where we were going to have it. "We know a doctor in Tokyo who has done a few of these reconstructive surgeries. Since our family lives in Japan, we are thinking we will just have him do it. I'd like to have your opinion about how to take care of Lily between now and the reconstructive surgery. I don't want her to get sick again."

When he spoke, his tone surprised me. It was as if his words didn't match his demeanor from only minutes before. "I've looked through the medical records and X-rays you brought. It seems they did the correct surgeries for her up until now, but five weeks in the hospital was completely unnecessary. If you had given birth in the U.S., we would have done the colostomy and vesicostomy surgery, and you would have taken her home after only a couple of days."

I was immediately on alert. He didn't need to speak to me this way. Why were doctors always making me feel awful for my decisions? Did I look like someone who was incompetent or, worse, negligent? We had done everything we could possibly imagine for our baby. She was struggling, but that was why we had traveled all this way. We were in this doctor's office because we needed his help.

I wasn't asking for confirmation of the quality of the care we had received in Japan. That was behind us, and Lily had been healthy up until a few days ago. I wanted his expert opinion about what to do going forward.

He continued to attack what the Japanese doctors had done. "This crazy tube sticking out of her bladder is ridiculous." He pulled on it, making the Tegaderm patch come loose. I jumped and put my hand on the sticky pad to hold it in place and make him stop. "We would never have put that in her." I thought he might pull it out. We had treated it with delicate hands for all these weeks so it wouldn't fall out. His behavior seemed bullish. "It is unfortunate they did this. How is that working for you?" His voice dripped with sarcasm.

"It is awkward and difficult to manage," I conceded.

"Well, of course, it is. If you had given birth in Minnesota, you wouldn't have had this long tube. I could perform an operation on her to eliminate the tube completely, and that would fix this issue for you."

I wasn't there for another operation. We were managing the tube, and it would be with us until we did the reconstructive surgery. We had a system, and it worked. I couldn't take more surgeries or hospitals.

"No, thank you."

"Well, at least let me change the tube for you. Did you know it is called a Balloon Catheter?"

I did not, remembering that at the NICU, they told me nothing. I shook my head.

132

"There is a tiny balloon inside of her. It is inflated, and that is what keeps the catheter tube in place. I can easily change it right now and at least give you a shorter tube." That sounded good; I nodded.

He left the room. I had to admit to myself I was hoping this doctor would have been amazed by what we had accomplished. I had hoped he would appreciate the fact we were able to navigate the Japanese medical system. I wanted him to reassure me that the future wouldn't be so bleak and that there was some hope for us on the horizon.

He came back with a catheter and tore it out of the sterile packaging. It was similar in diameter to the one Lily had protruding from her belly, only this one was a lot shorter. It would still dangle past her foot but wouldn't have to be wrapped around and around and held up with an S hook anymore. It would be an improvement.

He opened up Lily's outfit and then moved right in front of her, blocking my view. After only a few seconds, I heard a splat. I looked and saw the long tube and urine bag down on the examination room floor. The doctor continued to stand right in front of me, but within a few seconds, he backed away. He was done. There was a much shorter tube coming out of the hole in her belly. It would be less cumbersome. I didn't like his bedside manner, but he did help. "You said they gave you Bactrim to treat the urinary tract infection?"

"Yes."

"You said it was a powder?"

"Yes."

"I will prescribe a liquid form for you. You simply have to tilt her head back and put the medicine in her mouth through a dropper. That way, you will know for certain she gets the entire dose. Infection should be the only issue you will encounter between now and the reconstructive surgery. Her body is exposed to bacteria through the urine tube." He pulled on it again, more gently this time, but still enough for me to put my hand on her belly to protect it. "You can use the Bactrim if she gets a fever again. It should quickly take care of the issue. Do you plan to stay here in the U.S. now?"

"I live in Tokyo. My husband works for Northwest Airlines. Our home is in Japan. I badly want to go back. That is why Dr. Fujikawa, the doctor who did the colostomy and vesicostomy, seems like the right person to do the reconstructive surgery."

"Do you understand how incredibly complex this surgery is?" I was surprised again at his level of disrespect.

I could sense I better have a good answer, so he would stop treating me like a fool. I wished Fred was with me. "Yes, Dr. Fujikawa told us it was the single most complicated surgical procedure that is non-life threatening."

"That is correct, and do you know the credentials for this, Dr. Fujikawa?" I didn't. He was kind and respectful and told us he had done a few of these surgeries. At the time, that seemed like enough. Based on what Dr. Anderson was saying, it wasn't. "Do you understand what this entails? You have to have a precise, whip-smart, and incredibly knowledgeable doctor.

You need someone who is both a pediatric urologist and a pediatric surgeon, which is very rare.

There are only three doctors who I would trust to do this surgery if it was my daughter: Dr. Peña, Dr. Hendren, and Dr. Shaul in Los Angeles. The most famous is Dr. Hardy Hendren. There's a book written about him."

I nodded again. "Dr. Fujikawa mentioned Dr. Hendren in Boston and told us about the book." I had already asked my parents to find it, so I could read it while I was in Minnesota. Luckily, I thought to ask him, "Could you please give me the names and contact information of the three doctors?" He ripped off a piece of the waxy paper covering the examining table and walked out of the room. A couple of minutes later, he came back with the names written down. I safely tucked that piece of paper in my bag, knowing in the back of my mind how crucial it might be one day.

"Good luck. Ultimately, your daughter can live a full life. It will take many surgeries for you to get there, and it will be a difficult road ahead of you, especially if you go back to Japan. Make good choices." I felt like, with the information I had at each juncture, I was making good choices, but he was saying I wasn't. He also said, like Dr. Fujikawa had, that she could live a full life. I was glad to hear even this doctor thought it was possible.

"Thank you."

He opened the door and left. I put the medical records, X-rays, and prescription for the liquid Bactrim in my large bag next to the ripped piece of paper with the three contact names on it. I wrapped Lily back in her clothes, marveling at how much easier it was with the shorter tube, and then got us out of there.

As I pulled away, I allowed this doctor's tone and demeanor to seep into me. I became filled with guilt and regret. If only we had stayed in the U.S. for her birth, Lily would have been able to bond with us during those first precious weeks of life. If only we had stayed in the U.S., we could have easily solved the urinary tract infection. If only we had stayed in the U.S., we wouldn't have had to go through the fright of our last hospital stay at Joshi Idai. I had a long list of "if only." I sat with them as I drove.

As I neared my parents' house, it dawned on me why so many doctors treated me as if I had made so many mistakes and looked at me as if I didn't understand. Lily's little body was so unique and so complex very few doctors understood how to care for her, and even fewer knew how to fix her broken body. In the end, it would be up to us to find the right path for her. We were fortunate, in fact, because we lived in Japan and had international medical insurance. We could find the best doctors anywhere and could give Lily the best possible chance at a good life.

We were doing the best we could with what we knew. It had to be good enough.

One of the best things we did during those weeks in Minnesota was have a friend who was a photographer come over and take pictures of the girls. I wanted to create a birth announcement for Lily. With us in a safe place, it felt like the right thing to do. I had the girls wear similar outfits, and Emma insisted on holding her sister, with each of them grinning at the exact right moment for the camera. We had Lily's head tilted so her ear was tucked under and the photo cut off just above the urine bag. No one would be the wiser.

I took Lily to Saint Paul Academy to see my former colleagues. Many of them knew what had happened, but most did not. The head of school asked me to join them in the conference room and picked Lily up, awkwardly passing her from person to person with the urine bag hanging down. I cringed. I wasn't ready for people to see the reality of my world. I wanted to protect Lily and protect myself. It was at that moment that I realized that I wanted to hide Lily away from everyone. I didn't want anyone to see her until we knew what her future would be like.

My brother flew in from Alabama to meet Lily. Our friends welcomed us with open arms and warm hearts. There was kindness, excitement, joy, and laughter. They all held and loved Lily, tubes, missing ear and all, and gave Emma gifts and lots of attention. They marveled at what we were taking on and vowed to help however they could. It filled me with joy and courage to go forward with what was coming next for us.

After a month in Minnesota, I was ready to go back to Tokyo, to Fred, to the hope of a good life in Japan for our family together. I had gained confidence in my ability to care for Lily and was anxious to share that with him. We had the liquid antibiotic so we wouldn't have to go back to Joshi Idai. I didn't want us to be apart. It felt good to say that Tokyo was home. What had happened was behind us. We were making a life for ourselves in Japan, and I wanted to get back.

Chapter 22

At the beginning of September, Emma excitedly started preschool at a nearby international school. "Mommy, I'm learning Japanese words like you! *Arigato* means thank you.

Look! I can bow too." She lowered her entire body, bending her knees all the way to the ground. I laughed at her enthusiasm to embrace Japan. It made me believe even more that we had made the right decision to return.

Lily remained healthy, and I felt confident in how to care for her. We joined a playgroup of moms and babies who I met through the American Club. I did my best to hide Lily's differences from the group, but I saw them stare at her tubes and her ear, as they had in Minnesota. This time, instead of cringing, I decided we both needed to be out with other people. I was thankful for this group of supportive moms from around the world.

It was a relief to see that even after five weeks in the hospital, Lily could keep up with the other three-month-old babies. She nicely stuffed her entire hand in her mouth and blew happily on it. She jiggled any rattle we gave her. There were moments when I could forget about her bags and tubes and focus on how sweet she was.

The rest of the time, reconstructive surgery was on my mind. While I was in Minnesota, I read the book about Dr. Hendren. I was now keenly aware of the complexities of this complicated operation. A few years earlier, any child who had been born with Lily's condition, assuming the child survived, would have had a very slim chance of ever having urinary or bowel continence.

We had to decide who would perform the surgery and where it would be done. Dr. Anderson's pointed questions about us having Dr. Fujikawa do the surgery added a level of complication to this decision, but I felt obligated to see Dr. Fujikawa. He had been the one to save Lily's life. He said he knew how to do the difficult operation. We didn't have anything but his word to go on since he wasn't in a hospital anymore. If we worked with him, we could stay in Tokyo together as a family, and that mattered to us. I was certain that the new hospital where Dr. Fujikawa would be working would be different from Joshi Idai. It was time to call and find out.

I pulled out the piece of paper with the phone number and address he had given us before he left Joshi Idai Byoin. Not knowing if his smaller clinic had receptionists who spoke English, Fred's assistant had kindly called and set up the appointment.

Lily and I dropped Emma off at school and got in a taxi to the clinic. I handed the driver the piece of paper with the name on it. He brought me to a location about fifteen minutes from our home. I was glad to know it wasn't far away. As we approached the building, alarm bells started to go off in my head. The "clinic" looked like an old abandoned gas station. I was hesitant to get out of the taxi. The familiar fear raced down my spine. How could we be in such a strange medical place? This just couldn't be happening again.

I pointed to the paper Dr. Fujikawa had given to me and said, "*Wa doko des ka?*" It was an entire sentence, which I was very proud of, and I was hoping it meant, 'Where is it?' The driver looked at his own map, looked back at the address, and pointed toward the building nodding, indicating this was the clinic. Dr. Fujikawa had left Joshi Idai Byoin Hospital, the most prestigious level three trauma hospital in all of Tokyo, to work out of an old gas station.

The voice of Doctor Anderson in Minnesota was ringing in my head, "Do you know the credentials for this, Dr. Fujikawa? Do you understand what this surgery entails? You have to have a precise, whip-smart, and incredibly knowledgeable doctor." Simply based on the appearance of this clinic, it was not looking like Dr. Fujikawa could do this surgery.

I forced myself to get out of the taxi and then watched it drive away. I reluctantly went inside. It was dark in there. Not pitch black like no one was inside, but dark like they were trying to hide the fact that this was not supposed to be a clinic. There was no reception desk, and only makeshift curtains pulled along a hallway, separating the beds. I stood at the entrance, not quite knowing whether to stay or run back out.

I was caught and couldn't leave, just as I had felt so many times before. If we wanted to stay in Japan and stay together as a family, surgery with Dr. Fujikawa was our only option. I stepped forward. Since clearly, no one had heard me come in; I peeked my head around the corner of one of the curtains. I did have an appointment after all. I said, "Hello? *Ohio gozaimasu.*" I heard some rustling coming from the back of the clinic and saw some movement from the other curtains.

Dr. Fujikawa appeared. He was an unusually tall man with stylish black and gray hair. He had on dark suit pants, a white shirt, a dark tie, and a starched white lab coat. I immediately felt a rush of relief. I found him. He was right in front of me. He knew Lily. He knew our situation.

"Hello Dr. Fujikawa!" I bowed, hoping he could see and hear my enthusiasm and respect. Strangely, he didn't say anything.

I held Lily up for him to see. "Look how much she's grown." I knew he had been concerned about how small she was when she was born, so I added, "She has gained so much weight and is so beautiful." I wanted him to know everything we had done since we last saw him. "We went to the U.S. with her and saw a urologist." I left out the part about him insulting the long tube and about how he said Dr. Fujikawa was not the right doctor for the surgery. "We have been looking into the reconstructive surgery; that is why I'm here."

He was being unusually formal with me, standing still, not reaching out to touch or even look at Lily. He wasn't reacting to our visit the way I had expected. "Come with me." He summoned me down the hall, past the curtains, to one of the beds. He motioned for me to sit on the bed. It was the only place to sit in the tiny space, so I put Lily on it too. He stood in front of me while I awkwardly looked up. He spoke in a very serious tone.

"I have not found a hospital here in Tokyo where I can work, so I'm planning on moving to Dubai." *Did he say Dubai? In the United Arab Emirates?* "I have a very good offer there. I'm leaving soon and am wrapping up with my patients here. I am glad to see you before I leave, and I can certainly refer you to other doctors here in Tokyo who could help you with the reconstructive surgery."

Oh no, oh no, oh no! Whatever he was saying, I stopped listening. This surgery required the best surgeons in the world. This fact had been gnawing at me since we left the U.S. We would not be staying in Tokyo. We needed to speak with the three expert doctors recommended by the Minnesota urologist, and we needed to start that process very soon. I literally ran out of the clinic and hailed a passing taxi.

With Dr. Fujikawa not able to perform the reconstructive surgery, we had to look beyond Japan. We went back to the list that Dr. Anderson had given to me of the three doctors he recommended. Dr. Hendren, the one in the book we had read, had created most of the techniques for the reconstruction. The second doctor, named Alberto Peña, was also extremely instrumental because he had added his own procedure called a Pull-Thru, which made continence much more probable for these children. The third doctor on the list was Dr. Donald Shaul. He had worked with Peña and Hendren and had an outstanding reputation. Not knowing who to call first, we decided Dr. Hendren was the logical place to start.

I was still recovering from the shock of seeing Dr. Fujikawa, so thankfully Fred had the energy to figure out who would be the best surgeon. He started by trying to call Dr. Hendren in Boston. It turned out that speaking with him personally was next to impossible. Fred called the main phone number for the hospital, and they connected him to Dr. Hendren's office. Fred was put on hold for almost an hour, knowing every minute of the international connection was costing us a lot. Out of exasperation and exhaustion, he finally found a way to leave a message explaining who we were and what we needed. We never heard back. We moved on to Dr. Peña, and again Fred was unsuccessful in reaching him. We were worried we might have to fly to the U.S. just to interview the doctors. It would be a long and difficult trip, and one we hoped to avoid.

Fred called the number for Dr. Donald Shaul at Children's Hospital Los Angeles. He explained to the main desk he was calling from Tokyo and that he hoped to speak to Dr. Shaul. He was put on hold again. By now, he had grown used to it. But a minute or two later, a man's voice came on the phone. "Hello? This is Don Shaul." Fred was so surprised. He was actually speaking with the doctor.

"Hi, my name is Fred Deschamps. I'm calling from Tokyo, Japan, where I live as an expatriate from the U.S. with my family. My daughter was born four months ago in Tokyo with cloacal malformation. We have heard you are an expert in the reconstructive surgery she needs, and we are currently looking for the very best surgeon." Fred took a breath.

"I can only imagine how difficult these last few months have been for you," Dr. Shaul said, his voice kind. "I know many doctors in Tokyo and have a family connection with Japan. There are outstanding doctors there. You must feel good about the care you have received so far."

Fred was relieved. For the first time in our medical journey, a doctor in the U.S. understood what we had been through, where our hearts were, and how grave our situation was. "What other surgeons are you speaking with? You need to find the right person to work with your family. Not knowing your daughter's situation, I can only speak from my own expertise with cloacal babies, but this usually isn't one surgery; it is many. There should be a good bond and trust between your family and your medical team."

"We have been trying to speak with Dr. Hendren and Dr. Peña. Their offices have not returned our calls."

Without a second of hesitation, Dr. Shaul said, "Dr. Hendren is the best; he is the pioneer of the techniques I use for the surgery. I trained under Dr. Peña and have watched his expertise in action. They are both exceptional. You are right, though; they are difficult to see. I have done many of these cloacal repairs, not as many as they have, but I do know what I'm doing, and I have an outstanding team of doctors and nurses I work with here at Children's Hospital Los Angeles. You can contact me by email; it will be easier with our time difference. Please speak with your family and let me know. I need to get back to the operating room. I came out to speak with you because the main desk told me it was urgent. I'm so glad I did."

Fred got off the phone and came to see me. "I have a good feeling about Dr. Shaul. Let's go to L.A."

With each email Dr. Shaul sent to us, we became more and more confident and comfortable with our choice. He wanted us to come and see him in Los Angeles in December, and he asked us to send him Lily's medical records, so he could study her information in advance of meeting us. He said during our visit in December he would have several outpatient tests done so he could be clear about how her body worked in order for the reconstructive surgery to be a success.

We had a doctor. We had a plan. We relaxed.

Chapter 23

Fred and I wanted to explore Tokyo with the girls, but it took a lot of extra planning. Lily's medical devices and extra clothes had to be carried, and we worried about the stares and unwanted attention. We tried to plan outings where there were bathrooms with stalls that had closed doors because a changing table in the open was too public.

One weekend, with Lily strapped on Fred's front and Emma holding our hands, we decided we would visit Meiji Shrine, one of the most sacred places in all of Tokyo. After triple checking our backpacks, we took the subway and arrived at Harajuku Eki. We exited the station at Omotesando, the Champs-Élysées of Tokyo. It is filled with the highest of high-end shopping, fashionably dressed people, cars so outrageously expensive you have to look twice, and restaurants you could never enter without reservations months in advance. We walked with wide eyes down the boulevard, pointing out everything to Emma. We got her an ice cream cone and sat down on a bench to eat it. "Emma, look over there! Do you see that car's doors opening like bat wings?" We sat for a long time, enjoying our time away.

At the far end of Omotesando is Meiji Jingu Shrine. For as bustling and ostentatious as the city street is, the Shrine is a sanctuary for reflection and peace. At the entrance is a humongous Torii Gate made of towering tree trunks. Standing before the gate, we bowed to show our respect. Emma, of course, bowed the lowest. In front of us was a wide and long path covered in small pebbles on the ground and huge trees creating a canopy overhead. The walkway twists and turns as it goes. As we entered, we made certain Emma understood she had to be quiet and calm as we walked. "Emma, for as exciting as Omotesando was, here in Meiji Shrine, we have to show respect. You will see it is completely covered with beautiful green trees to shield us from the city, and you will hear birds if you are quiet. We are going to walk slowly and silently."

Emma nodded that she understood. She put her finger up to her mouth and said, "Shhhh."

Her commitment to serenity lasted for one small part of the path. She couldn't help herself. It was too tempting. Joyfully she shouted, "Mommy, Daddy, I'm a bird flying through the air! I'm going to reach the trees!" She was leaping and jumping with her arms flapping up and down. She started chirping like a bird.

We were again the out-of-control *Gaijin* (foreigners) disturbing the *Wa*. We weren't sure if we should claim her or not, but after a few seconds, Fred and I doubled over laughing. Emma's joy was contagious. We had not felt that kind of freedom in months. It was cathartic. Fred whispered, "I think this shrine will be accepting of our behavior; at least, I hope so."

We finished the long walk on the path and came to the entrance to the shrine itself. Emma had calmed down and was listening to see if the birds were responding to her calls. Fred leaned down to talk to her, with Lily waking up in the front pack as he crouched. "We are about to actually enter the shrine now."

"That wasn't it? The birds?"

"No, we will cleanse our hands and pass through another gate and then enter the actual shrine." He pointed to a covered area nearby with water flowing through a trough. She looked down at her hands.

"Let's cleanse."

As Fred stood up, his eyes widened in a way that told me something terribly wrong had just happened. I knew right away Lily's colostomy bag had just burst. We had been so caught up in the excitement of Omotesando with Emma that we forgot. We looked for toilets, but there weren't any. We were at the entrance to the shrine, so there wouldn't be bathrooms; they were many minutes back along the trail. Emma said in a loud voice, "Did Lily's bag burst again?"

Fred and I started looking for a place to change her and clean her up. We walked the perimeter of the pebbled pathway, checking behind some of the buildings nearby. We even stepped off the path into the trees. Finally, we decided on an area covered in stones. It was at least 100 feet from anyone or anything. The stones would be a good flat place to change her. Fred stood guard, Emma twirled, and I crouched down and started to change Lily. Fred looked everywhere, "all's clear. Go ahead." I took out an already-cut colostomy bag and several baby wipes to clean what I knew would be a disgusting mess on her stomach. I slowly unsnapped her outfit, pulled out her arms, pulled off the bag, and put it all in the plastic bag we had brought. As I was beginning the task of cleaning her belly with her colon sticking out, Fred gasped. "Watch out!" I jerked my head up and saw what he saw, a stampede of people all coming our way. It looked like hundreds.

In our search for the perfect spot, we had not seen a path coming out of the blanket of trees. We were directly in the middle of where the tour groups would walk. First, they came one by one, then ten by ten, and then we were enveloped with people parting as they walked on either side of us. Fred did his best to stand above us, but he was almost knocked over by the sheer volume of people. They craned their necks as they walked by to see what the foreigners were doing standing in what was obviously a main thoroughfare at the shrine. We were aghast but could not move with Lily so completely exposed and messy.

It seemed like forever before they stopped coming. The second there was a break, I quickly cleaned Lily up, put on a new colostomy bag and clothes, and picked her up off the ground. We were so shocked we didn't even think about how Emma was reacting. "Wow! That was a lot of people. They were noisy, not like me."

When we had recovered both our dignity and our senses, we proceeded into the inner shrine as if nothing had happened. In the Shinto religion, you make wishes and share your hopes and dreams. There are wooden plaques that can be purchased where you can write those wishes. Sometimes people wish for world peace, and other times people wish for good health. This time on my wooden board, I wrote that I was so sorry to always be disturbing the *Wa*, and I hoped we had not traumatized the Japanese visitors to this sacred shrine.

Chapter 24

And then, as quickly as we finally settled into the life we wanted in Tokyo, it ended. As December approached, it was hard enough to think about Lily having the extensive reconstructive surgery, but we worried about the disruption to Emma's life, the toll this would take on our family, and how much it would cost.

With all that churning in our heads, we flew to Los Angeles to meet Dr. Shaul at Children's Hospital Los Angeles. He came out to the clinic right away when he heard we were there. "Hi! I'm Don Shaul. I'm so glad to finally meet you in person." He shook our hands warmly. After all of the exchanges of emails in preparation for this meeting, I gave him a hug, with no bow needed. "How was your trip from Tokyo? I think I told you I have been to Japan before. My wife's family is originally from there. What an amazing country. So much to learn and explore." He leaned down to Emma and said, "Ohio gosaimasu." She enthusiastically responded with the lowest bow possible. He then turned to Lily, who was awake, cooing, and wildly shaking a rattle making certain we knew she was there too. "Hello, Lily. I'm happy to meet you. I'm here to help your body. We'll put the pieces back together again." A friendship blossomed between our family and his that would continue for decades.

Quite truthfully, he is one of the best people to ever come into our lives. Not only is he a top-ranked pediatric surgeon and urologist, singularly focused on extremely complicated cloacal repair, but he is the kindest, most compassionate, and most dedicated doctor. He believes that parents are an integral part of the care of these children, and he embraces the partnership. This felt so different from Japan.

He was the first American doctor to not only support but encourage our lives to continue in Tokyo. His wife has family connections in Japan, so he understood the culture and why we loved our new life filled with adventure.

He didn't scorn or belittle us. He invited us into the medical world and helped us find our way through it. We had no doubt he was the right person to give Lily the best possible chance for a full and vibrant life.

When he came into our exam room at Children's Hospital Los Angeles, his team had already met with us. They, too, were kind and welcoming and took the time to explain all that would be happening while we were there. The warmth continued when he walked in.

Upon our arrival, Lily was put through a battery of tests. An MRI, CT scan, ultrasound, X-rays, and more. At the end of all of the testing, we had a final meeting with Dr. Shaul. "We got everything we need from this visit to make the surgery successful. My team and I will put together our exact plans for the operation. My office will organize everything with you.

"We have not talked about this, but the recovery from this operation is as complicated as the operation itself. Lily will need to stay here in the hospital for many days and then in Los Angeles for multiple medical appointments until we can make certain she is healthy and can go back to Japan. You will need to be in Los Angeles for at least a couple of months." My body started to shake. I dropped my head into my hands. *No! Not again. Weeks and even months will go by, and we will be stuck in a hospital.* I wasn't sure how I could possibly do it.

Fred was devastated too. We had thought of everything except the length of time we would be required to be in Los Angeles. We hadn't anticipated it would be that long a recovery. There was no way Fred was going to be able to work remotely for two months. Los Angeles was neither the Minneapolis headquarters for Northwest nor his actual office in Tokyo. Medical leave for him was unthinkable. Fred had to keep his job, or we would lose everything. Even with our good medical insurance, Lily's bills and our time away from home were about to be astronomical. This time, it wasn't just about paying for gas to travel the streets of Tokyo in our big green minivan. We needed to rent a car for two months, a hotel for two months, and have food and activities for Emma for two months. It was about having every part of our entire lives uprooted, and each thing would cost money. I felt stuck.

147

Before we left Los Angeles for our winter holiday, we went to see Dr. Shaul's staff to schedule the surgery. The operation took a minimum of twelve hours. There would be an entire team of doctors and nurses in the operating room the entire time. It was a challenge to secure a date. We picked one at the end of January. Lily would be eight months old.

Kate, the office coordinator who we had spoken to several times as we got organized for the trip, casually asked us, "Would you like to stay at the Ronald McDonald House near the hospital for those two months? Since your family is coming from Japan for the surgery, you qualify for a room or even two."

I looked down at the floor. I had always thought of Ronald McDonald Houses as places for families of chronically sick children. I had seen and put coins in the little red houses at the front of every cash register at McDonald's. That money went to families with sick children. I didn't want to think of our child as chronically ill.

Fred was quick to react. He knew we couldn't afford a hotel for two months; anything other than the Ronald McDonald House would take any savings we had. "Yes, we'd like to stay there."

With Emma seated next to the window, already glued to her *Blues Clues* video screen, we flew from Los Angeles to Minneapolis-St. Paul, for Christmas, I said out loud what everyone else already knew. "Lily is sick, isn't she?"

"Yes, what do you mean?" Fred looked at me intently. I didn't realize that Fred had wanted to have this conversation with me for a long time, but he knew I hadn't been ready until that moment.

"I have spent so much time focusing on what Lily can do I don't think of her as sick. Even Dr. Shaul saw that she smiled, giggled, and even shook a rattle. She pees and poops, albeit differently from others, but she does them. She listens when I read endless books and rests all curled up in my lap. She has been on adventures with us all over Tokyo and is getting to know her world, like Emma. She needs operations, but they will go well, and she will recover. To me, she isn't sick."

Fred looked at me and smiled. "You are always the one thinking the glass is half full. How lucky for all of us that you are. But Sarah, the problem is that this time our reality is different. We have a daughter with a chronic medical condition. Lily is sick. Our family has a child that is very sick."

I pushed back, speaking a bit too loud, so the neighbor across the aisle turned her head. "I don't think about her that way." I looked down at Lily sleeping in my lap on the plane. I remained quiet for the rest of the flight, still not wanting to admit the truth. Fred had been thinking about this ever since he put his hand up and told Dr. Fujikawa, 'chotto matte kudasai' (wait a moment) while he took time to absorb the gravity of our situation.

Once we got to my parents' house, he took me aside and closed the door to our bedroom. "Sarah, we need help. I have to work while we are in L.A. Most likely, I will have long hours because of the time difference with Tokyo. I'll have to go back to Japan before you and the girls. I can't lose my job. Your parents are amazing and will come for the surgery, but they have to get back to work themselves. That leaves the burden on you of managing Lily in the hospital as well as taking care of Emma. It's two whole months. You can't do it by yourself." I knew what he was saying was true, but I couldn't bear to think about us being apart, nor about what we were about to go through. I rested my head on his shoulder and again cried, finally admitting to myself how much harder our lives would become. We had to find help.

We started the search for someone who would have superhuman qualities. The person had to be willing to be a part of our family at our most vulnerable time and be willing to move to Los Angeles and live with us at the Ronald McDonald House. That person had to watch our baby go through a life-altering surgery and be willing to step in when Fred had to go back to Japan. The most important responsibility for the person would be to take care of Emma, keeping her happy and busy, and showing her the parks and fun things for children to do in Los Angeles. To add to that, the person might move back to Japan with us once the surgeries are done.

Our dear friends told us about their babysitter, Siri, who was looking for a job and was considering being a nanny. They invited us over to their son's third birthday party to meet her. When we arrived, we didn't see her right away. They smiled and pointed outside. Siri was running around the yard, playing silly games with the kids and laughing and tickling them as they ran. One of the children tripped; Siri scooped him up and carried him in her arms while singing a rhyming song and checking to make sure he could still play.

In our wildest dreams, we could never have imagined someone like her could exist. She was a Macalester graduate ten years behind us who loved international travel, was kind beyond belief, gutsy, and creative. She was an extraordinary Mary Poppins. She had not decided what she wanted to do next after leaving Mac, so she told us she was flexible and wanted to join our family. She agreed to meet us at the end of January in Los Angeles when we came for the surgery. With confidence in having that decision made, Fred, Emma, Lily, and I flew back to Tokyo for the month of January. Once we arrived, all I did was count off the days until we had to go back.

On our last Sunday in Tokyo before leaving for Los Angeles, our friend from Macalester, Hiro, and his wife, Mariko, invited us to Nogi Shinto Shrine. They wanted us to have a place to make wishes, as we had done at Meiji Shrine, for a successful outcome of Lily's surgery. We accepted the invitation.

We took the subway on that cold January morning. There was a light dusting of snow on the ground, which made the shrine magical. We bowed as we passed under the Torii Gate at the entrance. Emma pointed to the basin of water just inside, "cleansing our hands!"

Our friends told us, "This water is to purify you and clear your thoughts, so you can be at peace in the shrine." We picked up the ladles and poured the water over our hands, shuddering with the chill.

Hiro, who is a very easy-going person, went to purchase the little wooden plaques where we would write our hopes for a successful surgery. I followed him over to the small building. I wanted to hear how to purchase the tablets in Japanese. There was a man at the open window ready to help. As I stood there, I heard Hiro say, "*EMMA*." He didn't say it once; he said it several times as he spoke to the man inside.

I felt awful interrupting him, but I also wanted to make sure we got the right tablets.

"Wait! We aren't making wishes for Emma's surgery, these wishes are for Lily. You keep saying, Emma."

He burst out laughing, "Sarah, *EMA* is what we call the wooden tablet. It is not about Emma's name or a wish for her; I'm simply purchasing 'EMAs' for all of us." I was horrified and didn't find it funny at all. I slowly backed away while he finished purchasing the EMAs. I could not believe it. The *Wa* had once again felt my disturbance. I hoped it would forgive me this time too.

He passed each of us an *EMA*. We walked over to the place where there were tables and pens. Emma stood next to me. With cold fingers, I wrote, "I hope Lily's little body will survive this reconstructive surgery, and I hope our family unites together behind the challenges of the next several months."

When I was done writing my *EMA*, I lifted Emma up to write hers. I asked her what her wish was for Lily's surgery. She scribbled circles and lines all over the tablet and said, "I'm writing that I want Lily to be happy, and I want to play with her when it is done." She paused for a second, looked over at Lily, all bundled up against Fred, and added, "I'm writing that I love her." We all placed our *EMAs* on the hooks, with our family's English writing standing out amongst the beautiful Japanese characters.

Fred and I didn't discuss what we had each written; we both knew we felt the storm coming our way. We thanked our friends for bringing us to the shrine and slowly made our way home.

Chapter 25

Three days before Lily was to be admitted to the Children's Hospital Los Angeles, we flew to L.A. This was the sixth time we had flown across the Pacific Ocean since arriving in Tokyo only nine months earlier. Emma was not amused at the prospect of sitting in an airplane for another twelve-hour flight. "Mommy, I think we need to stay in one place. I like my school and my friends. Why do we have to go?" I had been so focused on the surgery I didn't have an answer for a curious three-year-old. I hadn't thought of a positive parental response. I didn't want to go either. I picked her up instead and twirled her around, reminding her of all the new movies she could watch on her portable DVD player. She smiled, "Anastasia!"

The bills started mounting the moment our plane landed. We rented a car for two months, picked up groceries, and drove to the Ronald McDonald House. It was in a residential neighborhood one block from the hospital. The house was huge, with hotel-like rooms scattered around a large open atrium, and there was an industrial kitchen for all of the families to use off to one side.

Siri was waiting for us on the front porch. I exhaled, not even realizing how stressed I had been about this moment. She jumped down the stairs and ran up to Emma, giving her a huge bear hug, "I'm so glad to see you. I can't wait to spend time together. Come on inside, and there is a playground!" Fred and I exhaled.

On Super Bowl Sunday, January 28, 2001, Lily was admitted to Children's Hospital Los Angeles for her reconstructive surgery. We stopped at the front desk and received bright blue stickers saying 'in-patient.' As I put on the blue sticker, I turned to Fred, "it says we are inpatient; there is no indication we will be checking out." He grabbed my hand.

We were admitted a day before the surgery because Lily's bowel had to be completely clean for the operation. They told us it would take a full day to remove all of her stool but didn't tell us how they would do it. The first step was easy. The nurses hooked Lily up to the vital sign machine. I recognized it and nodded my head that I understood what we were doing. That was the only thing that was remotely familiar. From that moment on, Lily quickly plunged into a screaming, yanking, furious, angry mess.

The nurse quietly asked us to take a step back. "Could you please not touch anything while we do this?" *What could be so bad?* Another nurse approached Lily on the opposite side of the crib. She had a really long tube in her gloved hands. It was the thickness of an electrical cord. "I'm going to put this down Lily's nose. That is the only way we can get enough of this medicine in small babies." *What? A tube had to be put in Lily's nose and then shoved down her throat far enough that it reached her stomach.* The thought almost made me gag. I stopped breathing as they placed the tube near her nose. Lily obviously didn't know what was going to happen. Then, one nurse stood behind her and grabbed her head, and the other nurse shoved the tube in with one quick but forceful push.

What immediately followed was the loudest shriek I have ever heard. Lily was gasping and sobbing and continued yelping. She angrily started flailing her arms to pull the tube out of her nose. Lily would not calm down. She became more and more agitated and angry and kept trying to yank the tube out. Fred and I stood helplessly next to her, desperately wishing we could pick her up. Out of nowhere, another nurse came over to her and started to put restraints on her tiny hands and arms. I started to dive at the nurse to remove them, but Fred grabbed me and held me back. Lily continued to sob, and then so did I.

There is no way I could have prepared myself for this, and maybe it would have been better if I didn't know. I started to rock back and forth on my feet, keeping my arms down, cooing at Lily, "this is ok, you will be fine," when I knew she would not.

When Lily was restrained, they started dripping the clear medication into her through her nose. It was a laxative that would empty her bowel. Once it was flowing, and Lily couldn't grab it, the nurses brought in another tray of instruments. This time, they would be putting in an IV to hydrate her body before the surgery. I turned my head away, knowing I couldn't watch. I whispered to Fred, "The last time this happened, the doctor in the emergency room at Joshi Idai had to poke her so many times. She was crying; I was crying. Don't let that happen here."

Fred spoke up. "She is a really hard stick. Tiny veins. Please be really careful." With relief, they got it in Lily's arm on the very first try. One more step was done.

The nurses left, and Lily calmed down. They didn't warn us, but the awfulness wasn't over; in fact, it was just beginning. The medication started to work, and stool began to come out of the colostomy hole on her belly. It started slowly, so we had time to clean her off, put on a new colostomy bag, and even read to her. About two hours in, the stool started coming faster and faster, and it was more and more liquid. We tried to put on a colostomy bag, but there wasn't a break long enough to make it secure. Finally, we used rag after rag to catch the mess and get ready for more. It lasted for hours.

That evening, after Lily's bowel, was finally clean and she had fallen asleep out of exhaustion, Dr. Shaul came to her room. He gave us hugs and welcomed us back to Los Angeles. "My team and I are ready. I'd like to explain what we'll be doing since we will begin so early in the morning. First, we will put in a port." *One more hole.* He pointed above his heart. "It is a tube that allows us to give Lily fluids, medicine, and a blood transfusion, if necessary, during the operation." I had heard about ports, but I didn't realize Lily's surgery would require one. He paused, searching for the right words knowing he would be bringing difficult news, "what makes this surgery so complicated, apart from the need to reconstruct the bladder, bowel, and uterus, is that the baby has to be cut open from her belly button, all the way to the middle of her back."

The image of Lily being sliced open popped into my head. I shook it away. "During the surgery," he continued, "one of the most elaborate procedures we will be doing is to gently turn Lily over on the operating table, so we can reach each small system and can separate and reconstruct them."

I started to imagine what all of this looked like. A tiny baby lying flat on the operating table with so many instruments sticking out of her and so many complicated little parts needing to be separated and repaired, and then he mentioned turning her. The idea made me sick. I forced the image out of my head and focused again.

"I see both of you have donated blood here at the hospital." Fred and I had given blood right after arriving in Los Angeles, mostly because our family was about to receive so much from this hospital that giving blood seemed like a small gesture we could do. "We will have it in the operating room ready to go in case she needs a blood transfusion during the procedure."

I wasn't expecting that. Like the Ronald McDonald House had been a place I had always supported but had never thought I would need, giving blood had always been important to me. I was not prepared to think Lily would be the one who needed it.

"With the complexity of Lily's body, I'm planning on the surgery lasting between twelve to fifteen hours. I will not see you in the morning since I'll be getting ready in the operating room. I also have to conserve my energy because I will be leading the team of surgeons and nurses for the entire surgery. I want to begin as early as we possibly can. A nurse from our team will come to get Lily at 6:30 in the morning. You may walk down the hall with Lily toward the operating room but will not be allowed in. Another staff person will show you where parents wait during surgeries. We will have nurses come out of the operating room periodically during the day to let you know how things are progressing. Please plan to be in the waiting room the entire day."

This surgery, in 2001, was before there were pagers to tell you your child was done with the surgery. We were expected to simply sit all day long and into the night to wait for the surgery to be done.

Dr. Shaul reassuringly looked at us both, "I promise to take very good care of Lily. We will do what we can to ensure a healthy life for her going forward." He shook our hands and walked out of the room. We would not see him until the next evening after it was all done.

Fred stayed with Lily and me until 11:00 that night. During the next several hours, Lily remained calm. There was almost nothing coming out of her except urine through the tube into the bag. She was exhausted; most likely, the lack of food, the extreme stress, and the foreign environment had worn her out.

I was losing control of our baby again. This time was so much more than the surgery in Joshi Idai. I couldn't bear to think what her little belly and back would look like in twenty-four hours. Without asking permission, I did the only thing I knew how to do. I removed the arm restraints, which at least helped me to feel a little bit of control.

At about 2:00 in the morning, I lifted her out of the crib and tucked her into my arms on the bench where I was supposed to sleep. I ran my fingers over her belly and held her tight, memorizing what she looked like. "This surgery will change your life for the better," I whispered. "After this, you will begin to have a body that works the way it is supposed to work.

Daddy and I will take care of you no matter what. We will be there when you wake up after the surgery and will love you and hold you and make your life the best it can possibly be." I fell asleep with Lily held tightly in my arms. Fred gently kissed us both when he came back into the room at 6:00 am. Lily woke up and cooed at us. She wiggled her toes and smiled.

Fred picked her up and started talking to her about Emma and Siri. "They are sleepy, just like you. They miss you and tell you they love you." He continued to talk to her, and she continued to smile and coo back at him as I went to change into the clothes he had brought for me, brush my teeth, and splash some water on my face. By the time I got out of the bathroom, a nurse was standing there with him, ready for us to take Lily down the hall. It was 6:20 in the morning on Monday, January 29th. After everything we had been through, the day was finally here.

The nurse let Fred hold Lily as we walked down the hall. We got to a door that said, 'Operating Room ENTRANCE' and stopped.

"It is time for you to say goodbye to Lily. We will take good care of her, and we will let you know as often as possible how she is doing."

156

Lily was done cooing and wiggling. She was still in Fred's arms, hungry and exhausted by all that she had already been through. Maybe she knew what was about to happen. I couldn't bear thinking about it, so I focused on just walking down the hall. We kissed her on the top of her head and told her, "We love you." Another nurse came to help take Lily and all of her tubes and the IV pole through the operating room door. We stood transfixed, watching through the tiny porthole window as they walked with our beautiful baby down the hall.

A woman approached us in hospital scrubs. "I'm from the social work department. I'll take you to the parent waiting room." We reluctantly followed her, craning our necks to get a final look at Lily. We went down the hall, and the social worker motioned for us to enter a room. "It will be a long day, but the nurses will give you updates as often as they can. One of you always needs to stay in this room, but the other could get some food. You can bring it into the room while you wait. Good luck." She turned and left.

The waiting room was large but bare of any markings that this was a children's hospital. There were windows all along one wall, but it was so early was still pitch-black outside. There was a small television mounted up high in the corner with the sound turned off and rows and rows of uncomfortable-looking chairs. There weren't any other people in the room yet; I guessed most surgeries must start later in the morning. We picked two chairs on the far wall. This gave us a view of the windows on our right and the door on our left. Five minutes into the surgery, we were ready for our first update.

Fred went in search of food, and I fell asleep. He woke me up, and as my eyes came into focus, he triumphantly held up bags of food. "Look! McDonald's! They have one in the hospital. No fish eyeballs or candy bars for you!" I grabbed the bag and wolfed down the hash browns and pancakes. I blew on the hot cup of coffee, grateful for its warmth.

It was beginning to dawn on me that when we saw Lily again, come what may, this surgery would be behind us. I only had to wait the entire length of a twelve-hour airplane ride to see her again. I could do that.

After devouring McDonald's, Fred excitedly pulled a box out of his bag that had a DVD player and headphones. "I went to Best Buy yesterday, and

I have a surprise for you. I bought a portable DVD player and some badass headphones! Then, you will never believe it, I found every episode of *Friends!*"

We were not big TV watchers when we were first married, and aside from a moment of Sumo Wrestling on our first night in Tokyo, we didn't have any connection to international TV. The one thing we had loved to watch all those years ago was *Friends*. It was a real find and a true gift.

Those big headphones, bulging out far, brought back memories. The night I met Fred in his dorm with Hiro, he was banging away on his desk with drumsticks. He had enormous, very expensive-looking headphones over his cap from his school in Brussels. It was quite a sight, one that intrigued me enough to get to know him more. Music had always been a passion of his, and quality equipment was a central tenet. Over the years, I watched, admired, and listened to his music. "I thought you might like to disappear into another world while we wait."

I gave him a giant hug, ripped off the wrapping, and put the headphones on. Immediately, Ross, Joey, Phoebe, Rachel, and Chandler took me away from that room and unexpectedly made me laugh out loud.

After hours of episodes on that little DVD screen, I looked up and saw the Parent Waiting Room was full, with almost every chair in the room taken. I slowly lifted the headphones off and discovered the room was quiet. I had been laughing out loud for a long time. All of a sudden, I worried. Maybe like in Japan, I was disturbing the *Wa*, and this time I was in my own country. I could never get it right.

At 3:00 in the afternoon, after sitting for eight hours and watching family after family come and go, with most surgeries being two to three hours that day, we were still there. The fun of *Friends* had worn off, and the anxiety about Lily was now pulsing through my body.

A nurse entered the room, we looked up, and she came over to us. She bent over and whispered, "They are still working on her. Dr. Shaul wanted you to know it is going well, but he still has a long way to go. The morning shift of nurses is leaving, and the evening shift will soon go into the operating room to assist. All of the doctors will be there until the end." I was exhausted. How could the doctors possibly sustain themselves for so long? Could they concentrate that long? Did their backs hurt? Did they take breaks? Was Lily safe for so long under anesthesia? It didn't matter what I thought or worried about, they just kept operating, and we just kept waiting.

At 5:30 that evening, when the waiting room was completely empty again, Fred said, smiling, "Hey, I have a great idea! How about McDonald's for dinner?"

He returned after a few minutes with two supersized French fries hot out of the oil and a nice, greasy chicken sandwich. It went down quickly. "I put twenty dollars in the little red Ronald McDonald house box in front of the cashier." This time, we personally knew and cared about where the money went.

At 7:30 that night, way after the sun had set, a nurse came to see us. "The surgery is done." It had been close to thirteen hours, and for that entire time, I just sat there. I hadn't been able to move, except for one time when I ran down the hall to get in and out of the bathroom as quickly as I could. I was worried that a nurse would show up and tell us that something had gone terribly wrong. It was easier just to sit. I wiggled in the chair, just to make sure my bones still moved.

"They are finishing up in the operating room, and Lily will be taken to the Pediatric Intensive Care Unit. Dr. Shaul will meet you there. I'll be back to get you in a few minutes." She didn't say if it had gone well, but she didn't say there was a problem either. Just like when I was pregnant with Lily, I decided to believe that it was going to be fine.

Cell phones were blocked in the hospital, so Fred ran downstairs and out the front door of the hospital and called our parents to report the news.

With the nurse guiding us through the hallways, we approached the PICU. Was it going to be like Joshi Idai? Locked door? Nurses on guard? Gowns? Hairnets? Slippers? Antiseptic that made your nose curl? I held back.

Fred recognized my hesitation and went in first. He motioned that the door was open, and I should follow. We did put on hand sanitizer, but that was the only thing that resembled Japan. The room was large, with curtains separating each of the twin beds and regular chairs, with backs on them, next to the beds. Straight across from the entrance, the nurse pointed to Lily. I was startled. I couldn't believe we were going to see her.

Dr. Shaul came in right after us. He looked tired but seemed relaxed. Fred shook his hand. I gave him a hug. He smiled. We stood a few feet away from her bed. I glanced at her. Lily didn't look like Lily. She was three times her tiny size. Dr. Shaul could sense my hesitation.

"She is very bloated because she had to have the IV fluid pumped into her for over twelve hours. As she recovers, she will return to her normal size. You can see she is receiving oxygen through the ventilator on the wall. It is pumped in through the tube in her mouth and down into her lungs. That will be removed when the swelling goes down. As I mentioned, she has a port above her heart. We used it to give her fluids and medication during the surgery.

"Fred, we did need to give her blood. We used yours. Your daughter has a bit more of you inside of her." He smiled. "It helped to keep her going during the operation."

I reached for Fred's hand. "She will need to rest," Dr. Shaul said. "And I'm guessing so, do you. You can bring Emma and other guests in here." He must have sensed we didn't know when we could visit Lily.

I was expecting him to tell us, just as was the case in Japan, there were strict visiting hours in this PICU. "There are no specified times you can be here; you can come and go as you wish. I would like to see you tomorrow. Let's plan to meet in the afternoon, around 3:00. Would that work?" We nodded. "I can assure you, she did very well. I am pleased with how this went. I'll look forward to speaking with you tomorrow." He shook both of our hands, then left.

Fred and I walked over to Lily. It looked like a balloon had been placed inside of her and had puffed her up. Her face, legs, hands, even fingers were bloated. Her eyes were taped shut, maybe to protect them during surgery? "Oh my God, look at her." It dawned on me we could only see the medical instruments, not anything on her body. I blurted out, "This is only temporary. The bed, the room, tubes, doctors, it won't last." Fred's face didn't look at all like this was going to be temporary.

I leaned over the large bed and kissed her forehead. Fred did the same. I didn't uncover the blankets; she needed the warmth, and Dr. Shaul would explain what he had done in the morning. For today, I wanted Lily to know we were there with her and we loved her. Fred and I got on either side of the hospital bed, and each held one of her puffy hands. We stood there for a few minutes, then both of us could feel the momentous stress of the day falling away and our bodies giving in to the fact that this reconstructive surgical nightmare was over. "It's done. She is alive. We all survived." My wishes, made at the Nogi Shrine in Tokyo and written on an *EMA*, seemed to be coming true.

We went back to the Ronald McDonald House and found Siri watching over Emma, who was peacefully sleeping. She had already become a part of our family, so we hugged.

"Guess where we went today?" Siri asked with her usual joyfulness.

We could not even fathom a guess. "We were at the Science Museum of Los Angeles all day." She explained that Emma loved it disassembling and reassembling each exhibit. She said Emma was inquisitive and seemed thrilled to use her intellect to explore the museum. "We had a great time."

We were reminded the world did go on even though we were not a part of it. Siri pulled out a bright red children's book about the human body. "Emma could not get enough of this book today," she said. "She tried to understand each body system. I know she'll want to read it with you tomorrow." We were certain Emma was drawn to this book because she wanted to understand Lily's surgery. We had explained it to her, pointing with our finger at her own belly, but we knew after the surgery Lily wouldn't look anything like any belly or internal organ in that book. We hugged again. Siri went to her room, and Fred and I each gave Emma a kiss and promptly passed out on our bed, still fully dressed.

The next morning, Emma woke us up early, showing us the bright red book about the human body. "Mommy, look what I got yesterday at the science museum. It has lots of information about bodies. You have to see it." My three-year-old's enthusiasm was contagious.

We read it together, with her pointing out the body parts she had learned the day before.

The three of us got ourselves up and dressed and went to get some breakfast. We told Emma, we would take her to see Lily. "Did her body get fixed? Can I play with her today?"

I gently brushed aside her questions, "Let's all go to the hospital; she can't wait to see you."

When we arrived, Emma was thrilled to wear a bright blue badge. In-patient didn't bother her one bit. She proudly told the people at the desk, "I'm going to see my baby sister, Lily!" Before entering the PICU, she happily slathered on the sanitizer. Since the beds were high, we picked her up and pointed across the room to Lily's bed. The curtains along the window were opened up, and the sun was streaming in. I desperately hoped all of the bandages and tubes and pumps would be gone so Emma wouldn't see any of it. Of course, it was all still there, and she looked more swollen than twelve hours before.

"That's not Lily. That isn't a person." Emma looked horrified. She turned her head, looking to the other beds trying to find her sister. It startled me. Emma was articulating what we were thinking. Lily didn't look like a human. She had no neck, her eyes were tiny slivers, and her little rosebud lips were so big they seemed to overshadow the rest of her face. She had tape all over her face.

And then there were all of the wires and tubes protruding from under the covers on all sides. It looked bad. There were different colored tubes with different colored liquids all pumping into her body. There was a machine loudly pushing air into her lungs, and a vital sign monitor was buzzing and beeping. Lily lay still, obviously so full of sleeping and pain meds she looked like she was in a coma.

As we had done in Lily's bassinet at Joshi Idai, we brought some photos to place inside her PICU bed. Emma helped us to pick them out, so I asked her where she wanted to put each one. She placed a photo of herself right next to Lily's head. "When Lily wakes up, she will be so glad to see my smiling face."

After we stood next to Lily's bed for a few minutes arranging the photos, Emma said, "I can see her now. She is inside there, Mommy." We knew this was hard on Emma. We had tried to shield her from the tragedy and worry, but seeing Lily like this made what had happened to her sister a reality. She hadn't been allowed to come near her at Joshi Idai, so this was the first time she could visualize why Lily had to be away from us for so long when she was born. She could tell Lily would never have a body like hers. Emma was struggling to understand, and it was going to get even more difficult as time went on than it already was.

I let my guard down a tiny bit, swallowed my tears as best as I could, and said, "Yes, Lily is inside, resting and recovering; she will be out soon. She is better. She has lots of tubes and is so puffy, but she will be back to playing with you very soon, I promise." I didn't actually know if that was true, but I couldn't take away the hope either.

Emma bent down and placed a very timid kiss on Lily's forehead. She whispered, "I love you, Lily." And then we took Emma back to be with Siri.

That afternoon, Dr. Shaul told us exactly what he and his team had done the day before. With Fred standing next to me, I knew we could understand it all and discuss it later. I tried to listen, but Lily's puffy body kept getting in the way. "We had to turn her over twice during the procedure. She lost a lot of blood, that is why we gave her yours. The colostomy and stoma for urine will remain while the reconstructed tissues heal. She will have to have two additional surgeries in the future to close each of these stomas." That one I heard loud and clear, two more grueling surgeries for Lily to endure. Two more times are coming from Tokyo to Los Angeles. Two more times, that would put unbelievable stress on our family.

"I'd like to show you the surgical sites, so you can see where the healing will take place." Now I was fully alert.

163

"Before you see her, I want you to know this was a successful surgery. It went exactly as I hoped it would. It will look awful for a long time, but I can assure you she will heal well." He then pulled back Lily's blanket and opened up her little hospital gown. The machines were going wild as he touched and moved her. I knew that, like at the hospital in Tokyo, nothing could possibly prepare me for what I was about to see, and then there it was. Lily's belly was completely covered with stitches and staples and bandages, and dried blood. The stitches crisscrossed her tiny body. They went up and down and side to side. I forced myself not to look away.

"The most critical of the incisions is this one," Dr. Shaul said, moving his finger up and down along a cut that went from above her belly button to the bottom of her pelvis. "I won't turn her over now, but she has a similar incision from her bottom that continues up her back. It is through those openings we were able to separate her bladder, bowel, and uterus successfully." He pointed without touching her since she was so swollen. "We created a hole for the stool to exit, as it should from her bottom. That is called the Pull Thru procedure, the one created by Dr. Peña. Nothing will come out of that hole in her bottom yet because we kept Lily's colostomy. We cannot remove it until everything heals in the new passage for the stool. As I said, the colostomy will be closed in a separate surgery."

Pointing to a spot below her belly button, he said, "The original vesicostomy opening, as well as the tube and bag for urine, are gone. We closed that hole and created another one that allows the urine to drain directly from her bladder into a diaper without going through a tube. This isn't a urethra; it is just an opening in the bladder so urine can come out. There is still a risk of infection, but we have eliminated the tube, which can breed bacteria." All of a sudden, I remembered this was what Dr. Anderson, the urologist in Minneapolis, had wanted to do for Lily all those months ago. Now I understood the unnecessary burden of the urine bag and the risk of infection we had carried all those months. Back then, when Dr. Anderson had proposed the minor surgery, I could not let anyone else touch her. I didn't have the courage to let her go into anyone else's arms or have anyone do anything to her body. I was fearful they wouldn't return her to me.

164

Now, with more confidence and clarity, the removal of the urine bag was reason enough to have the surgery. It would radically alter how we could pick up, hug, carry, and interact with Lily. This was fantastic news and would improve her quality of life tenfold. This was a sign that things would get better for Lily. I must have looked relieved, so Dr. Shaul paused for me to take in this positive news.

"Within a few months, when the swelling and tissue recovers, the colostomy can also be removed." I implicitly now trusted Dr. Shaul and was glad to know he had a plan. I also knew I had no other choice but to follow what we were told. Dr. Shaul started to cover Lily's abdomen and place the blankets snugly around her swollen body.

He stepped away from her, obviously having something critical to tell us. "As you can see and hear, she is still connected to the machine that is keeping her lungs working. We cannot continue this machine much longer because we don't want her lungs to stop functioning on their own. Tomorrow they will be removing the breathing tube. It is an extremely delicate procedure. If it isn't timed right, the swelling in her throat may close in and cut off her breathing when the tube is removed. If that happens, we will need to perform a tracheotomy, so she can breathe. A specialized doctor, an ear, nose, throat, or otolaryngologist, will perform the procedure along with a team of trained nurses. You will want to be here for it."

Are you kidding me? A tracheotomy, an ENT, death again? I could not fathom that this was happening. I was about to be sick.

"I have one final piece of information I think you have heard from others; Lily has a single kidney. We were able to confirm that during the surgery. There has been and will continue to be, stress on that single kidney because the bladder is not functioning properly. We will monitor it going forward, but for now, it seems to be properly filtering her blood. Do you have any questions?"

Even though Lily was clearly not in a position to leave at all, my question for every doctor in every hospital was always the same. "When can she leave?"

165

"Lily will be here in the PICU until she is stable and the sutures all seem to be healing properly. I think it will be at least a few days. She will then be moved to a regular room in the hospital and will stay for another week or so. As I mentioned yesterday, you may come and go from the PICU as you want, and you may have other visitors so long as they come with you and check in at the hospital's front desk to get a visitor's badge. Once she is moved to a room in the hospital, you can stay with her in the room overnight if you like. I will be stopping by to see Lily each day around this time. I don't need you here when I examine her, but if you have questions, it might be good for us to check-in. Once she is discharged from the hospital, we will want her to visit our clinic each day. After that, we'd like to see her a couple of times a week, and assuming it all progresses normally, we can then see her once a week. As we discussed, you should plan to stay in Los Angeles for at least the next six weeks to two months."

Dr. Shaul paused. He looked at Lily, then at Fred and me. "This is a marathon for the two of you and your family, not a sprint. It started the day Lily was born and will continue for many years to come. It is taxing. I have learned a difficult truth through my years of practice; this is very hard on most marriages. I have seen couples go through this. Many don't survive this kind of constant, chronic medical trauma. It is relentless, and the toll on the family often becomes too much to bear. Take care of each other. Take time for each other. It will be important."

I blinked, opened my mouth, shut my mouth, and stood there, bewildered. Couldn't he see Fred and I were on the same team, working together, supporting each other, and doing our best for our children? We weren't like everyone else. We deeply loved each other and were making this work. We were going to continue to make this work. Even if it was relentless, falling apart was not an option for us.

We didn't talk about what he said; we didn't have the courage.

166

Chapter 26

When we arrived back at the Ronald McDonald House, Emma and Siri were ecstatic. Emma tried to speak but tripped over her words. "Mommy, Ronald McDonald is coming here!" Siri jumped in and explained there would be an actual visit from the King of Hamburgers himself in a few minutes. They had been told he would be reading children's books, and Emma could bring one if she wanted. Emma was holding her new bright red science book about the body and could not wait to give it to Mr. McDonald.

Sure enough, he walked in the door. "Howdy to all of you beautiful people!" There was an explosion of cheers and happiness and gleeful screams. He brought balloons and gave them to outstretched hands. It was mostly siblings at this event. The Ronald McDonald House knew, more than we parents did, how much they needed to be showered with attention.

He told the children to gather around him in the atrium of the House, and he would read them stories. Someone handed him Dr. Seuss' *The Cat in the Hat*. He read it, enunciating words as he read, and all of the children gleefully followed along, many of them knowing the story and delighted to have it read by such a famous person.

When he finished, he asked, "Does anyone else have a book for me to read?" Emma couldn't wait. She stood up and put the book right in front of his painted red nose. Emma was excited because the red book matched. He slowly opened it and started to read. "The human body is made up of many different systems. The first is the digestive system. It provides nutrients to our bodies by making our food give us energy." Ronald looked out at the little children who had happily listened to Dr. Seuss only minutes before. They didn't look so amused. Emma, on the other hand, had her legs crossed, her hands folded in her lap, and her neck pushed straight out, taking in each word. She had already memorized the book but thought having Ronald McDonald read it would bring it a whole new meaning. All of the children started to wiggle, and he looked like he was a bit worried he might lose their attention. He gently closed the book, passed it back to Emma, and said, "This, young lady, is an incredibly interesting book. I can see why you love it so much. You are obviously very talented and smart. I hope you continue to read it and grow up to be a doctor one day." Then, he looked away from her and said, "Now, does anyone have another story to read?" Another child handed him Eric Carle's *The Very Hungry Caterpillar,* and that was the end of Emma's love affair with Ronald McDonald.

The next morning, Fred and I casually made the walk back to the hospital. We were sure everything would be better today. We sterilized our hands and entered the PICU. We stopped at the door. We could see ten doctors and nurses surrounding Lily's bed. I had never seen so many together at one time. The intensity in the room was electric. This was not better. As we approached, no one turned to greet us or move away. Fred whispered, "This must be the team to take out her breathing tube." My heart was racing. Fred and I could see what they were doing, and it didn't look good.

At the bottom of Lily's bed sat a large metal suitcase. It was open and had shining medical instruments meticulously pressed into black foam. A nurse was kneeling on the bed, crouching over Lily. Her gloved hands were suspended about five inches above Lily's mouth. On the other side of the bed, another nurse stood with her hands up near Lily's face. There was a doctor behind the nurse, and he looked like he might be in charge. With the team frozen in place, he said authoritatively, "On my count, three, two, one." The nurse standing on the floor quickly peeled off the tape that was holding the tube in Lily's mouth. Once that was done, the nurse hovering over Lily's head reached down and, with one swift jerk, pulled out the tube. There was an audible gasp, and the entire group leaned in further to either hear her breathing or to grab a knife to make a hole in her throat so she could.

My eyes were riveted on the metal suitcase. If they needed a knife, it would be coming from there. I held my breath, thinking that might help. The nurse's hand was inches above Lily's head, and the breathing tube was now swinging back and forth in the air. It had been three seconds since the tube was pulled out. All heads were now staring at the doctor. He was intently watching both Lily and the vital sign monitor to see if there were signs of her breathing on her own. The doctor said something we couldn't hear. The metal suitcase was folded, the nurse got off the bed, and then the entire medical team seemed to melt back into the room. They neither acknowledged nor spoke to us.

We had been standing statuesque and finally realized it was over. We ran to her. I hoisted myself up onto the side of the bed with the bedrail cutting into my stomach. I put my ear tight against her nose. I had to hear for myself if there was air coming out or not. I heard nothing. My heart was racing; why had they all left? Lily was dying. Fred tapped lightly on the back of my head and pointed to the vital sign monitor. All of the squiggly lines were moving fluidly and evenly. Not a beep or a blip in sight. "I think if you move your head away from her nose, she might be able to breathe a little better," he said in his deadpan way.

"Very funny." I put my feet back down on the ground. We moved to what was now a familiar position, Fred on one side of her bed and me on the other. We both thoroughly scanned her body. "You know, aside from these red marks where the tape was ripped off of her face, she looks pretty good." We cautiously touched her little face. It was red and puffy. We both leaned in and gave her a kiss on her forehead, the one place we could find without scratches, puffiness, or stitches. We whispered, "We love you dearly. You are a fighter and survivor." Then we left her sleeping.

Over the next few days, Lily got better and better. The swelling went down, so she returned to her normal size and shape. We saw Dr. Shaul several times. He was happy with her progress. She was healing and responding better than he had expected.

At the end of the week, Lily was well enough to be moved from the PICU to a regular pediatric hospital room, where they predicted she would stay for a week. She was back to smiling at us and would even wave a toy in the air. We no longer had a concern about her surviving the surgery, but the healing process had only just begun.

As things got better for Lily, they got more difficult for Fred and me. We were exhausted and not sleeping at night. We tried to be with Emma as often as we could. Fred was working every minute he wasn't with us, and he had to return to Japan very soon. Each of us was doing what needed to be done and nothing more. With Dr. Shaul's team, there wasn't a language barrier as there had been in Japan or any concern about her medical care. The worry this time was that she would have to finish her healing with me at the Ronald McDonald House, and I didn't have five weeks to figure it out. I only had one.

Taking care of Lily after this surgery would be complex; it felt far beyond what I could manage. There were staples, stitches, and different holes in her body, and I couldn't see inside to know if it was healing well. I was terrified I would harm her and ruin all the progress we had made. I asked multiple questions each day. *How are the stitches healing? What antibiotics are you using? Is her system working as you hoped? How will we know if something is wrong?* I wrote every answer down in a notebook I had started months before so I would have something to refer to when I was overwhelmed and needed help.

Emma was tired too. "Mommy, I want to go home. I want to learn more Japanese. I miss my toys and my bed. I miss my friends. I miss you reading stories to me." She liked routine, and this was not that. She had more questions than we could answer. "Why can't Lily leave the hospital? When will she be better? Let's leave. I want to go home."

A few days later, the moment came that we both dreaded. It was crushing for us to think Fred couldn't stay in Los Angeles any longer. He had to get back to his job in Tokyo. He had to leave us behind, and we were not in a place where we could be left. He had kept up with the relentless workload at Northwest, but his work was in Tokyo, not Los Angeles. He ran an operation with hundreds of planes flying in and out of Japan that went all over the world. It didn't stop, so neither could he.

I slowly walked with him to the taxi waiting outside the Ronald McDonald House. We hadn't talked about what Dr. Shaul had said to us about couples not making it through the nightmare of endless medical issues. With the urgency of the taxi driver sitting and the meter running, I broke that silence, trying as always to be optimistic. "I believe we are going to survive. We are going to stay together. We love each other, and we have a good life in Tokyo. We will make it." I was searching desperately for confirmation and added, "Look at all that we have already been through!"

Fred tilted his head down. I could feel that he had been thinking about what Dr. Shaul had said as much as I had. He could see the reality of our situation better than I could. I was so wrapped up in learning how to care for Lily. My focus was on everything turning out well, us being back together, and continuing our life back in Japan. I couldn't see what was happening to us, nor would I let myself. Fred whispered, "We don't know what is in front of us. This is hard. Really hard." We hugged tightly, kissed each other, and he got in the cab, and it pulled away. I sat on the steps all alone again, and with the warmth of the sun on my cheeks, and sobbed. We wouldn't see each other until I brought Lily and Emma back with me to Tokyo an entire month later.

Chapter 27

After almost three weeks at Children's Hospital Los Angeles, Lily was discharged. As I had predicted, that day was very different from the one when she came home from Joshi Idai Byoin. Instead of her being completely healed, she still had metal staples, black stitches, and white bandages covering her entire belly going around to her back. She had a deep red scar above her heart where they had removed the port used during surgery. She had lost weight.

Like before, she had her colon sticking out and needed a colostomy bag, and now there was a new hole in her belly for urine with no tube attached. Wearing a diaper was no longer done to emulate all other babies. It was done to catch urine from a hole in a place where there shouldn't be one.

I wanted her at the Ronald McDonald House with me. She was my baby. I loved her. I needed her, but I also knew this would be hard. My questions were answered and thoroughly explained. "Sarah, there is still a worry of infection." They pointed at the stitches. "There is still a worry the bandages might come loose too soon." They showed me how they were taped and where they might loosen. "There is still a worry she might get sick when you bathe her, but you need to." I couldn't see how to put even a drop of water on my baby, let alone immerse her in a bathtub.

The nurses prepped me for what would be on the discharge orders that were fifteen pages thick. They focused on the fact that there would be multiple bottles of medication that were mostly to be given through droppers directly into her mouth. "You'll want to watch that because these can be tough on her stomach, and the taste is pretty foul. Expect her to either spit it up or throw it up. She needs them, though, to fight infection and to heal, so do your best to keep them in her." All I could think about was her vomiting and her stomach splitting open.

172

In Japan, I had arrogantly complained out loud that I wanted my baby at home, that I was the best person to care for her, not a hospital, not doctors and nurses. Here, I was searching for that same conviction, that same arrogance. I had to admit now I understood why the Japanese medical system excluded parents from the care of their children. At that moment, I craved exclusion.

I got my blue badge for the last time and took the elevator to her room. With the nurses watching patiently behind me, I started to take off Lily's hospital gown. My hands were shaking so badly I couldn't unsnap the top. I put my face near Lily's, trying to hide my fear. "Hi beautiful, we are going home. We are going to see your sister." She smiled, thank goodness. I put a shirt over her head. I had bought one four sizes too big, so it didn't touch anything, and I pulled it down. Even though it was chilly outside, I didn't have clothes to put on her legs. How could I put anything on them if they had to be snug around her stomach? I put one hand behind her head and one hand under her bottom and gingerly picked her up as I had done to breastfeed her for weeks. This time though, there weren't any tubes or wires sticking out; it was just Lily. I leaned in, and she bonked my nose with her little fist. I allowed a tiny part of me to think maybe I could do this.

As I placed her in the car seat, I put a hat on her head and blankets over her. I slid all of the paperwork into my backpack and unceremoniously left. The reconstructive surgery was behind us. Unfortunately, that meant only one surgery was done; there was so much more to fix.

I knew walking out that I would be right back in the next morning, but this time I would be getting a yellow badge which was only for a doctor's appointment. It felt like an upgrade. Cloacal babies have multiple issues beyond their tangled abdomens. Lily still needed to be evaluated to determine what those other medical issues were. We knew about her missing ear and missing kidney, but we had been told multiple times we had to expect more.

Lily was developmentally on point for everything social, emotional, sensory, and cognitive. She had started to eat whole baby food before the reconstructive surgery. She babbled and said a few words, she interacted with us, and she listened to Emma's stories. Everything was going well, but she was hitting none of the physical developmental milestones. She was in the 10th percentile for weight and height. She wasn't sitting up, crawling, or rolling over, and for eight months, I hadn't cared. In fact, having her make any motion at all would have been a nightmare with the mess it would have created from the colostomy bag and from the bag of urine that would have trailed behind her. Today though, it seemed important. She was behind.

Our first appointment was with a craniofacial doctor who, because of Lily's missing ear, evaluated her for head or brain deformities. She had none.

Doctors had worried her sweet, rosebud mouth looked like it might be a problem. There had been a concern her mouth wouldn't be big enough for all of her teeth. The oral surgeon concluded it was cute and little, and we had nothing to worry about.

Lily went to an audiologist to find out how much she could hear. She had 100% hearing on her left side, where she had a fully formed ear. On the right, where the outside ear was missing, she had ten percent. With that balance, it was confirmed she could hear well enough, and neither hearing nor speech would be an issue.

We had to see an otolaryngologist or ear, nose, and throat doctor. "The missing ear is called microtia. There are surgeries that can be done to try to improve hearing from her 10% level, but they are invasive, including creating a hole into the skull, and may not bring quality hearing at all. It is something that can be decided later." I liked the word later. As in, maybe never. He continued, "The good news is plastic surgery can create a prosthetic ear that will match the ear she has. Right here in this hospital, there is a marvelous doctor who can make an ear for Lily. I'm writing a referral for you to see him." I had no idea that such a surgery was even possible. She could have a second ear. I was elated.

Next on the list was an orthopedic surgeon. Lily's right thumb was half the size of the left. It looked a bit more like a finger than a thumb. She held things, played with toys, and grabbed a spoon as Emma had done. I knew the thumb was smaller, but I didn't pay attention to it because it worked just fine. I didn't know anything was wrong, so I wasn't prepared when the orthopedist uttered that dreaded word, surgery.

174

"Her thumb is part of the cloacal malformation she has. It is called hypoplastic. It means it never formed properly. There are five types of hypoplasia, all increasing in complexity. Lily's is type two, near the easiest level to fix. We will need to perform a surgical procedure that stabilizes a joint in her thumb, and then we will strengthen it with already existing tendons. Ultimately, it should function like her other thumb. We should do the operation around age three; that is when the thumb and tendons will have grown enough."

I stared at Lily's tiny thumb, now being held in the doctor's large hands. I heard him say age three for some surgery for a problem I didn't even know existed. When he was done with all of the medical words that I wasn't paying attention to, I grabbed Lily's car seat and raced for the front door of the hospital. I was desperate for fresh air.

Outside, when I started sobbing in the hospital's Contemplative Butterfly Garden, I realized the doctor had confirmed my worst fear. This was not going to end. In fact, we had just begun. I took out my notebook and wrote a huge number one. Next to it, I put colostomy closure, age ten months. In the next line, I wrote number two, the closing of the hole for the urine, date unknown. Below it, I wrote number three, thumb enhancement surgery, age three.

I finally admitted what the doctors had been telling me since she was born. We would be spending the next several years planning for hospital visits, traveling the twelve hours to Los Angeles for never-ending surgeries, recovering in a hospital bed, and then traveling twelve hours back to Japan. This was now my life. I could not believe this was happening to me, and we still had one more dreaded doctor's visit.

The next morning, I forced myself through the door of the hospital again. In the only act of defiance I could think of, I slapped my yellow doctor's visit badge upside down on my shirt, then we went straight to McDonald's. I got a supersized order of French fries, wolfing it down so fast the hot oil burned my tongue. I had some baby food in a jar for Lily. She was as hungry as I was. She had pureed chicken. I was proud that one of us was eating something healthy. Lily and I then went to see Dr. Reinisch. He is a famous plastic surgeon who specializes in the reconstruction of ears in small children.

As early as the 1950s, ears were made out of rib cartilage. Doctors would take a piece of the child's rib, mold it into the shape of an ear, and then graft it onto the side of the child's head. It was a difficult procedure, and the results were not always optimal. The child had to wait until at least age six because the ribs had to grow big enough for the surgeon to use them.

Dr. Reinisch changed everything. He perfected a procedure that uses a prosthetic plastic ear. It is grafted onto the side of the head and is done at the early age of three. The results are as close a match as possible to the child's other ear. It really is a miracle.

Since he is world-renowned, seeing him is nearly impossible. Appointments are taken, but you can count on at least a three-hour wait, which we had to do, staring at a huge fish tank the entire time.

The moment he finally entered the examination room, I understood why the wait and fame were deserved. He looked at Lily like she was the most important child he had ever seen. He firmly shook my hand but looked past me at her. He gently put both of his hands on either side of her small head and said, "You are a beautiful baby. I'm so glad to meet you." Lily shook her head from side to side, making him remove his hands.

He patiently took the time to explain to me the procedure he would use to make a new ear for Lily. He placed his finger on the smooth part of Lily's skin where an ear should be, running it from top to bottom. He was speaking to me with actions, not words, and for the first time in a long time, I could understand what was being said by a doctor. "When Lily turns three, and her other ear is fully formed, we will create a prosthetic one that matches Lily's left ear as closely as we possibly can. There are two surgeries needed to make the ear." Luckily, he didn't pause for me to react.

"The first surgery takes the prosthetic ear and attaches it to Lily's head by using a subcutaneous layer of skin that basically shrink wraps it around the prosthesis." He drew a line with his finger along the top of her scalp and made the motion of scooping out some skin. As I imagined the blood and gore and potential brain matter being exposed, he continued. "This is what holds the prosthesis in place. Lily will be able to actually feel her ear with the skin we use. It is living tissue and looks completely normal and will match her skin tone because it is her own skin. We then take skin grafts from behind her left ear, and from her lower abdomen, below where she has had her surgery." He pointed to each spot. "This is like a tummy tuck because we harvest the skin and then pull it tight along her belly. We place all that skin in pieces around the ear to make it match and blend together. Once this surgery is complete, the ear is set, will not move, and looks like any other ear." I focused on the fact that the stub was going to go away, and a real ear, one Lily could feel, would appear.

"The second surgery is done as soon as three months after the first. It is more cosmetic but completes the illusion of a real ear. It creates a tragus, the small piece of flexible skin that covers the hole to our inner ear." He was wiggling the one on Lily's left ear. She reached up with her little hand and touched his wrist as he moved her ear. We do this by pulling the skin up from the cheek, like a facelift." He pulled upwards on her cheek to show how he would have enough extra skin to make that flap. Next, he jovially said, "She will have a tummy tuck and facelift by age three. She will be the envy of all of her friends!"

I smiled for what felt like the first time in weeks. He proceeded to show me many pictures of children who had ears he had created. The photos of before and after were miraculous. I never imagined this was possible.

After our appointment with Dr. Reinisch, I got out my notebook and wrote number four, creation of ear, age three, and finally, since this was truly our last appointment, number five, making of a tragus, age three years and three months.

I called Fred. I explained about all of the surgeries she had to have; then, I heard words slipping out of my mouth. I didn't even know they were there. "I have been thinking about whether the surgeries are worth the time, effort, and expense. The reconstruction was critical; she couldn't have a full life if she didn't have it. I know we must close the colostomy and urine hole, and they will consume the next few years. I'm worried about how all this disruption and stress is taking over our lives. I hesitated because I wasn't sure I actually believed this. But needed reassurance that we were willing to make this sacrifice for our daughter and our family. Maybe the ear and thumb surgeries could be delayed?" What do you think?"

He didn't hesitate for a second. "There is no question in my mind, we will do all of these for her, and we'll do them when the doctors allow us to. We want her to have the best life possible, and we can provide that for her. Since we sold our home in St. Paul, and Northwest is paying for our housing here in Tokyo, we have extra funds that can be spent on surgeries, hotels, car rental, and food in the U.S. We will do this for her, and we'll do the best to protect our family."

I knew he was right, but the burden of those five lines in my notebook, each filled with surgery, verified for me how much of my own life would be poured into making the best life possible for our daughter. It took my breath away. I would lose my own life so I could save hers. I shoved those thoughts deep inside myself. I was her mother, so I would do this for her. And that was that we would proceed with our lives knowing Lily would need to have five invasive surgeries over the next two and a half years.

Six weeks after the reconstructive surgery, in early March 2001, Emma, Lily, and I went back to Japan. Lily was well. She was finally gaining weight and sleeping through the night. We had gotten her a seat for her car seat on the plane, and she happily entertained herself by jabbering to me, smiling at Emma, and shaking her prized rattle at all who stopped by to look at her. The staples and stitches were gone. Bandages were minimal, and medication was reduced back to Bactrim only. Emma was so excited she couldn't contain herself, "Mommy! I get to go back to school! My friends are waiting for me. Let's get on the plane! Come on!" She literally pulled me down the jetway.

By then, I was confident in how to care for Lily. In fact, it was not much different than before. I carried colostomy bags and colostomy scissors, and extra clothes. I had diapers that became wet and had to be changed. I understood all of it and could do it, so we went home.

Chapter 28

With Lily healing and Emma happy at school and back into her routine, we were able to expand our lives further into the culture of Japan. Sometimes it was just by going on a walk, to a new restaurant, or we found a new park or ice cream shop. Other times, the ones that excited us most were those that took us far beyond our comfort zone and made us realize the true excitement of living in Tokyo.

One of the adventures that thrilled us involved baseball. Northwest Airlines was a sponsor of multiple organizations and events around the city of Tokyo. One of them was Japanese Major League Baseball. A little more than a month after our return, Fred's name came up as the person from Northwest who had to throw out the first pitch at a game in the Tokyo Dome. The only problem was Fred was Belgian and had no understanding of, nor interest in, the game, let alone how to hold or throw a baseball.

We went to work to figure it out. The first phone call we made was to my dad, a lifelong Minnesota Twins fan. I excitedly said, "Hi! Guess what? Fred has been chosen to throw out the first pitch at a Japanese Major League Baseball Game in the Tokyo Dome." There was a long pause; I could hear my dad laughing harder than he had in a long time. He obviously could see our dilemma.

"Dad? Are you there?" My dad and Fred had a very good relationship, but early on, there were some cross-cultural conflicts. My dad loves baseball. He remembered, not very fondly, that he had taken Fred to a Twins game when we were first dating. Fred sat through the game with his fist on his chin and his elbow resting on his knee, completely floored by the extreme boredom of the game. Unlike soccer, which Fred loved, the ball was too small. It didn't get touched by many people, and it didn't move a lot on the field. On top of that, the yellow alcoholic beverage he was given to drink was nothing like the

300 different kinds of Belgian specialty beers he was used to savoring at home. A hot dog? What was that? It looked disgusting to him.

I allowed him to have his moment to laugh uproariously at our predicament. "Dad? Can you tell me how far it is from home plate to the pitcher's mound?"

My Dad proudly said, "Sixty feet, six inches."

"Okay, what do you have to do to throw a strike?"

"Practice!"

The next morning, Fred and I went out into the vast yard behind the Northwest apartments. We triumphantly held our trusty kitchen mitts and a tennis ball. We put the girls on the swing set. We thought we were pretty hot stuff and were ready to pitch and catch baseballs.

Fred counted off what he was certain was sixty feet, six inches. He added a few more steps just in case. He threw down his black jacket and proudly marked that spot as the pitcher's mound. I crouched with my back to the apartments because that was what I had seen catchers do. I thought my light blue kitchen mitts were very professional; they even had rubber coating to catch the ball and hold it tight. I was set, and so was Fred.

By the time we had gotten ourselves situated in the yard, our friends and Fred's colleagues in the apartment building had all heard our commotion, and had come out on their terraces, pulled up chairs, and were going to watch. We didn't care. We knew we had this one down, easy.

Fred stood on his jacket and wound up, or at least kind of pulled his arm backward, and then he dropped the ball. It was not a good start. He picked it back up, pretended to brush it off like in the big leagues, and then pulled his arm back again. He whipped the ball so forcefully that it went over a very high wall and into the neighboring apartment complex. There were cheers from the crowd behind me.

I went back into the apartment and grabbed a second tennis ball, noting we only had one more, so Fred needed to improve fast. When I came back out, Emma, now three-and-a-half, was cheering, "Come on, Daddy, you look great!"

"Hey," I said. "How about coming in about thirty feet so you might get the motion down first? Then you can slowly back up." Fred picked up the black jacket and moved the pitcher's mound. I threw him the tennis ball and crouched.

This time he wound up and threw the ball directly at me. I screamed and covered my face, so I wouldn't end up with a bloody nose. Instead of catching the ball, I batted it away. I yelled out, "Strike!" The crowd erupted, clapping and cheering. Emma started screaming. Lily even lifted her arms. That was enough practice for us; we knew we were ready for the major leagues.

The big night came. As we exited the subway, we were startled by the size of the enormous Tokyo dome. This was definitely not a joke. We had splurged and had purchased a real baseball glove, so Fred at least looked the part. We were welcomed at a special back door. Lily, Emma, and I went with Fred through the tunnels to the waiting room.

After only a few minutes, a security guard came and got our family, and we walked out onto the field. Lily was on my hip, having a great time watching the crowd. The Jumbotron, those towering screens all over the dome, showed Fred in his red Northwest Airlines Polo shirt so all 40,000 fans could see him. This was a big game, Yomiuri Giants versus The Nippon Ham Fighters.

They motioned for Fred to come out to the pitcher's mound, and for some strange reason, he grabbed Emma as he was heading out. The screens projected his slow walk of sixty feet six inches to the pitcher's mound. Outside of the dirt, he put Emma down, and on the big screen, you could see him shaking his finger, most likely saying, "Stay right here." Lily and I waited and watched, standing to the side of the catcher. We definitely had a front-row seat.

As Fred was given the ball by the umpire, the mascot for the Ham Fighters came out of the dugout, heading straight for Emma. It was gigantic and pink, and a bird, and it was waving to the crowd but walking toward her. She freaked out! She forgot completely about what Fred had told her and started running around on the field behind Fred with the cameras and jumbotron catching it all. The crowd started to roar.

The screen turned to him. You could see the determination on his face. He wound up keeping the ball in his hand and even bending his knee like a pro. He threw the ball with everything he had.

The catcher and the umpire, and Lily and I were watching and waiting. "STEERIKE!" The umpire said it in English, or at least I heard it in English. I couldn't believe it! How did my Belgian baseball-hating husband throw a strike in a Japanese major league baseball game?

Fred stood stunned for a second about what he had done, and then he turned and saw Emma screaming behind him with the massive pink bird still chasing her around. He casually scooped her up and walked triumphantly off as if he had thrown the final pitch in a tie game to win the pennant, or at least that is how my dad likes to tell the story. It was one of the best moments. We felt we belonged in Japan.

Chapter 29

Only a few weeks after the baseball game, we had to go back to Los Angeles for Lily's colostomy "take down" surgery. We decided Lily, and I would go alone this time. Fred would work and be with Emma at night, and Siri was still willing to spend time with our family. She flew to Tokyo to be with Emma during the day. The entire process would take ten days.

Lily and I flew the twelve hours, mostly on autopilot. We rented a car and went back to the Ronald McDonald House. That next morning, she was admitted to the hospital.

"Hi, checking in for Lily Deschamps." I got my blue badge.

In order to close the colostomy, her bowel had to be emptied. Again. Tube in the nose. Screaming at the top of her lungs, including flailing arms. Restraints. Bowel cleaning solution flowing. Poop everywhere. No sleep. Extreme jet lag.

They came for Lily first thing in the morning. I had been so focused on the preparation and execution of this surgery that it wasn't until Lily was safely out of my arms and in the operating room it dawned on me that the colostomy bag would be gone. Lily would poop like everyone else. She could learn to sit and stand and walk and run and play, no more bag on her belly to worry about.

I didn't watch *Friends* this time. I just sat. I didn't think or reflect or even read a book. I was too tired, too worn down.

At 11:30, they told me Lily was out of surgery. For the first time after an operation, I didn't hesitate. I ran over to her. She wasn't puffy and didn't have a tube in her nose, or her eyes taped shut this time, so with conviction, I pulled back the blankets and lifted up her hospital gown. There was a large white bandage that covered another long set of black stitches, but I knew the colostomy was gone.

I can't think of a single time in a parent's life when you would ever wish for it, but there I was sitting, waiting for Lily to poop. I was even excited. At 3:20, it happened. I whipped out my camera and took a picture. I believed our lives had radically changed for the better.

I had a whole pack of baby wipes, diapers, and baby powder ready to go. I put them beside me, ready to clean her up. A nurse walked in. "What good news, Lily has passed stool."

I thought that was a bit formal for our situation. "I brought you a product for diaper rash. It is called ILEX, and it is quite helpful when babies first start having stool come out after the removal of a colostomy." She put the tube on the crib. I opened it up and squirted out a little bit onto my finger. It was white, like Zinc oxide, and extremely thick. I thought it would coat her bottom and never come off. I was definitely not going to use it. My arrogance from our time in the NICU in Tokyo took over. I could manage this; I knew how.

"Thank you so much for this. I'm sure it will come in handy sometime." I proceeded to put it in my bag. I cleaned Lily up and then lightly powdered her bottom as if she was a queen and needed primping. The nurse left, saying she was going to get Dr. Shaul. She looked worried as if she needed backup support from the doctor for whatever had to be said.

Right after the nurse left, more poop came out. I wiped, and then more came out. It wouldn't stop. As my disbelief started to grow, Dr. Shaul walked into the room. He leaned in near me, staring at Lily with her diaper filling again. He spoke calmly, "Lily's body didn't respond the way we wanted it to. She wasn't born with a sphincter. That is the muscle that constricts her bottom to keep it closed so she can be continent. When we created the hole during surgery, we tried to create a sphincter, but it wasn't working properly. There is nothing to stop the stool from simply coming out all the time."

What the fuck was he talking about? Diarrhea twenty-four hours a day? "How can that be? I thought the reconstructive surgery solved this. This

184

surgery was supposed to be a success and make life infinitely better for her. No more colostomy bags."

"Sarah, Lily's body is complicated. We can fix many of the problems, but not all of them. You will have to change diapers often and use the ILEX cream the nurse gave to you." I looked down at the ILEX sticking out of my bag, willing it to disappear and for Dr. Shaul to go away.

He was ruining my happiness. "Lily will need to have another operation to fix this." I gasped and started weeping, tears dripping onto Lily's body. He looked away from my face. "We can fix the stool issue, but not now, not for several years. Lily is healthy, and the new passage to eliminate stool is working, even if it has no valve to stop it from coming out. It will be tough for the next few years, I know."

Next few years! Few YEARS?

I let my mind wander to the future that was in store for us. In order to attend preschool, children had to be out of diapers. She couldn't be five minutes without a diaper. Now she couldn't even go to school because of her body. How would she have playdates? How would she sit? How could she sleep at night? Why did we take away the colostomy? Why not leave it? At least the poop was hidden. It was impossible for me to grasp what he was saying.

"Please know this was an important correction. It eventually will make it possible for her to be continent, just not now." He didn't explain how he was going to make her continent; he said someday in the distant future, she could be. What did that mean? I didn't have the courage or energy to ask.

In a more businesslike manner, he said, "You will be returning to Children's Hospital for Lily's reconstructive ear surgery with Dr. Reinisch and for the thumb surgery when she is three, in about two years. I will see you then to discuss the next steps. In the meantime, you need to find a pediatrician in Tokyo who can see and work with you. Lily may develop urinary tract and bacterial infections more frequently, and having a doctor available to treat her will be critical.

Lily is on track to have a full life. This is one more step along the path."

I thought Dr. Shaul could fix all of Lily's issues, make her whole, and send her on her way in life. He was the best; I knew he could do anything. It was then that I had to admit there was no prescribed roadmap for Lily. We were on this unknown path together, and it was now my turn to take over. Dr. Shaul gave me a hug and walked out. I wouldn't see him for another two years.

I blew my nose, wiped my tears, stood up straight, and said, "God damn it. So be it." I looked at the nurse and said, "I gotta go downstairs." I went to the pharmacy in the hospital. As I went down in the elevator, I was thinking about my visit to the "pharmacy" at Joshi Idai all those months ago. I was pretty certain this one would be dust free, would have lights, and most likely would have clearly labeled medical supplies. It did! It even had chocolate bars.

I bought twenty-five tubes of ILEX and another five packs of diapers. The pharmacist who helped me acted as if he had seen these kinds of purchases every day, and maybe he had. A few days later, we were discharged from the hospital.

The Ronald McDonald House in Los Angeles had been our home. We had mostly kept to ourselves, protecting Lily from others but also hiding our own difficulties. Most families in the House were that way. They had come not only from all over the United States but from all over the world. Children's Hospital Los Angeles is world renowned for treating many complex medical problems. Ronald McDonald House was a safe place to stay and made the harrowing experience of having your child in the hospital a little less so. It was a place where we could speak openly and also could keep silent. We were accepted as we were.

We didn't make friends, but we did get to know a few people. One of the most poignant relationships we had developed was with a family who had come all the way from Asia, like us. They spoke English fluently and knew Los Angeles better than we did. Their situation was agonizingly difficult. They had been at the House for over a year. They were waiting for a new heart for their sweet little girl. They remained there long after we had come and gone.

As I was packing our things to go home, I did not know if I would ever be returning to the Ronald McDonald House, I wanted to show my gratitude. Instead of going back to the McDonald's in the hospital to deposit something in the little red house at the cashier; I pulled out my checkbook and wrote a check to the foundation; it was the least we could do.

Ten days after the surgery, I was now changing Lily's diaper and coating her bottom with ILEX every thirty minutes. It was gross and frustrating, and she didn't like it a whole lot more than I did. If I didn't do that, she would get a raging diaper rash within minutes, even with the ILEX in place. Traveling for twelve hours on an airplane with a baby who needed to be in the bathroom 24 times during the flight made me laugh more than cry. I had done so many strange and unusual things. What the hell! Add this to the list.

Chapter 30

We did survive the flight. We tried each and every one of the ten bathrooms we could find on the plane and did the rounds twice. That way, I figured no one saw us near their seats more than two times. I rationalized, as I had so many times in Lily's life, that this made me look like any other mother trying to change a baby's diaper on a long flight.

I was dragging as I walked through the arrival doors at Narita Airport with Lily on my hip. Fred stood there, bursting with good news. He hugged us tightly and took our bags and Lily in his arms to give me a rest. He seemed gleeful, not at all what I expected, and certainly not how I felt because it had been more than thirty minutes since Lily's last diaper change; she was stinky. I was beyond tired, and I needed to find a bathroom.

My mood didn't dampen his. I could see he was filled with excitement. "Sarah, guess what?" I couldn't guess. "We get to move into the Northwest Airlines Azabu House!" I stood still. That was pretty exciting. I had heard the story of the creation of the house. It was legendary. In the 1960s, a Minnesota-based Northwest Airlines vice president was asked to move to Tokyo and run the Asian operation. He was reluctant and ultimately refused to move unless the company built a replica of his large suburban Minneapolis home. For some reason, they agreed.

The house was magnificent. It had five bedrooms, a large office, a living room that could accommodate over 100 people for receptions, and an enormous kitchen. It was at least 5,500 square feet of indoor space, but the most defining feature of the home was the high brick wall that surrounded the large, meticulously landscaped garden. The garden had grass to play in and Japanese flowering trees and bushes. All year long, even in the dead of winter, the yard sparkled.

It didn't have Emma's forest, but it would have plenty of places for adventures.

The best that Tokyo offered was around the corner from the Azabu House: a famous city park, a grocery store, Baskin Robbin's ice cream, two coffee shops, and our favorite bakery.

There was even a Shinto Shrine nearby.

The house had been empty for years. The company had only used it for occasional events when the executives came from Minnesota to Japan. That meant that this beautiful property was falling into disrepair. Fred, as the ranking expatriate in Asia, asked if our family could move in and begin to take care of the property.

So, in May of 2001, exactly a year after we had relocated to Tokyo, we moved into the Azabu House.

Right down the street, we finally found a pediatrician for both girls, Dr. Sung. Emma loved to go and see him. "Dr. Sung, can I hear my heart?" He let her have the stethoscope. "Dr. Sung, look at my boo-boo. Do you have a superhero band-aid?" He pulled Superman out of his cupboard. She even brought him her red book about the body. He patiently read the book with her and showed her the medical instruments that he used to examine the human body.

Dr. Sung understood Lily's situation. "I will keep you out of the hospitals here. Joshi Idai Byoin is an outstanding facility, but I also understand your reticence about going there again. Doctors here believe they know best, and parents are secondary when it comes to medical care. I won't do that with you. We have to be in partnership. I can send reports to Los Angeles if necessary. He kept Lily on a low dose of Bactrim, the medication that protected her body from urinary tract infections. I was relieved someone understood.

Unfortunately, even with the antibiotic, she continued to have infections. Lily would spike a fever, and I'd pick her up and literally run down the hill from our house to Dr. Sung's office, sweating by the time I arrived. "Dr. Sung, Lily has an infection again. Can you help us?" With expert care and different antibiotics, he kept Lily safe and healthy. We no longer had to worry about Lily's care. Life could be almost normal, which changed everything for us.

Fred and I spent more time with our friends, feeling confident leaving the children with babysitters when we went out to dinner. We began to take family outings further and longer from home. In the winter of 2002, when Lily was a year and a half, we decided it was time to travel as a family somewhere other than Los Angeles. The Snow Festival was taking place in the Japanese city of Sapporo on the island of Hokkaido, and we wanted to see it. They create life-sized sculptures out of snow, and each year there is a theme. That year, since it was the year the Euro was created, the theme was a celebration of all things Belgian. We could not believe our good luck! We pulled out our Minnesota snow pants, mittens, jackets, and hats, and off we went on a plane to northern Japan.

Upon arrival, we first cleaned Lily up in the airport bathroom and then went to the festival. They had everything Belgian, including the famous statue of the little boy peeing. When we saw the Manneken Pis, Fred and I burst out laughing. It seemed to emulate our personal life, pee flowing everywhere, even in the snow.

In addition to Belgian sculptures, there were snow slides, castles, and climbing structures. All made out of snow and ice. We spent a day like no other screaming down slides, hiding in castles, and laughing, playing, and running free from all of our daily stress. Lily's body cooperated enough that there wasn't too much of a mess, and she didn't get a fever. It was a taste of heaven.

After such a fantastic day, Fred and I agreed we would not try to figure out a Japanese restaurant for dinner. We were all hungry and wanted fast food, which for our family meant McDonald's. I glanced at a map of the area and thought I had seen there was one nearby. It seemed we could easily walk. It turned out I didn't remember the map very well. It got darker and colder, and we walked up and down more streets, looking and hoping we would see those Golden Arches.

I saw a local policeman who looked like he might be able to help us. I went up to him and said, "*McDonald's Wa Doko Des Ka?*" (Where is McDonald's?) I was so proud of being able to ask a full question in Japanese, and I was absolutely certain he had to know McDonald's, so I thought we would be on our way in no time.

The policeman stared at me. I asked more slowly, "*McDonald's Wa Doko Des Ka?*" Again, blank look. Fred was standing far enough off to the side that he was unable to hear me and was wondering what was taking so long. I looked pleadingly over my shoulder for him to save me. He walked over and spoke to the policeman.

"*Ma-ku-do-nal-do, Wa Doko Des Ka,*" he said. The policeman got a smile on his face and pointed; Fred said it correctly. We lowered our heads in shame, saying *arigato gozaimasu*, thanking the policeman, then turned and ran to "Ma-ku-do-nal-do."

Chapter 31

Now that we were stable at home, Lily and Emma were both thriving. Lily did learn to roll over, crawl, and, by sixteen months, walk. She was talking and certainly expressing her needs. She was sleeping through the night and playing with the other toddlers in the playgroup we were a part of in our neighborhood. Mostly, she got in Emma's face and took all of Emma's toys which annoyed Emma to no end. "Mommy, Lily is stealing my toys. As a family, we don't steal," she said indignantly one day with her hands on her hips. She did have a point. Lily had been such a cute little sister when she was immobile.

Poop and pee were a problem. "Diaper blowouts" were disgusting and almost daily.

ILEX became my best friend, but Lily's bottom had a rash more often than not. I simply couldn't keep up with the endless stool that came out of her body. I wished the stool surgery was next, but it had to wait. Urine kept coming out of the hole in her belly and then spilling over the top of the diaper. When we were with other people, I tried to casually brush it off as a "wet" shirt. But mostly, I was relieved that life seemed normal and that the girls were both thriving.

The summer of 2003, however, was going to be intense. It had taken almost an entire year to plan. Lily would have three surgeries in four months. The four of us would fly to Los Angeles for the first surgery, then spend three months in St. Paul for healing. We'd fly to Los Angeles for two more surgeries, stay for a week to heal, and be back in Tokyo before Labor Day for the first day of school. I had it planned down to the smallest detail. Flights, done. Hotels and apartments were booked. Car rental, reserved. Summer camps and time with Grandma and Grandpa for Emma were organized. All of the complications of moving an entire family halfway around the world for an extended period of time were lined up and ready. Since I couldn't control the outcome of the surgeries or the daily mess created by Lily's body, at least I could control the overwhelming complexity of our summer plans.

The brilliant Dr. Reinisch would make her ear, and an outstanding orthopedic surgeon would strengthen her thumb. In May, she would have the first surgery to actually create the ear.

Then, three months later, would be the second ear surgery and also the operation for the thumb.

They would be done on the same day in the same operating room.

The four of us landed back in Los Angeles the last week of May 2003, two weeks before Lily's third birthday. We were staying at a hotel this time since my parents were joining us. "Grandma!" Emma yelled as she raced down the hall and into grandma's arms that were filled with presents. Emma beamed back at Fred and me, "This is going to be a great vacation!" At least one of us thought it was going to be great!

Two days after arriving in Los Angles, Fred, Lily, and I reluctantly went through the front door of the hospital. Lily immediately walked over to the fish tank in the reception area. "Mommy, look at the orange fish; it is Nemo!" We had gotten a DVD of the film for the trip, and it was a hit. Do you see Dory?" She walked around and around the tank, partly to find Dory but mostly to avoid going into the hospital.

At the check-in desk, we received our badges, outpatient orange this time. We knew it was a risk to take her home immediately following a five-hour surgery, but Dr. Reinisch insisted it would be fine. Since I was again brimming with over-confidence, I thought I could take care of any issue myself in our hotel room. We agreed not to have Lily stay in the hospital overnight.

Nurses brought us back to an examination room, where they checked all of Lily's vital signs, and we changed her into a hospital gown. Lily had developed quite a vocabulary by age three, and she used those words to express her anger about being in a hospital. She put up a fuss, telling us, "No, no, no. I don't want this. No sur-gar-y. No doctors. No ear!" She touched the little stub.

Dr. Reinisch walked in and came over to Lily, cupping her face. "My, you have grown so much since the last time I saw you! You are so beautiful! I am going to make an ear for you, and it will radiate your beauty even more." Lily stared at him, not quite sure what to say or do, so she didn't say anything.

He used a purple pen to mark her tiny nub of an ear to signify this was the side he would be operating on as if you couldn't tell. He looked at us, "Do you agree this is the side where we will create an ear?"

Fred and I both said, "yes." Lily remained quiet.

"Let me explain again what we will be doing." He was pointing to Lily's head. He retold the details that I had memorized. I winched at words like subcutaneous and prosthetic ear and tummy tuck. "The stunning part of all of this is that Lily's new ear will have feeling in it because of the skin we use. It isn't the same feeling as her other ear, but it will have feeling."

I sheepishly asked a question I had been wondering for a long time. "Will Lily be able to have pierced ears?"

"Why yes! It will look like a real ear." He then went into more detail, "The surgery is about five hours. You can come and see Lily in the recovery area when she is done, and you can take her home tonight."

I had been tormented over the last two years about how the result of the colostomy closure surgery had gone and the daily implications that it had on our family. Each step I took toward this hospital, this room, and another doctor, made me worry more about the outcome this time. Having something go wrong on her glowing face would be more than I could take. This surgery had to be a success. This time we had to get it right. Unable to take another moment filled with this dread alone in my own head, I said, "Dr. Reinisch, you have made hundreds of ears, but today, please make the best one you have ever made."

He smiled, nodded, and said he would see us after the surgery.

The hospital had renovated the entire operating and waiting area during the two years we had been away. They had pagers now that allowed us to go anywhere in the hospital instead of having us endlessly sit in the sterile and uncomfortable waiting room.

Fred and I smiled at each other and said, "Ma-ku-do-nal-do?"

The day started well, but the five-hour mark came and went. Then another hour passed. I started to imagine all of the horrible things that could be happening in the operating room. Why did they say five hours when it was now six? Was she even still alive? My hands started shaking with the fear my mind was creating. We could do nothing. We had to sit and wait. After six and a half hours, our pager finally beeped. We ran, breathlessly arriving at the recovery room door. Lily was still asleep.

I'm not sure what I expected after ear surgery, but once again, nothing prepared me for what I saw. Fred and I both gasped. My eyes bulged, and my mouth dropped open. I didn't realize what I was thinking was actually pouring loudly out of my mouth, "Lily looks like a mummy!" Her entire head, including her neck, was shrouded in white cotton fabric. The only opening was a little round hole cut out for her eyes, nose, and mouth. The fabric was holding two large white cups, one over each ear. She was lying immobilized in the bed, making the image even worse. Unfortunately, that was not the worst part.

There were two long tubes, the diameter of a pencil, coming out from under the mummy cap, exiting at her neck. They hung down at least two feet on the bed, next to her hips. At the end of the tubes, there were plastic balls about the size of my hand, and there was bright red blood collecting in them. I almost threw up. *What had we done to our daughter?*

Seemingly out of nowhere, Dr. Reinisch approached her bed and enthusiastically declared, "Lily will have a gorgeous ear! She did great. She can go home in an hour or two."

How the hell are we going to care for that?

"These long tubes have to stay in her for a few days while you are still here in Los Angeles. They are draining the blood that is coming from the subcutaneous layer of skin we removed. It looks gangly right now, but not too much blood should accumulate. Don't knock the tubes; we don't want them to come out." *Was he kidding me? Don't knock them? How do you carry a three-year-old, except if she is catatonic, without knocking them around? What if Lily starts pulling them out? What kind of an asinine decision had we made?* I was desperately regretting my happiness about those orange outpatient hospital badges.

Dr. Reinisch pointed to Lily's head. "We put this cloth over her head because we don't want the new ear to be touched. She also has a cup covering her other ear. We removed some skin from behind that one. She probably won't hear very well for a couple of days, so you'll have to talk loudly to her."

Great, the mummified little girl became deaf too. "We'll take that cup off of her good ear in a few days, and her hearing will be good as new. He paused. "The new ear needs quite a bit of time to heal. Since you will be in Minnesota, we will keep the white cloth on her head and the plastic cup over her new ear until you return in August." He smiled a big smile. "You can wash her hair through the head covering. Make sure to avoid getting the new ear wet."

How is that possible? I remembered trying to bathe Lily after the reconstructive surgery. It was awful. I decided Lily would have very dirty hair over the next few months.

Before he left, Dr. Reinisch said, "I'll see you in our clinic in a couple of days to check on things and to remove the cup on her left ear. If you have any questions, you can call the number on the discharge papers. She did great! You'll be so happy."

Happy we were not. Nervous. Scared. Overwhelmed. Those came to mind, but nothing remotely close to happy. Lily didn't feel happy either. Moments after she woke up, "Mommy, Daddy, this feels yucky," she said, pointing to the mess that was now her head. Not long after that, the nurses said we could go.

Fred gently picked Lily up off of the bed with me trailing very closely behind, like I was holding a wedding veil, except I was holding two-foot-long dangling tubes of blood. "Sarah, stay close to me. Don't let the blood balls get jerked." What kind of a new vocabulary was this?

When we entered the hotel, I was so glad I had forgotten to remove my bright orange badge from the hospital. Blood balls and headdresses with bulging plastic ear covers were going to be impossible to explain.

The next day, Fred had to get back to work in Tokyo, so without too many spoken words, we said our goodbyes. We would not see him until we all reunited in Los Angeles at the end of August for Lily's next two surgeries. It would be almost three months.

After so many times, and so many years, it was just a simple fact that we would be apart.

We didn't talk about it; we just lived through it. We resolutely accepted our individual roles. It meant Fred lost touch with the daily care and issues with Lily and Emma, and I lost the ability to talk to him about his job, and most importantly, we lost touch with each other.

This time when he left, I felt something I hadn't felt before while we were apart, jealousy. The idea of him having an exciting cultural experience while he was away in Tokyo upset me because I had none. I had no time to myself, no break from the stress, and never a full night of sleep. All I could do was put one foot in front of the other, hoping it would land on the floor.

I remembered what Dr. Shaul had said; maybe he had been right. This is a marathon, not a sprint. It is taxing and very hard on marriages. It is relentless, and the toll on the family often becomes too much to bear. He told us to take care of each other and take time for each other. He said it would be important. We hadn't done that. All of our energy had gone into our children, to save Lily's life, to give Emma the happiest childhood. As a couple, for the first time, it felt like we had lost our way. We weren't taking care of each other, and we were each barely surviving.

During that week after the ear surgery, keeping Lily still was excruciating. She wanted to go swimming and play with Emma or run up and down the halls of the hotel. My parents tried to entertain Emma away from the hotel, but she wanted to be with Lily to play. Sitting, with absolutely no movement, was not possible. I found a way to securely hook the blood balls to her shirt, but even with that, every movement jerked them up and down. It might have been funny if I had been able to think beyond the fear of racing to the emergency room if they ripped out. I counted the minutes until we got to see Dr. Reinisch.

After only waiting for two hours past our scheduled appointment time, Dr. Reinisch walked into the examining room and said, "You look great!" The blood balls had dried dark blood in them. Lily's face was black and blue, and her hair was matted and greasy, all ragged under the mummy cap. As he approached her, she burst into uncontrollable tears. She held out her hands and said, "Stop! Don't come here!" Who could blame her?

He approached anyway, without much fanfare. With tears streaming down her face and me standing helplessly beside her, he took off the cotton shroud. Dr. Reinisch then removed the blood balls from under her skin. In awe and relief, I watched them bounce on the examination table and looked to see if blood was pouring out the back of her head where they had been removed. Luckily, nothing. Next, he took off the plastic cover on the left ear and let her hair fall down over the black stitches behind it. With the mummy veil off and the plastic cover over the surgical new ear still in place, I could see Lily's hair had been completely shaved off, and half of her head was bald.

Dr. Reinisch saw me staring. "In order to get to the subcutaneous layer of skin, we had to shave her hair on this side entirely." He was pointing to the long, red, thick gash with black stitches on the side of her head. "You can't see it because of the plastic protector, but the new ear is also completely covered in stitches. Each small piece of harvested skin was meticulously sewn over the prosthesis. She needs to keep this on to protect the surgical area for the summer." While he said it, he put a new mummy cover over her head, which mushed the hair on the left against her good ear, and shrouded her bald spot, bright red scar, and bulging plastic protector on the right. "I'll see you in about twelve weeks!" He turned and, over his shoulder, said, "She will be fine."

Nope, not fine. Reluctantly, I collected myself and my disfigured daughter. *Was this worth it?* Bewildered, I walked out of Children's Hospital. We had completed only one of the three surgeries of the summer.

I called Fred when we got back to the hotel. "She looks horrible. She is completely bald on the side of her head with the new ear. She has black stitches sticking out from behind her good one. He removed the bandages, so you can now see her tummy has a cut that goes from one hip all the way to the other side, where they harvested the skin. Dr. Reinisch quickly looked at the prosthetic ear, but he didn't let me see it. I can't imagine what we'll see below. He put a new mummy cap on her head. Not only is it hard to have her covered like that, but her hair will be so greasy and gross by the time we get back here in August."

"That sounds awful." I cut him off, "I'm worried about taking the flight to Minnesota with the girls. It is so uncomfortable to walk in public with her. Everyone stares at me. I'm sure they think I beat her, and that's why her head is covered. I'm worried someone will call child protective services."

"Lily is so lucky to have you as her mother," he said calmly. "You have saved her life and have made the quality of it astronomically better. Who cares if others see her and stare? Unlike in Japan, you aren't disturbing the *Wa* this time. Don't guess what others are thinking. Maybe they are in awe of what you have done to protect your child. Sarah, you are a strong and courageous woman. I don't know anyone who could do what you have done for their child. I love you." We hung up.

I felt better after talking to Fred. I knew there was so much love and tenderness between us, but he was far away, and I still had to pack to get the three of us on a plane to Minnesota.

It was going to be a very long summer. I forced a smile on my face, held Emma's hand a little too tight, and walked down the jetway onto the plane. The stares were fewer than I thought they would be; thank goodness, at least something went well.

Instead of staying with my parents, we chose to have a place of our own this time. We would be in St. Paul for three months, so I decided it would be too long to be guests in their home. We rented a cheap apartment a block away. I had arranged for Emma to be at summer camps at the Science Museum. "Mommy, I got to make Play-Doh and bubbles, and tomorrow we will make cupcakes!" She was excited by the science and happy to spend so much time with Grandma and Grandpa.

Our dear friends had a small third birthday party for Lily with candles on a homemade cake. Lily loved it. While dancing around the room, she sang in a sweet voice, "I am beautiful. I am a queen. I am wonderful. It is my birthday!" It made my own heart sing to know that she felt like any other three-year-old. She was full of confidence and pride, and happiness. It was a joyful day. We took several photos of her in a pink flowery shirt, with a big smile. Her cute little face was peeking through the white shroud over her head. I started to think of her as a Teletubbie. That cute space creature with bubble ears and a cover over its head. Anything was better than a mummy.

I was so focused on her ear I lost track of her intense need for me to care for her bladder and bowel. A few weeks into our stay in St. Paul, Lily developed a very high fever. Without a doctor in Minnesota, I had to take her to the emergency room at the Children's Hospital. I was relieved to see the word "Emergency" plastered in glowing red letters above the front sliding door. I headed straight to the reception desk, which was clearly marked by the sign above it which said, 'Reception Desk.' I was relieved it had no resemblance at all to the emergency entrance at Joshi Idai.

The woman behind the desk did stare at us. She saw the black stitches on the side of her head, the now filthy head cover, the plastic ear cup, and the bald spot now blatantly peeking through. The lady was definitely not channeling my Teletubbies image. Instinctively shielding her head from the receptionist, I said a little too forcefully, "She had ear surgery, but that isn't why we're here. She has a urinary tract infection." The woman had a look on her face that conveyed she had heard everything before, but this was definitely new.

"Well then, I'll let the doctor know you are here."

"Thanks."

Within a couple of minutes, we were hurriedly ushered to an examination room where a doctor was expectantly waiting. I had been rehearsing how to explain in as few words as possible what the problem was. "Thank you for seeing us. This is my daughter, Lily." I put her on the bed in front of him. "No, I didn't hurt her; she had plastic surgery on her ear in Los Angeles a month ago. We aren't here for the ear." I was actually not 100 percent sure we weren't there for the ear, but I didn't want anyone but Dr. Reinisch to touch her ear, so I was taking a bet, and hoping I was right, that the issue was Lily's bladder. Her urine had started to smell funky. It was cloudy too. Dr. Reinisch had put Lily on another, stronger antibiotic to fight infection in the ear, so he had taken her off of the Bactrim. I had a hunch she had a urinary tract infection.

"We live in Japan, so we don't have a pediatrician in the U.S. She has cloacal anomalies, which means she has a reconstructed bladder and bowel. She was taken off of her prophylactic dose of Bactrim for the ear surgery. I think she now has a UTI. Please could you take a urine sample?" I had lifted Lily's outfit and was pointing to the hole in her belly where urine comes out. "Her pee slowly drips out of this hole; you will need to collect the urine as it drips." The doctor's face lit up.

"This is so great! I'm excited to meet you." It was not the greeting I was expecting. "I'm starting my pediatric residency, and it is not very often, especially in an emergency room, that you can see such an interesting patient." You would have thought he had hit the jackpot of patients. "Yes, we'll get a sample of urine. Have you noticed any change in it?"

"Over the last two days, it has turned cloudy, and it smells. That's why I knew this was not connected to her ear."

It turned out, thankfully, I was right. Lily had a urinary tract infection. I got the prescription for Bactrim, enough to last several months, and proudly walked past the receptionist with a bit of a strut. All of my learning and time in hospitals and endless medical appointments was paying off. In a warped and strange way, it felt good.

At the end of August, it was time to go back to Los Angeles. Emma had grown weary of endless science experiments and of living in a strange apartment. She was tired and cranky and wondered why Daddy wasn't with us. We had a chart in our small kitchen that counted the days until we saw him. The only problem was it also counted down to when Lily was going to have two more surgeries.

Emma was now relentless. "We still have 10 days until we see Daddy! That is too much. Can't we just go home?" Part of the problem was I had started mentally preparing to be at the hospital. I was distant from the girls, temperamental, and focused on nothing but what was coming our way. I wasn't a model parent.

My parents and our friends knew the escalating dread I had. They tried to help, but as much as they all loved and cared for us, we were headed to Los Angeles for more surgery, and they were headed back to their own lives. There was a disconnect, so I pulled inside myself and resolved that this, too, would be behind us soon.

These two surgeries would be hard as if we hadn't already experienced that. Dr. Reinisch would make the tragus, the small piece of flexible skin that would cover her ear. As he told me before, he would do it by pulling the skin up from the cheek, like a facelift. The orthopedic surgeon needed to stabilize the joint in her thumb by strengthening it with Lily's tendons.

I spent countless hours trying to make it possible for Lily to have the two surgeries at the same time. I thought of everything I could to argue my point, including that the anesthesia used during the surgery was exhausting to recover from afterward. I honestly don't know why they agreed to it, except maybe for my dogged refusal to take no for an answer. They would do the surgeries one after another in the same operating room. When I had gotten my wish, I hoped I hadn't made a mistake by asking.

In late August, twelve weeks after the first surgery to create the ear, we all flew to Los Angeles. Fred came from Tokyo, and Siri, Emma, Lily, and I came from St. Paul. Emma was thrilled to be reunited with Siri and gave her a big hug as we entered the plane. "Siri! Where have you been? I missed you!" She jumped into her arms and was carried beaming down the jetway holding tight to Siri's hand all the way. Lily looked a little worse for the wear. Her hair had only been washed through the head cover all summer, and the cap was anything but sparkly white.

Lily was less than thrilled about being at the hospital again. "Daddy, I want to play today. Let's run in the park. Please. Not here." It broke our hearts to know she now knew what was happening, especially since there was no way out. We reluctantly walked through the sliding glass doors.

We got our orange badges for outpatient surgery from the smiley front desk people. I had asked Dr. Reinisch and, thankfully, had been told there would be no blood balls this time, so I knew we could take care of Lily at the hotel that night. Since she would have the double surgery, we met both the orthopedic surgeon and Dr. Reinisch in the examination room. They told us they were actually pleased to be sharing the operating room and had worked out how to coordinate their individual procedures. I was relieved.

As they were wrapping up their pre-surgery questions and were about to leave, I stood up and, without thinking, put my hands together, as I always did in Tokyo, and bowed deeply. "Doctors, you have done so much extra work for Lily, and that's before you even begin this surgery. Thank you for your kindness and willingness to go above and beyond for our family. We appreciate it."

Dr. Reinisch said he would see us after his part of the surgery. The orthopedic surgeon brought out the now infamous purple pen and marked Lily's little right thumb. He held it up and said, "You will have a strong and powerful thumb when we are done. We will put a cast on your arm during the surgery; what color would you like?"

"Orange!" Lily shouted.

I was caught off guard. I had worked on so many details but had obviously forgotten to ask how they immobilized the thumb after the surgery. I wasn't prepared for a cast. How long would she need to keep it on? We would be headed back to Tokyo soon. I guessed she wouldn't have it off before we left the U.S. The nurse came in minutes later to get Lily and prepare her for the operation. This time Fred and I knew the drill. Lily did too. She had stopped talking, which seemed to be her way to cope. She was fixated on the snap on the hospital gown. Open, close, open, close. A fidget to keep her mind and fingers busy. We leaned down, kissed her, told her we loved her, and we watched as she went down the hall in the nurse's arms. Lily looked back at us with no words or tears but with a face that was pleading with us to take her away. I broke down right there and stood still in the hallway long after she was gone.

Fred and I found a quiet place to sit for the five hours we were told the operation would take. I reluctantly asked a question I'd been thinking about the entire summer. "Do you think Lily knows what is happening to her? When we talk to her about the surgery, she seems so disinterested. I stood in front of the mirror with her, showing her what was under that cap. She turned away, almost in disgust. I held her two thumbs in my hands and pointed to the bigger one saying the other would be big and strong as well. She didn't say anything. I just don't know what goes on in her head about all these doctors and hospitals." She was three, into everything, and a curious child. She was extremely talkative, but when it came to hospitals, you could watch her physically shut down.

We tried to talk about how this was affecting Emma. That one we knew. The guilt and feeling that I was abandoning my oldest daughter weighed so heavily on me. "I try to hide all of this mess as much as possible from her, but I'm fooling myself. Emma is keenly aware of what is happening around her. She notices that I'm gone with Lily or distracted entirely because I'm planning what comes next. We bounce from city to city. It doesn't make sense to her. She has nothing stable, and she needs it. This is harming her too, but in ways, we still don't know."

"Sarah, we're almost done. This has been the summer from hell, but in a couple of days, we leave Los Angeles and get to be at home as a family. You'll see Dr. Shaul before you leave next week to know what is next for Lily's bowel issues. Once we know that, we can finally return home to Tokyo." As he spoke, tears dripped down my face. I realized the weight of the summer was about to be lifted.

After two hours of waiting, the orthopedic surgeon came out with his scrubs, hairnet, and his mask pushed up over his forehead. "I just finished, and it went well. She should have the full range in her thumb, like her other one. I understand you are headed back to Tokyo soon. She needs to keep the cast on for eight weeks, so assuming you will not be returning here, you can have it taken off by an orthopedic surgeon in Tokyo. I don't foresee any issues with the recovery, so a follow-up with me will not be necessary."

In some ways, I was grateful he wasn't going to make us return to Los Angeles in eight weeks but finding an orthopedic surgeon in a Japanese hospital where they might speak English seemed like finding a needle in a haystack. The doctor shook our hands, we thanked him, and we never saw him again.

Late that afternoon, after waiting another four hours and worrying that Lily was dead, as I always did when surgeries took longer than I expected, our pager beeped. The first thing that popped out at us when we saw her was an orange cast covering Lily's thumb and arm. It went all the way up, holding the elbow in place, and continued almost to her shoulder. Her arm was awkwardly positioned in an L shape.

Since it was Dr. Reinisch standing in front of us, I tried to look away from the neon cast and focus on the ear. He said, "It is perfect." We couldn't see a thing. Lily had another plastic cover over the new ear and another fresh mummy cover on her head. "It looks fantastic. I'm so pleased."

Before he left, he said, "Instead of coming back to Children's Hospital for the removal of the stitches, I want you to come to my Beverly Hills office. It is less chaotic. You won't have to wait so long, and the final removal of this cap on her head won't take long at all." He handed me a business card. Beverly Hills office?

After Lily had woken up, we got her dressed in a rainbow-striped outfit. One of the colors in the rainbow was bright orange, which matched the cast. I tried to be cheery, "You look so pretty. Isn't it great how bright the cast is? Your all-time favorite color, orange."

Just then, we got the answer to our earlier questions about whether or not Lily knew what was happening to her. She started screaming and shrieking, "I hate it! I want it off! I want out!" She had gone in quietly, gently opening and closing a snap, and come out ready to rip off the cast and maybe even her own head. She told us what she thought, and I agreed with her entirely.

Fred distracted her, "We get to go to our hotel now. You have videos, and Siri and Emma are waiting for you. You can eat anything you want. Ice cream for dinner? French fries? Should we stop at McDonald's on the way out?" He talked until she calmed down. As we left the hospital, tears streamed down her face. I could finally see how this was fixing her physically but harming her emotionally.

As always, after surgery, Fred left for Tokyo. During his short visit, when we weren't focusing intensely on Lily's recovery, talking about how much this was costing, or spending time with Emma, we each tried to prepare for what came next. We were beyond exhausted and hoped our return to Japan would heal the distance between us.

Chapter 32

Even though we had gotten through three grueling surgeries that summer, Lily's medical issues were not even close to being over. Six surgeries down, at least one more to go. We had to see Dr. Shaul before we left.

For two years, Lily's bottom had been fiery red. Even when we changed her diaper every thirty minutes during the day, she still had to sleep in that mess during the night. We couldn't keep up. Things she loved, like swimming pools, were off limits, and prolonged activities that took her away from my side were too.

If that wasn't enough, as her body grew, the amount of urine she produced did as well. It became harder to hide the wet spot, and there was nothing we could do to stop it from leaking all over her front. I tried to put her in darker clothing to make it less obvious and sometimes even put a tiny piece of tape over the top of the hole in her belly to direct the pee downwards into the waiting diaper, but nothing was foolproof, so more often than not, she was wet.

I had built up this surgery in my mind as the one that would finally restore Lily's body to the place it should have been when she was born. The ominous dark shadow would be gone. I craved the next step for her, for us. I was fairly certain the surgery Dr. Shaul was proposing would allow her to go to the bathroom like everyone else. The moment for the conversation about this huge life-changing operation had finally arrived. I couldn't wait to see him.

We walked into the examination room, and he gave both of us a hug. I put Lily up on the table, and without saying a word about the bright orange cast, the cup on her ear, or the white cover on her head, he asked her, "Lily, can I look at your belly? She nodded, shocked back into her hospital silence. He gently lifted her dress. "You look great; all of the scars healed well, and it seems the hole for urine functions properly." I thought to myself if urine leaking everywhere is functioning properly, then it works just fine.

"I have some good news for you. Now that she is three, she can start a regimen to empty her bowel that will keep her continent. It should work most of the time with fewer rashes." *Wow!* There was something we could do right now. We didn't have to have surgery to make the poop stop. I couldn't believe this. It was going to be life-changing for all of us, and it would happen now without another surgery.

"The procedure is to do a daily enema." *What did he say?* I had only remotely heard that word. It had something to do with emptying the bowel. "You need to purchase Fleet's Enema for Children. It is a liquid in a small squeeze bottle." *Squeeze bottle? Excuse me?* "You will inject it into Lily's colon, through her bottom, and that should empty the bowel enough to last for a good part of the day." I couldn't picture in my mind how this was going to work.

"The procedure is complicated. She has to cooperate, and you have to have time and patience." He sighed deeply like he was about to deliver bad news. "Each evening, you will inject the Fleet's enema into her bottom. Keep her still on her hands and knees with her head down; the liquid must go as far as possible into the colon to loosen the stool. She needs to remain in this position for at least five minutes."

Now I could see the picture in my head. It didn't look good. "You'll probably want a few towels under her because sometimes the stool leaks out before you are ready."

Gross.

"After five minutes, flip her over onto a toilet, and let her empty her bowel into the toilet. Take a lot of the Fleet's enema solution with you. I don't think you can buy it in Tokyo. This will help to give her independence, but it is a temporary solution to her bowel issues. It will improve her life significantly for now."

I was supposed to do what to my child each night? Lily was like a whirling dervish; she never sat still. How was I supposed to get her to lie down, with her bottom in the air, and let me inject a solution inside of her that would make her poop into a toilet for who knows how long each night?

Dr. Shaul wasn't finished. "Sarah, let's sit down. Lily, you can get off the exam table. I have some fun toys for you here." He pointed to the corner of the examination room. She jumped off and ran to the toys. She picked up a plastic hammer with a peg board. She raised the hammer dramatically over the board and hit each peg with such force they flew out the bottom. We laughed. I turned back to him. I was full of anticipation and hope.

"As I told you before, Lily needs to have another very complicated operation that will permanently address these issues. We have to wait until she is five and can tolerate such a large surgery. There are four really important parts. These are critical and can all be done in one surgery." I tried to refocus because this was what I had been waiting to hear for two years.

He became very serious and leaned in toward me. "The first part is that her bladder is still too small. It needs to be enlarged to capture the capacity of urine she will make as she grows up. To do that, she must have her bladder augmented. We will take part of her small intestine and make a bladder." He was staring straight at me. I realized even though I had desperately wanted this conversation, I wasn't really concentrating after the enema news. He was talking, not drawing, showing, or moving. I was in trouble, and we were only through the first of four parts of the surgery. I wrote down the words as best as I could in my notebook to dissect with Fred later. He kept going.

"The second part of this surgery is to remove the current hole in her belly where the urine exits her body."

Hallelujah!

"In the surgery, we will strengthen the urethra at the bottom and will stop the urine from coming out that way. In order to have 100% continence for urine, we need to create a Mitrofanoff."

A who? How do you spell that? I was now madly taking notes. I hoped I could read them later.

"We will use her appendix to make a passageway from the surface of her skin into her newly augmented bladder. Urine will not come out the bottom but out through a tube, a catheter that will need to be inserted in the hole on the surface of her skin. She will then be able to empty her manmade bladder straight into the toilet. She will pee through the tube going forward."

I could not focus. *What was he saying? Would she never pee like everyone else? Would she pee through a tube? Wasn't that going backward?* I thought this surgery was supposed to fix everything. It sounded like it would make it worse.

"We also need to protect her kidney, so we will need to re-implant the ureter from the bladder to the kidney to make certain there is no reflux of urine which damages the kidney. Her kidney has to be protected at all costs since she only has one."

I was lost. *Wait! Are we talking about a ureter or a urethra? Which one was which? I thought I knew that one was something with the kidney and the other came from the bladder. Which one did she have? Which one did she need?* I was screaming in my head, but I remained silent.

"For the final part of the surgery, we need to stop the stool from leaking all the time." *Amen!*

"During the reconstructive surgery, we had hoped the colon and rectum would close enough to stop the flow of stool. That didn't happen. We don't want to go back to a colostomy."

No, we definitely don't want to do that.

"We have to create a way to make her 100 percent continent for stool. Doing the Fleet's enema for the next two years will be fine, but it isn't a long-term solution to achieving bowel continence. We need to construct an ACE or Malone. We will create a separate hole through her belly button that will connect to the top of the colon. She will use another catheter to inject solutions, like the Fleet's, into the hole. Because this will work from the top of the colon, she has the potential to be continent 100 percent of the time. She will no longer have stool accidents. Once we do the Malone, she will simply sit on the toilet, put the solutions through the catheter, and then she will go to the bathroom like everyone else."

That definitely did not sound like everyone else to me. It sounded very foreign, very scary, and very precarious. I didn't ask the questions or state the worry that was raging through my head. I let him talk. When he was finished, I knew it was time to say something.

"I'd like to say out loud what you said so I can tell Fred." I recited as best as I could what he had said. He nodded, I had gotten most of it, and he agreed. When I was done talking, I scribbled that I needed to purchase another entire suitcase to fill with Fleet's enema solution.

"So, in two years," I said, "you will do another larger surgery. You'll make a bladder and make it possible for her to be continent for both urine and stool. Is that right?"

"Yes. We will do what we can to make certain Lily is able to hold stool and urine all day long with no accidents and no more wet dresses." He slowly gestured to the growing wet spot on the front of Lily's clothes where her diaper had slipped, and the pee was flowing onto her front. I hugged Dr. Shaul, not knowing how else to communicate my gratitude. As we parted ways, I realized it would be another two years before I would see him.

A few days later, we had an appointment with Dr. Reinisch. I was still a little perplexed about meeting him in Beverly Hills. Looking closely at his business card, I realized his office was on the iconic Rodeo Drive.

As I got out of my tiny rental car, it dawned on me I was out of place. I had on an "I don't care" wrinkled T-shirt and my unusually dirty jeans that came with the smell of *Eau de bleach*, compliments of our multiple visits to the hospital. It was an understatement to say I was not Rodeo Drive chic. Since my daughter wore a white cover on her head and sported a neon glowing orange cast, we definitely screamed Beverly Hills misfits.

Dr. Reinisch's office building had a gigantic glittery white door that matched the Prada and Louis Vuitton stores down the block. I heaved it open. In front of me was a beautifully appointed elevator complete with a fancy bench and glass mirrors. There was soothing background music coming through the speakers. This was not a children's anything. Dr. Reinisch is a plastic surgeon and is famous for his pioneering pediatric reconstructive ears, but right here, in this office, there were no children's ears being made.

There was dark cherrywood paneling in his waiting area and very fancy white leather benches. There were two young, very thin, stunningly beautiful women with long, flowing hair in the waiting area. They were dressed in what I guessed was the latest haute couture, and there I was with Lily. I felt so out of place.

The person behind the desk was perky and didn't seem fazed by my arrival, but she didn't have us sit down in the waiting area either. As she pointed to the door to enter the offices, she said, "We have a variety of beverage choices. Would you like Perrier, Coke, Diet Coke, Ginger ale, orange juice, water?"

"Perrier would be wonderful."

She bent down to Lily's level, "And what would you like, beautiful little girl?"

"Orange juice, please."

She told me to sit in what looked like a dentist's chair. I put Lily on my lap. She closed the door, and I swiveled the chair around and stared at the spectacular view of the entire city of Los Angeles. What a view! My Perrier arrived in a tall glass with little ice cubes clinking as it was set down on the very expensive-looking wood table next to me. I watched the bubbles rise up in the glass for a few seconds before taking a long sip. It felt decadent to be pampered. Lily gulped down the juice and loudly placed the fancy glass on the counter.

In walked Dr. Reinisch, "Look at you, my beautiful!" he said, staring at Lily. She smiled, thank goodness. "I'm so glad to see you here in my office!" Not even acknowledging the kind of clinic we were in, he said, "No three-hour wait here." He seemed genuinely pleased we were there.

"I know you are going back to Tokyo," he said casually. "Well, I'm headed to Australia next week. Since I created this ear procedure, I have been invited to show doctors in Australia how to do it. I'm looking forward to it. They have many doctors coming to watch and learn." As he spoke, he reached for Lily's head cover.

I stopped listening to him. This moment was one I had simultaneously looked forward to and dreaded for over three months. With Lily sitting mutely on my lap, he removed first the mummy cap and then the cup on her ear. I gasped. She was facing the doctor, so I was looking at the back of her head. I saw she had no hair at all on the right side of her head. Nothing had grown back in the three months since he shaved it off. On top of that, the right side of her head was covered, literally covered, in black stitches. They went across the top of her head, behind her ear, and they were all over the prosthetic ear itself. They went up and down and sideways. The stitches were obviously attaching all of the pieces of the skin he had taken from her belly and behind both ears. It looked like he had fit puzzle pieces with black string together to make her new ear. No matter what the future would bring, right now, she looked like a very disfigured version of Frankenstein.

I was so glad Lily couldn't see my face. While I was becoming more alarmed behind her, Dr. Reinisch was staring at Lily's head from the front, looking from side to side to see how the two ears matched. He said, "You'll see the new ear is a bit bigger than the other one. That is by design. Lily's head and real ear will grow a bit more, and the new ear can't. Once her growth stops, they'll match."

He turned to Lily, "I'm going to take out your stitches. You will only feel a tug, nothing more. It shouldn't hurt. Do you understand?" Lily nodded her head. I held her tight around the belly, and he began the process of meticulously removing each and every stitch.

I had Lily turn around, and if I had not been shocked enough already, this time, I gagged. It was not an impressive parenting move. She looked awful. This was beyond what I could have ever imagined. Even with the stitches gone, the new ear was completely swollen, looking two or three times the normal size of an ear. Dr. Reinisch jumped in. "It is swollen, but that will slowly go away." Confidently he added, "You will see in a few months, it will

213

all grow together and will look like her other ear. You will not be able to tell it is a manmade ear. Her hair will grow in, don't worry."

I sighed. *What had we done?*

Before we left, I hugged Dr. Reinisch, trying to swallow my anguish, and wished him luck in Australia. He hugged Lily telling her one more time how beautiful she was. She smiled weakly this time, and he walked out of the room.

With Lily now looking unimaginably worse than when we walked in, I was horrified to think we still had to get out of the office. I slowly opened the door to the posh waiting area with all the fancy, strikingly beautiful women. I shivered, thinking how different we looked. As the waiting room door closed behind us, I didn't know why or where I found the strength, but I held my head up high. I had a compelling and poignant reason to be there, and I needed to see Dr. Reinisch too. I intentionally put Lily down so she could stand on her own. Full of pride about what we had accomplished that summer, we exited the fancy building and walked down Rodeo Drive.

We got back to the hotel, and I promptly gave Lily a bath. I used a hearty shampoo and fully washed what was left of her hair. I found some barrettes that Emma had used and combed Lily's thin blond hair over the bald patch and new ear. It looked silly, but silly was better than shocking.

We flew back to Tokyo with only a couple of days to get over jet lag and get organized before the first day of school. Emma would be starting kindergarten, and Lily would be starting nursery school at the American School in Japan. The director of the school had admitted Lily even though she was not continent, something that went against the hard and fast rule. The director patiently listened to the story of Lily's life and felt compassion toward her. She wanted to give this very intelligent but physically handicapped little girl the opportunity to attend such an outstanding school. Siri was amazingly still willing to continue to be with our family since she didn't yet have plans for herself. Instead of having me visit each day, we agreed that it would be more discreet to have Siri come and change Lily's diaper, which was full of urine.

Unlike all of the dressed-up children on their first day of school, Lily started with a bald head, funky-looking ears, a bright orange cast, and a questionable ability to be continent. On the first day of school, jitters didn't begin to capture the emotions at our house.

Chapter 33

After dropping off the girls at school, I realized that we would finally have a break. We were going to have two years with no surgeries, no trips to Los Angeles, and no organizational nightmares to pull off so Lily could survive.

We solved the urine leaking problem with larger diapers. Through Dr. Sung, we found an orthopedist who took off her cast. It was not so bright orange by the end of the eight weeks, but her thumb now functioned as it should. Lily's hair slowly grew out over the new ear, and the swelling and crisscross stitch marks faded. A real, true ear started to peek through. I thought less and less about it and more and more about how far we had come to give Lily the best possible life.

Doing the enema at first was another nightmare. Lily didn't want to lay on the floor with her rear end in the air, and she absolutely didn't want the Fleet's enema squeezed through her bottom into her colon. She hated sitting on the toilet and refused to cooperate. Fred and I only added to the stress because we had no idea what we were doing. After several very messy days, we became more comfortable, and Lily started to trust us. She was old enough to realize if she stayed clean, she felt much better. We tried to be creative about how to fit it into our daily lives. Reading bedtime stories moved from while she was in her bed to while she was on the toilet. We read a lot more books that way.

Emma blossomed at school. She had an outstanding kindergarten teacher; she made friends and was happy. She was so glad to be back to a routine that made sense to her. One afternoon after a particularly wonderful day at school, she stood in front of me, counting on her fingers the things that made her happy. "Mommy, I love my school. I love my teachers. I love my friends. I love Japan, and I love my family!" As she said each one, she held out a finger and proudly showed me there were five whole things. It was exhilarating to hear her speak with such conviction after all she had been through.

Our life blossomed the way we had hoped it would. Lily and Emma started playing soccer at a local school. Emma was quick on the field and liked the competition. Lily, on the other hand, at the tender age of three, preferred whatever place on the field she could stand where there was little chance of the ball coming her way. She picked flowers and grass and liked to stand quietly or even sit in the sunshine. The girls also practiced Aikido, a Japanese martial art. It was Lily who loved to throw the sensei master over her shoulder.

Our friendship circle grew. The more confident we became about how to care for Lily, the more time we allowed ourselves to venture away from home, just the two of us. After three years in Japan, we developed many strong friendships both in the international community through the girls' school and in the Japanese community through Hiro. Once Lily's enema was done, Fred and I could go out together. We went to New Year's parties, birthday dinners, and wine-tasting events.

I became the president of the parents' association at the girls' school, and I served on the board of trustees. I created a book club and a parenting group. It felt good to continue my work in education.

With all of the sacrifices that Fred had made for so many years to excel at his job, it finally paid off. One winter evening, Fred came home and surprised me with wonderful news. "I am being promoted to Vice President of Asia!" It was a coveted position and one he deserved. With that level of responsibility, we would gain some much-needed financial flexibility, and with Lily's body was stable, and we could travel with him around Asia. Our family could finally explore again.

"Girls, Daddy has to take a trip to Beijing, China, next week. We are all going to go together!" Emma loved to travel. At first, Lily was less excited since, in her mind; a plane ride landed her in the operating room.

During those two years, with no surgeries, we visited ten countries. Every time the girls had a break from their school schedule, or when there was a long weekend, we traveled. We created family experiences and lasting connections. We were recovering.

One of our best memories came during a trip to Sydney, Australia. Someone Fred worked with invited us to go on a yacht into Sydney Harbour. There were eight colleagues and friends from the Sydney office of Northwest and Emma and Lily onboard. It was a glorious day. When we walked on, I went with the girls to the back of the boat. "That's the Sydney Opera House." I pointed in awe and disbelief.

"Mommy, look at the bridge! We are going under it!" We passed under the Sydney Harbour Bridge. It was thrilling to experience that with the girls.

We pulled up to a dock near the restaurants in Darling Harbour for lunch. We were told we would be getting lunch there. After a few minutes, a waiter with a white shirt and black apron approached the boat. Above his head, he carried two platters bursting with every kind of seafood imaginable.

As he set them down on the tables, he said, "These were brought in fresh this morning. You can't get better than this." He stepped back on the dock, and we pulled out again. I was worried. I was certain the girls would hate it. They liked all of the food we ate in Tokyo, including all types of sushi, but on that platter, there were eyes and tails still attached, reminding me of my hospital meals.

As I stood there wishing that I could have ordered something specifically for the girls, the captain called us to the upper level. "Hey, everybody, come on up! Take a look at the harbor from up here!" Emma and Lily stayed behind. After a few minutes, we started to slowly find our way back downstairs to get some lunch. I was stunned by what we saw.

Lily had pulled a chair up to the table with the seafood. She stood on the chair, hunched over the platter. In each hand, she had a huge lobster claw. She feverishly dunked a claw into the melted syrupy butter, opened her mouth as wide as possible, and stuffed the meat into her mouth. Butter dripped all the way down her fingers and arms and onto her shirt. It even covered her shoes, the chair, and the deck of the boat. She still had another lobster claw in her right hand and was ready to dunk. I suppose I should have rushed over and removed the expensive lobster from her hand. Instead, I stood there staring at her glowing, radiant smile as the Opera House disappeared in the distance. With the eight adults and Emma now staring at her, she finally took her eyes off of the claw and saw us. She paused and rubbed her belly with her dripping hand, "Yummy, yummy in my tummy! Mommy, I love lobster and especially the butter sauce. We should try this at home." At that point, I was bent over laughing. I saw Lily's sweet and mischievous personality shining through. It was a happy, joyful moment, even if we had less lobster to share.

Our need for travel and adventure went beyond what we had done in our early days of marriage or even when Emma was little. During those two years without surgeries, we became obsessed.

Aside from seeing Asia, we spent a month in the summer of 2004 in Belgium and France with Fred's family. Then we spent a month seeing family in St. Paul and friends in San Francisco and Austin, Texas. We didn't think about whether or not it was good for our girls to be moving all the time because, for Fred and me, it was rejuvenating. Travel and exploration were things we still wanted. It brought back the excitement for a life together that we had felt when we were first married.

We traveled so fast and so far, it was as if we were running away from what we knew was coming. If we stopped, we felt like the hospitals and surgeries and Los Angeles might catch us, so we kept moving.

Then, one day, our lives came to an abrupt halt. The travel and the friends, and the fun had to end because we had to go to Los Angeles for surgery number seven. This was going to be the surgery that would determine the kind of life Lily would lead. Would she be fully continent with urine and stool? This was the question we had waited five long years to find out.

Chapter 34

We pulled the girls from their school in late May 2005, a week before the end of the year. Lily was almost five and was finishing Pre-Kindergarten at the American School. She was so happy at school and screamed at us about leaving. "What are we doing? I don't want to go. I won't go. I don't want another operation. You can't make me do it."

We had switched Emma to a different school for first grade, The Montessori School of Tokyo, and there was an end-of-year special celebration she had to miss in order to get to Los Angeles on time. "Mommy, as you know, I have a starring role as a flower in the play this year. I have to be there. I can't miss it. There are only three flowers. It won't be right if I am not on stage. The entire world will notice." Both girls were keenly aware that only bad things happened in Los Angeles. This was going to be much harder with older children.

Despite their protests, we got on the plane. We were beyond numb to the trip. It now signified we were headed to a place that brought anxiety for all of us. We checked into the same hotel we had stayed in two years before. Emma reluctantly entered the hotel room and went to the corner, and sat. Grandma and Grandpa were there, and that added a sense of relief, but Emma was already waiting for this to end, and it hadn't even begun.

Two days later, Fred, Lily, and I walked into Children's Hospital Los Angeles. We got our blue badges and went to Lily's room. Bowel prep was a misery again. Lily cried, and then I cried. We didn't sleep. Fred stayed with us late and then came back for the 6:30 am operation.

The surgery lasted almost eight hours. Dr. Shaul and his team of surgeons and nurses had to reconstruct, once again, Lily's convoluted body parts so they would have a chance to function like everyone else's.

When we saw Dr. Shaul after the operation, he said he was very pleased. "The surgery went better than expected on all counts. I think Lily has a very good chance of being completely continent." I cried.

As we sat there in the recovery room for Lily to be stable enough to go to her permanent room in the hospital, we peeled back her covers to take a peek. Forgetting how it had been so many times in the past, I was shocked all over again. "I completely forgot. She has two more tubes." One came out of her belly button, and one came out through a small hole in the lower side of the abdomen where her appendix used to be.

"Remember, that is what we were told to expect. Two tubes."

"I know, but it feels like we are going backward again." I rested my head on his shoulder.

I never left Lily's side during her entire week in the hospital. Since she was older, I didn't want her to ever feel alone. That meant I slept on a thin, blue plastic chair that barely reclined. I pulled it as close as possible to Lily's hospital bed and mostly watched her sleep and kept an eye on the nurses that came and went. It was exhausting to the point of debilitating.

Fred walked in one morning and paused, not looking at Lily but at me. "What the heck, Sarah. You look like a ghost. I know sleep is tough here, but wow. Have you eaten any food?"

I mumbled something incoherent, and then Fred saw behind my head the window ledge where I had stored my stash of "food." You could see the wrappers of a few Snickers bars. There were some potato chip bags and the leftover malted milk balls from the previous night's most-needed sugary treat. I guessed by the look on his face I wasn't doing well. "Okay, let's get you a shower, and you can put on these new clothes I brought for you." He handed me nicely laundered pants and a shirt. I noticed the very pleasant smell of lavender dryer sheets. "There is a shower down the hall for families. Go and run some hot water over yourself; it will feel good. I'll get us some real food while you're gone." I picked up the clothes and grabbed my shampoo. I was certain they would provide some type of soap and a towel in the family bathroom. I locked the door behind me and started to feel extremely fortunate I was about to take a private shower. I was certain Fred was right; this was what I needed.

After getting undressed, I realized the towel on the shelf was tiny, and there was only one. It made me think of my *SHAH-WAH* after giving birth to Lily in Tokyo. I quickly decided if I could get dry with that one, then I could do it with this one too.

The shower itself was one of those plasticky stalls where the entire thing was pressed into a shower shape and then pushed into the corner. There was a wooden pulldown bench bolted to the side of the shower for use if necessary. I turned on the water, then stood there and waited and then waited some more, but it never got warm.

I forced myself to get in and was glad to realize there was a dispenser on the wall, the kind you push to get liquid soap. I pushed it a few times and then vigorously rubbed the liquid all over my face. Within seconds, my face was on fire. I bolted out of the shower, stuck my head under the cold water in the sink, and started scraping my face with my fingers to get off what I realized was hospital disinfectant. I was panting, standing in a pool of water, and starting to shiver. I yanked the tiny towel off of the shelf, but it was tinier than expected.

I was desperate, so I started running back and forth in the small bathroom, flailing my arms to see if I could dry off. By the time I got back to Lily's room, my cheeks were breaking out in hives. Fred was sitting next to Lily's bed with what looked like a nice warm meal. "Hi! Did the shower feel good?" I winced.

Before being released from the hospital, Dr. Shaul explained carefully how we were now expected to care for Lily. "For the next month, the two tubes you see will remain in place. Lily's urine will constantly flow out of the hole in her lower abdomen. She will have a urine collection bag like before." He reached down below her hospital bed and pulled out the bag. "We'll make the tube shorter to go home." He pointed to the second tube sticking straight out of her belly button. "This is the new passageway that connects to her colon. You will now use a syringe to inject the Fleet's enema directly into that tube while she sits on the toilet. You will not have to put any more liquids straight into her bottom. No more flipping her over. You will need to come

222

back the week of the 4th of July, and we'll remove the catheters." He handed me a bag filled with all of the medical equipment we now needed. It all looked fairly familiar. I felt confident in how to care for her.

This was an improvement. No more leaking holes in her belly. No more lying on the ground and injecting a solution into her bottom. Once both of the tubes were removed, she would go to the bathroom like everyone else, so long as she had two catheters and lots of solutions and could spend 45 minutes on the toilet each day, which was definitely not like everyone else.

When Lily was discharged, Fred went back to Tokyo. Emma, Lily, and I went to St. Paul for a month. We didn't think about the separation this time. I felt confident that I could handle Lily's medical needs, and we were actually looking forward to a month with my parents in St. Paul.

On the fourth of July, Lily and I flew to Los Angeles to have the tubes removed. Emma stayed with Grandma and Grandpa. It was supposed to be a simple office visit with Dr. Shaul, so we both proudly received a yellow "office visit only" sticker this time. Lily slapped hers on her shirt. "Mommy, yellow. It is the same as my dress."

Lily knew that the two tubes would be removed at this appointment. We had talked about how great it would be to have them out. She jumped up on the exam table, a place she was very familiar with at this point. I had brought a few books for her to look at, so she leaned back onto the table, took out the books, and tuned us out. She didn't want to participate even though this was all about her body.

After about two minutes of pleasantries, asking Lily about her summer in Minnesota and what books she liked, Dr. Shaul got down to the particulars. He lifted her little dress and touched the tubes. "I'm going to remove both tubes." He started to clip off the stitches that held the pee tube in place. As he cut, he said, "Lily's bladder is small because it was made out of her intestine. Over time, it will stretch. For now, it needs to be emptied every 30 minutes." He slipped the tube out of the lower hole on the side of Lily's belly. I had been focused on the stretching of the bladder part more than the every 30 minutes part. He kept talking, so I kept following.

"Sarah, you will need to put a 10 French catheter into the hole."

Oh no. A what?

He then pointed to the hole on the side of Lily's belly and held up a floppy tube for me to see. It was about two feet long. "Once you put KY Jelly on the end of the tube, you will insert it into Lily's bladder every 30 minutes to drain it."

KY Jelly? Wasn't that for sex? Great, now I have to buy sex products for my five-year-old daughter.

"She should stand over the toilet and let the urine drain through the tube into the toilet. Make certain you drain the new bladder every 30 minutes, or it might rupture." Lily looked even closer at her book.

Did he say ruptured bladder?

He had now moved onto the tube protruding from her belly button, the Malone thing. As he cut through the black stitches holding the tube in place, he said, "For the enema, you will again use a 10 French catheter."

I got that part, the floppy tube.

"You will put some KY Jelly on it and insert it into the hole."

More sex products understood. "Then, tape it to her stomach, so the tube stays in place, and using a syringe, you will inject the Fleet's enema and a salty saline solution into the catheter while she sits on the toilet. From there, it is exactly as you have been doing for the past couple of years." I was used to fitting an enema into our life each night. I knew the sacrifice that had to be made.

A nurse came into the room and brought a box of catheters. In big black letters, it said *10 French* on the side. She also handed me a tube of the infamous KY Jelly. In a plastic bag, there was some medical tape, loads of syringes, and bottles of salty saline solution. It reminded me of when I had dumped my bag of medical devices on the floor at Joshi Idai, and Dr. Kawasaki had helped me to interpret what I had.

Lily had been sitting quietly the entire time Dr. Shaul was touching and pulling on her belly. Then, the nurse approached her. "Lily, can you please hold still?"

Lily was clearly done with the appointment, and it looked like she wanted to hit the nurse. "I'm going to put the tube into the hole right here on your side." She pointed gently, showing Lily what she was going to do. She put a small pea-sized amount of KY on the end of the tube and then seemed to gently, slowly push the tube into Lily's belly. You could see it snaking through the top layer of her skin, disappearing little by little into the inner folds of Lily's body. It almost made me throw up.

The nurse turned to me and smiled as pee started to come out of the tube into the cup she had set on the examining table. "See, it flows out. It is a bit tricky at first to know how far you need to push in the tube. Go slowly. Once you see the urine, that is your indicator to stop." She gently pulled out the tube. Lily didn't flinch. I couldn't speak. It was gross. I weakly smiled, hoping I conveyed confidence in my ability to take on my new task. *No problem, I could do this.* There was a problem, though, I had been distracted by how the tube looked going along Lily's skin, so I didn't pay attention to how to actually push in the tube.

"It is almost the same routine for the enema." She used another 10 French catheter, putting KY Jelly on the end, and again, she seemed to effortlessly find a little opening in Lily's belly button and push the catheter inside. It went in about three inches. She stopped. "I have reached the top of the colon here. You will have to be careful because if you go too far, you will damage the colon."

I was still back on exploding her new bladder, and here she was, suggesting I was going to rip apart her colon.

As we were getting ready to leave the hospital, I went back to something Dr. Shaul had said. Lily's new bladder had to be emptied every 30 minutes. He didn't say during the day or up until bedtime. He said, "every 30 minutes." That meant twenty-four hours a day. I was never going to sleep, and neither was Lily. Then, I started to panic. I realized as I left that the nurse had inserted the tube in the urine hole ten minutes before I left the hospital.

225

I had 20 minutes before I had to do it again. The hotel was 20 minutes away. I knew I wouldn't make it, and Lily would explode. I picked her up and sprinted. I said to myself, "I can do this, I can do this, I can do this."

Lily was a tiny five-year-old little girl, and from the very first second she saw me coming at her with a 10 French catheter dripping with KY Jelly on the tip, she shrieked and ran and hid under the bed in the hotel room. After much coercion, I coaxed Lily into the bathroom, got her clothes off enough that I could at least see the hole for urine, and then I tried to shove the tube straight in. No luck; the tube bounced off the surface of her skin, bending as I pushed. I tried again, but nothing.

"Lily, please stand this way." I turned her a bit more toward me. She was standing on one side of the toilet bowl, and I was on the other. "Can you move that way?" I tried to poke her again. "Let me see, maybe if I hold the catheter at a different angle, let's see if this works." I pushed the catheter, tilted my head, and put on more KY, then less. I held the catheter with two hands, then one. I stood above the toilet, then crouched both in front of it and then on the side. Nothing. I never even got it in a tiny bit. I had discarded a large number of catheters that were now accumulating in a pile on the floor of the bathroom because I was certain they were defective. I had used almost an entire tube of KY. It had been flung off the catheters and was clinging to the bathroom walls and floor. Some of it was on my shirt and Lily's shoes. I was frantic and sure I would ruin her urine hole, pop the new bladder, and then she would die from toxic urine build-up moments after leaving the doctor's office.

The time was ticking by, 30 minutes, then an hour, then an hour and a half of us standing over the toilet with me trying and trying to get the goddamn catheter in, just so she could pee. I dissolved into tears, crying so hard I couldn't even see the catheter. I had to figure this out. I left Lily standing over the toilet and raced to get all of the paperwork the nurse had given to me. I frantically flipped through the pages, finally landing on the emergency phone number for Dr. Shaul's clinic. "Please, please, can I talk to a nurse or doctor for Dr. Shaul? I have an emergency!"

They put me on hold; then, a medical fellow got on the phone. I started screaming into the phone, "I can't have her pee; the tube won't go in. I have been trying and trying for almost two hours. The bladder is going to burst, and I have no way to get the pee out! Please, please help me. I don't know what to do!"

He was calm and not riled by my hysterical voice. "Hi, Sarah! Why don't you come on over to the clinic? We'll be here a few more hours. We'll let the front desk know to let you in right away. Does that sound all right?" Before he finished his sentence, I dropped the phone, grabbed Lily and the pile of catheters I had discarded on the bathroom floor, ran to our car, and drove like crazy to the hospital. I was absolutely certain her new bladder would explode, and she would die.

They were ready for us, and we went back to see the nurse immediately. I was a mess. I was sure I was failing parenthood. Anyone else in this situation could stick in the catheter and have their child pee. It was me, only me, who could not. I was incompetent, and my daughter would die.

The nurse who had helped us only a couple hours before grabbed one of the catheters that were like snakes wiggling in my hand. As I let go, I looked down and saw that Lily and I both were covered in globs of the KY sex jelly. Another success in my brilliant parenting.

The nurse was unphased. She put a touch of the KY on the end of the catheter, not the fistfuls I had been using only minutes before. She then showed me the exact angle I had to use to put the tube into Lily. I bent over and put my face right next to the hole. Lily was absolutely still, unlike how she had been standing over the toilet for the past two hours. "Think of the hole as a clock. First, find three o'clock," she said as she lightly slid the tube a tiny bit into the hole. "Then, you need to move the catheter to six o'clock." She pulled it ever so slightly down. "There is a turn in the pathway we created inside of her so urine won't leak out through the hole." *Oh.* She gently pushed the tube in about four inches, and pee started flowing into the paper cup she had on the exam table. I stood there in awe while she was clearly marveling at the technique that

Dr. Shaul had used. "Lily," she proclaimed, "you are a real trooper."

Then she turned to me, the basket case, "Now you try." With my hands now wobbling and my fingers almost raw from holding the catheter for many hours, I followed her exact directions. Three o'clock, a tiny bit in, move straight down to six o'clock, and gently slide it in until you hit the pee. I did it! To see it flow was like getting liquid gold.

With my head held high, Lily and I walked out. When I had her all clicked into her car seat, it dawned on me I had no idea what the magic clock angles were to put in the tube for the enema tonight. I was toast.

At the hotel, I shoved some food into both of us, knowing I had to empty her bladder again in a few minutes. After being so sweet with the nurse at the clinic, when I tried 30 minutes later to repeat the procedure, Lily revolted. My sweet, kind, adorable, agreeable child was apoplectic about me inserting a catheter into that pee hole. Since I had spent so much time pushing on the hole, she was now raw, and it hurt her when I put it in.

"Lily, sweetie, it will only take a minute. I know how to do it now. See, you stand right there next to the toilet; it will be quick." I spoke to her gently. "Lily see how great it is that we get to practice while we are here in Los Angeles? We will have a fun time and will make this work. Isn't it wonderful to be the two of us?" She put her arms straight out in front of her. I was clearly supposed to keep my distance.

"Mommy, nope. Not happening. I don't want you to touch me anymore. You are not allowed in my space." She made a full circle with her arms straight out. I was not getting in.

I tried again in a nice calm voice. "Honey, this is going to help you. You can now pee like everyone else. No more pee dripping from your belly! No more diapers!" I said it as enthusiastically as I possibly could. "Look, you are a big girl now."

I could feel the tension and worry, and frustration building inside. No matter what I said no cajoling was going to work. I lost it. "Lily, we have to do this! You have to stand still. If we don't, your new bladder will burst, and we will be right back in the hospital for another surgery." She finally stopped flailing, came to the toilet, and stood.

I found the hole, stuck the damn tube in, a tiny bit of pee came out, and I removed the tube. The whole thing took less than 30 seconds, yet I knew I would be doing it again in 30 minutes. It was time for her to go to bed, but the idea sent tremors throughout my body. I was a mess. All night long, I sat on that bed watching as the minutes ticked by on the red digital clock.

At first, I had her stand up at the toilet every 30 minutes, then I put a plastic bag in the garbage can, stuck the tube inside of her, and had it drip into the trashcan. I tried not to wake her up.

The next evening, in addition to the pee, I had to do the enema. I was terrified. I'm certain it was sheer luck, but on the first try, I got the tube in – at least there was one thing that went according to plan.

After three days of this routine of fighting with Lily by day and not sleeping at night, I was desperate. Sometimes Lily was so upset that it took an hour to get her to do it. We basically stood next to the toilet for the entire day. I had not slept, not even for one minute, out of fear of missing the next round. Through my sleep deprivation, I came to the realization that I could not keep this up.

On the fourth day, I blurted out, "Lily, I will buy you a present each time we have to insert the tube to pee. You can have whatever you want from the gift store at the hospital. I don't care, just don't fight me anymore. Let's work as a team." The reality of what I had promised obviously did not dawn on me until the words were out in the room, and Lily was starting to nod her head in agreement. This was going to mean every 30 minutes; I was promising to buy her something. I had uttered those words at 11:00 at night, and the gift store at the hospital opened at 8:00. I would be getting eighteen separate items by the time the store opened, and that was only for half a day. I didn't know how long we had to do this, and I didn't know how long it would take for the bladder to expand, but for today, every single time felt like an eternity, and this was going to help.

She cooperated, and I kept my promise. We bought one of everything in the gift store. She picked out teddy bears, toys, cards, candy, music boxes, earrings even though she didn't have pierced ears yet, rings, bracelets, presents for Emma (which I thought was very kind), and endless other items she brought to the counter. "Mommy, do you think I should get the orange teddy bear or the purple one? I also like the blue one, feel it on your face, it is so soft and cuddly. Mommy, why don't you get something for yourself? You deserve it." I pulled out a Snickers bar, remembering my own time in the hospital.

I paid for it all, hoping the same person was not working each time I checked out and that the credit card statement would not appear for at least a month. We bought so many things I had to buy two additional suitcases in order to get all of them back to Tokyo.

Each day, as Lily spent time picking out item after item, I got a break. I found a bench outside the store and had a moment of peace and quiet all to myself. That was also a gift. I didn't have to interact with her or touch her. I rested my mind, not thinking about anything at all.

At the end of those fateful days at the hotel, Lily began to trust me. I learned how to put the catheter in properly, and she learned how to stand at the toilet and let her bladder empty. We slowly pulled back from doing it every 30 minutes. We had learned her bladder, in fact, didn't explode and kill her if we went a couple of hours. The enema tube was much easier to navigate, and since doing the enema had been awful up until that point, it was actually pleasant for Lily to sit on the toilet 'like everyone else.' None of that made it easy, we still fought and hated it, but it was now possible.

We spent the rest of July and all of August in St. Paul. It wasn't an easy summer. Emma went from sad to angry about having to spend yet another summer away from Daddy and Tokyo, and my attention was on Lily, not on her. I was sleep deprived and overwhelmed, and I was bordering on irrational.

One day, through my fog, without more than a minute of thought, I said, "if you girls want, we can get a puppy when we get home at the end of the summer." The girls couldn't believe what I said. They stopped screaming and throwing stuffed animals at each other across the room and started jumping for joy. What had I done? I actually didn't know. I had never had a dog.

But that bribe was a success. All I had to do was say the word "puppy," and magically, the girls paid attention. "Hey, you need to sit down in the restaurant so our puppy will see you have good manners." Lily sat down.

On the first of September 2005, Lily, Emma, and I arrived back in Tokyo after getting the all-clear from Dr. Shaul. Thankfully, Fred was ready for anything when we landed. We schlepped our multitude of suitcases through customs and headed straight to the pet store.

We picked out the cutest, sweetest, and gentlest puppy. Lily cradled it in her arms, and Emma wrapped hers around Lily. It made me cry. They, in fact, did need a puppy, and maybe I did too.

All the way home, we enthusiastically discussed what to name it. In the end, I won. I desperately needed a cup of coffee, so our little tan and white colored Shih Tzu was named Coffee.

Chapter 35

In the fall of 2005, we felt relieved and grateful. Lily was continent. She joined Emma at the Montessori School of Tokyo for kindergarten, and right away, both girls made friends. Emma was a second grader enjoying the atmosphere of the Montessori program. Fred's job was stable, and I accepted the position of Assistant Head of School at the girls' school, which meant I could help Lily with emptying her bladder throughout the day. Working again felt second nature. I was back in an environment I knew and understood. Children and schools, and administrative work brought me joy and peace. After five difficult years, we were settling into a routine and a good life for all of us.

That Thanksgiving, we wanted to celebrate. We were grateful and wanted to express it.

We invited our friends and Fred's Northwest colleagues to our home. We had a stupendous Thanksgiving buffet with tables for 70 people placed around the Azabu House living room. It was a feast. It was filled with succulent turkey, moist stuffing, smooth gravy, and even steaming apple pie.

Fred and I stood at the front of the room. He raised his glass, "Thank you for coming. It has been a remarkable five years for our family. Thank you all for your kindness and support. We raise our glass to you. *Kanpai!*" There was a glow in the house that day. It was powerful and positive.

The next morning, someone knocked on our door. The tables were crooked, tablecloths stained with gravy and stuffing, and napkins wrinkled on the tables. We wondered if it might be the caterer coming back to pick everything up. It wasn't, and that knock would change our lives forever.

"Fred, how are you doing?" The man forced his hand out, and Fred shook it. It was the Chief Financial Officer of Northwest Airlines. He had flown all the way from Minnesota.

Fred hesitated, "Hi. Come on in." We looked at the mess strewn all over the living room, realizing this was not our home. It was Northwest. Fred quickly said, "We had a Thanksgiving party yesterday. We invited the entire Northwest team. I wish I had known you were here. We would have loved to have you join us."

The CFO entered the house and took a few steps past Fred. I was surprised to see he was dressed casually in jeans and a wrinkled plaid shirt. This felt unusual, nothing like the formality of the office. He was surveying the entryway, not paying any attention to us. "Can I take a look around the house?" It was Northwest's house, but it still seemed like such a strange request. "Sure, be our guest."

He disappeared for about 10 minutes. Fred and I stood motionless at the front door, not sure what to do.

When he returned, he said, "Thanks! See ya," and walked out.

"What was that?"

"I have no idea."

Fred had known the CFO for a long time; he had been his original boss at Northwest in Saint Paul fourteen years before. Maybe he wanted to see the house since it was such an iconic part of Northwest's history.

Within days of his visit, the real reason became clear. Northwest Airlines declared bankruptcy. Fred knew the company had been in trouble, but bankruptcy? How could that be? The peaceful life we had finally created for ourselves would disappear. If Northwest went bankrupt, our lives went with it. Something that had sustained our family enriched our lives, and given Fred such an amazing career would no longer be the same. Even our home would disappear. With the company in bankruptcy, all assets, including the Azabu House, would have to be sold. We would have to move out. It crushed us because it was one more thing, in an already endless list of them, that caused turmoil in our lives. Our sadness was not only for our family but for Northwest too. It was devastating to see it falling apart.

Instead of growing and supporting the Asian operation as Fred had done for so many years, his job quickly became managing it through bankruptcy. He had worked tremendously hard to create a positive spirit within a group of people who needed it. Bankruptcy mandated the opposite. It meant division, separation, letting people go, and presentations filled with carefully crafted words that brought hardship and frustration. Fred tried to bring dignity to a process that had none. Working for an American company abroad became precarious for everyone. Managing bankruptcy in any situation is difficult, but this was agonizing.

It would be hard on a professional level for Fred but even more so for our family. We relied on Northwest's commitment to us living abroad for us to stay. Our home was their home, and Northwest had to continue to believe that Fred was the person who could pull off this difficult process. We were afraid of what the future would bring for our family.

Reluctantly, we started to look for a new place to live. Northwest had to sell not only our home but the Daikanyama apartment building as well. We searched and searched for months. Heaviness set in as we realized that nothing could replace the Azabu House. It had a meaningful history for Northwest and now held our family's stories and life. This made the process even more painful. We settled on another house in our neighborhood. It would always be a house and never our home.

Our lives were filled with worry and confusion. I allowed myself to think that maybe we just needed to move back to the U.S. Fred and I talked about it a lot but were on opposite sides of what to do.

"I think it is time to consider leaving. We need a life that is stable that we can depend on, and this life now doesn't have stability. This is so difficult for me. Fred, I don't want to give all this up. I just feel this isn't a place for us to live anymore."

"Sarah, I don't know what to do. I have to stay and continue with negotiations and settlement for the bankruptcy. My job is here, not in Minnesota. I don't know how long this will take."

For more than a year, we went round and round about what to do. I couldn't let go of the belief that there had been enough upheaval in our lives. I had to have stability; I craved it. That didn't help Fred and me. With the intensity of his work, we were forced to split the tasks of our life again. Fred worked all day in the Tokyo office and all night with headquarters, and I managed everything else. I finally couldn't do it anymore. As much as I treasured the life we had, I was ready to leave Japan. Fred reluctantly agreed and resolved to find a way to make it happen.

On June 6, 2007, seven years and one month after we arrived in Tokyo and one day before Lily's seventh birthday, we left. I flew with the girls, and Fred stayed behind. He would fly back and forth between Japan and Minnesota until the bankruptcy was done. I needed the summer to find a new school for the girls and to put our lives back together in Minnesota.

We watched as the movers packed our belongings and took our carefully acquired Asian treasures out of our house one by one. It was the carefully chosen tansu cabinet from the 1800s and the golden screen with cherry blossoms dancing across the middle that choked me up the most. I was heartbroken to undo the life we had so painstakingly put together.

The girls were still young, nine and seven, but they could feel the heaviness in our hearts as we stood and watched the moving truck fill. Fred and I wondered if they would remember their Japanese, how to bow and show respect when greeting people, how to take off their shoes when entering a home, or the beauty and wonder of Japan and the rest of Asia. We hoped they would recall the majesty of snow-capped Mount Fuji and the food meticulously prepared in restaurants for us. The most important memory we hoped they would take away was the precious time we spent bonding as a family.

Lily was done with her surgeries. Each one of the seven painful, tedious, horrifying operations had brought us closer to giving Lily a fuller life. We thought she was ready to enter the life that waited for her in Minnesota.

235

After the moving truck pulled away, we heaved our suitcases into our green Toyota Estima. I smiled to myself as I thought about bouncing like a pinball to the back and rolling out the trunk as I arrived at Joshi Idai that fateful first time. We had successfully survived even those difficult days of fish eyes for breakfast and baby prison hospitals and life and death decisions to save Lily's life. This I knew for certain.

As we drove to the airport for the last time, I gazed out upon our adopted city. This time I knew many of the shops and restaurants we had patronized and dined there. We passed multiple shrines, each symbolizing hope and wishes for a good life beyond the protection of Japan. We sped by the taller buildings that had been our bank or were the apartments where our friends lived. We knew this city. We had made it our own.

We entered the airport with our big green van, parking it just outside Narita Airport. We checked our bags and headed to immigration. The Northwest agents had given Fred a pass to come with us to the plane. Every minute together was important. We stopped at our favorite tonkatsu restaurant and waited for the pork cutlet and steaming rice to arrive in the perfectly organized bento box.

The girls wolfed down their food, and I pushed mine around. I didn't want to be separated from Fred again. He was certain he could be back with us in only a couple of months, but it was once again painful to say goodbye. I tried to be positive. Looking down at my food, I said, "we made it. We had our adventure; we are together as a family; we did it." I didn't have a speech prepared or a toast written to our success at living in this foreign land. I was too full of emotion to actually express what I was feeling. Fred had been silent and finally spoke.

"Sarah, look what we did. We beat every odd. We surpassed every expectation. We made our dream of living in a new country with our family happen. We should have no sadness or remorse. We should feel pride and a sense of accomplishment. Look at our children!" We looked and burst out laughing because Lily's use of chopsticks was still precarious, and rice was dribbling down her chin and had managed to stick to her shirt. "Well, you know what I mean." I grinned, and she gave us a toothy smile.

"I love tonkatsu! Mommy, we have to make this in America. I want it to taste just like this one." She clamped down on a piece of the pork that had been perfectly cut into small square pieces just right for chopsticks. She had a strong grip on it and slowly brought it up to her mouth. She popped it inside and proudly chewed with gusto. "See! I'm a champion chopstick holder! I only want to eat with them forever." She was now waving the chopsticks above her head in triumph. The three of us burst into applause, complete with whoops and cheers. The entire restaurant looked at us. Yes, we were once again disturbing the *Wa*.

I looked back at Fred. "I know how much we have changed. I only knew one word when I arrived seven years ago, and look at my Japanese!" I was exceptionally proud of my language at that point. I could carry on simple conversations and get us almost anywhere we needed to go. Fred continued, "Look what we did! We took these sweet kids with us all over the world. We challenged ourselves as parents and showed them how to not only accept differences in other people but to thrive in a place where we look and act different from everyone else."

I instinctively put my arm around Emma, "maybe they *will* remember this as they grow up?"

Emma lifted her head and joined our conversation. "I will. I'm going to tell everyone about our life. I'll remember." She fumbled with something in her pocket and pulled out a Japanese five-yen coin. She held it up above the table so we could all see it, and she touched the hole in the middle, "I'm going to make a necklace out of this when we get to America, so I'll remember. I'll always remember." She gently stuck it back in her pocket, shoving it in as far as it would go.

It was then that I started to cry. When we were in the middle of the tragedies and difficulties, it was so hard to see that this had amounted to anything beyond survival. Emma helped us to remember it.

We paid for lunch and slowly walked down the concourse. Fred grabbed Emma's hand and squeezed tight. As we approached our gate, Emma jumped into his arms and wrapped herself tightly around him. "Daddy, I love you. I'm going to miss you so much." Fred reached into his own pocket. He pulled out a little box and whispered into Emma's ear. She pulled her head back, gingerly took the box, and hopped out of his arms, ready to walk down the ramp to the plane.

Fred pulled me in, and we hugged for a long time, not wanting to let go. "We did well. I'll be there as soon as I can. I love you so much." The tears started again, and I just let them fall. I had been holding Lily's hand, and he snatched her up and gave her a twirl. She squealed. "See you soon, little bug." I picked her up, wanting to hold her close as we left. We walked down the jetway, turning around as we slowly saw the door of the plane approaching. I lifted Lily higher and higher into the air so that she could wave to Fred. She silently and then, with gusto, started shouting, "Bye-bye Daddy, we love you, bye-bye! We are going to America. *Sayonara.*"

We disappeared from Fred's view entering the plane and settling into our seats. I grabbed both girls' hands and held them until the plane was high in the air. Emma wiggled her hand out of mine, shaking it to get the blood flowing again. She reached into her pocket and pulled out the beautifully wrapped box that Fred had given to her minutes before. She gingerly pulled each piece of tape off so she didn't rip a single corner. She took out a silk-covered box, unclasped and slowly lifted the lid. She gasped and reached into the pillowy soft fabric on the inside of the box.

She dangled a delicate piece of glass by a string. She held it up to the airplane's window. Through the light, we could see a painted image, and it sparked back at us. Emma held it up to her face. "Mommy, it is a beautiful green mountain with the sun peeking over it. Our mountain, it is our mountain." This time, Emma grabbed her sister's hand. "Lily, it is the mountain we moved while we lived in Japan!"

Acknowledgment

The idea for this book started when Lily was born in 2000, but it wasn't until 2016 when Fred encouraged me to write that I started to tell the story. I'm forever grateful for his support.

A few years ago, Lily asked why I hadn't written our family's story. She said it might help others to understand what a child who is born with a rare disease has to go through to survive. I have done my best to tell what happened.

Emma, now all grown up, is a brilliant writer. I aspired to tell our story using words as carefully chosen as the ones she uses when she writes.

My parents, brother, and in-laws all lived through this with us. They kept us going and picked us up when life was so difficult. When I wanted to write this book, they were enthusiastic supporters. How lucky I am to have them all in my life.

There were over thirty friends and family who read versions of this book. Thank you for believing it was worth your time. Your encouragement kept me writing.

Siri Eggebraten loved our children and cared for them as if they were her own. Her positive, joyful outlook brought goodness and happiness to our entire family.

I'm not a writer by training. It was through many classes and individual coaching from Lisa Wroble that my ideas began to take shape and make sense. She believed in my book from the start.

Just when I thought I could revise the manuscript no more, I met Kate Hopper. As a developmental editor, she helped me to rewrite the entire book again. Thanks to her, it became stronger and more meaningful.

We are so thankful that Joshi Idai Byoin hospital in Tokyo kept Lily alive during those first frightful weeks. Dr. Shaul put Lily's little body back together again. There aren't enough words to express our gratitude. Thank you to all of the nurses and doctors at Children's Hospital Los Angeles who touched our lives and changed Lily's forever.

About the author

Sarah has a master's degree in education from Stanford University. She is an educator, a school administrator, a multimillion-dollar fundraiser, and editor for a widely-distributed medical newsletter about her daughter's condition. Through her twenty-year career in education, she has developed relationships with cross-cultural organizations and with families all over the world. Sarah and Fred live in Minnesota, both of their daughters live nearby.

Email: sarahdeschamps@mac.com

Made in the USA
Monee, IL
06 June 2023

55ddaffe-7048-403a-85f1-263ee1753608R01